C000263826

Charles and Jill Hadfield

WATCHING THE DRAGON

Letters from China
1983-85

Impact Books

First published in Great Britain 1986
by Impact Books, 112 Bolingbroke Grove, London SW11 1DA

British Library Cataloguing in Publication Data

Hadfield, Charles
 Watching the dragon: letters from China
 1983–1985
 1. China—Social life and customs—
 1976–
 I. Title   II. Hadfield, Jill
 951.05′8′0924   DS779.23
 ISBN 0-245-54390-2

Printed and bound in Great Britain by
Biddles Ltd, Guildford and King's Lynn

Acknowledgements

We would like to express our gratitude

to the people of China, for the two richly rewarding years we spent in their country, and in particular to our Chinese friends, our colleagues, and our wonderful students for their warmth, affection, and humour;

to Lewis, Andy, and Ian, for sending us there in the first place;

and to those without whom there would have been no book – Malcolm, Felicity, Hugh, Anne, John, Janette, Michael, Jill, Susan, Tom, Adrienne, Graham, Allan, Sarah, Alex, John, Anna, Birkhild, Hildegard, Franz, Becky, Erszi, Barbara, Hugh, Betty, Jim, Shelagh, Bert, Jenny, Jim, Sheila, Lynn, John, Claire, Jean-Yves, Henri, Danielle, Christiane, Derek, Suzanne, Debby, John, Dilys, Jonathan, Rod, Jerome, Val, Bruce, Tony, Jenny, Steve, Rita, Linda, David, Angi, Sue, Roger, Tom, Chris, Elin, Gill, Dave, Margaret, Bill, Gerry, Mary, Peter, Kyoko, Kurt, Moni, Gabi, Jon, Anne, Halina, Lesek, Jeremy, Jean, Norman, Jon, Mon, Steve, Betty, Adrian, Margaret, Maggie, Steve, Pat, Patti, Michael, Christiana, Paddy, Strix, Ralph, Julia, Roger, Pat, Chryssoula, Yann, Ann, Philippa, Michel, Lesley, Teddy, Elizabeth, Joan, Chris, Ben, Ruedi, Brigitte, Conny – the recipients of *China Newsletter*. Our thanks for their affectionate and supportive letters, cassettes, and deeply appreciated parcels of coffee, cheese, books, thermal underwear, and Christmas puddings!

Sources

Letter Three: Anecdote about Qu Yuan: from *The Songs of the South*, David Hawkes ed., Penguin 1985. Letter Four: Chinese lesson: from *Colloquial Chinese*, P.C. T'ung and E.E. Pollard, Routledge and Kegan Paul 1982. Letter Six: Poem by Li Po (Li Bai in text) from *Li Po and Tu Fu*, Arthur Cooper, Penguin 1973. Letter Thirteen: References to short story, *The Marriage Bureau,* by He Xiaohu: published in *Contemporary Chinese Short Stories*, Chinese Literature, Beijing 1983. Extract from *Kite Streamers*, by Wang Meng: from *The Butterfly and Other Stories*, Panda Books, Chinese Literature 1983. Marco Polo's quotes: from *The Travels*, Marco Polo, translated by Ronald Latham, Penguin 1958. Letter Fourteen: Quotes from *The Teacher*, by Liu Xinwu, *Sacred Duty*, by Wang Yaping, *Melody in Dreams*, by Zong Pu: all from *Prizewinning Stories from China 1978–79*, Foreign Language Press, Beijing 1981. Quote from *A Spate of Visitors*, by Wang Meng: from *The Butterfly and Other Stories*, Panda Books, Chinese Literature 1983.

To our parents

Map

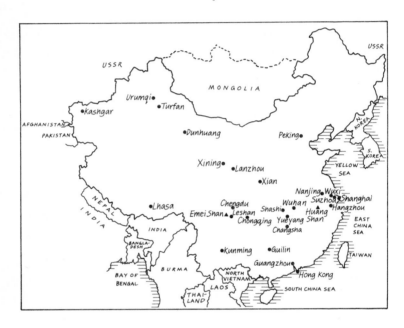

Contents

Foreword

From 1983 to 1985 we lived and worked in China. We were sent there with eight other teachers under a development scheme funded by the World Bank. Our aim was to teach English to postgraduate scientists from all over China, who would then study abroad for a year or two before returning to their own institutes. At the same time, we were to train a team of Chinese teachers who would work alongside us as colleagues, and gradually take over the running of the centre as the project ended, and foreign aid was phased out. This book is based on the 'newsletters' that we wrote home to family and friends while we were there. We would write these letters over a period of days, or sometimes weeks, and send duplicated copies every couple of months. We wrote in turns, one of us typing until tired or interrupted, and the other taking over where he/she left off. We have tried to make clear where authorship changes, though we cannot ourselves always remember who wrote which parts. So the letters have a composite authorship.

It is, in some ways, a naive book. We have no specialist knowledge of China, and do not claim to offer a sophisticated analysis of its culture or politics. There are many things about China that we do not, and probably never will, understand, and we hope that our Chinese friends will forgive us for any misunderstandings or misinterpretations of their country and culture. We should point out some very large gaps in our experiences there. We were working in an educational setting with privileged, educated people, near a huge city. Any observations we make are based on contact with a tiny percentage of the population, as 80% of the people work on the land as 'peasants'; with these people we had very little contact, yet the 'real' China one occasionally hopes to glimpse through the clouds of unknowing, probably lies with them, as it always has. We have tried, simply, to give an honest and straightforward account of both what it felt like to be a Westerner living in Chinese society, and of the great changes and developments we witnessed in that society during the time we were there.

Each letter records what we observed and felt at the time of writing. Early impressions and observations are sometimes modified by later experience, and our feelings about and reactions to the country change with the passage of time. When editing the letters, we have left these modifications and fluctuations unchanged: the book is, in a sense, the record of a journey – a journey into deeper knowledge of and friendship for a great country and its people. The reader is invited to accompany us on that journey.

Letter one

ARRIVING

Letter one
ARRIVING

1 June 1983

10 pm and 90 degrees! And there's more to come they tell us. Wuhan has been variously described to us as 'One of the Three Ovens of China', 'The Furnace of the Yangtze' and 'Stove City'. Apparently we haven't seen anything yet!

I'm sitting here in the living room of our two-room flat, typing in the dingy light of one forty-watt bulb, bamboo chairs, straw mats on the floor, fan whirring in the background, green fly-screens over the windows to keep out the mosquitos, crickets chirping outside. Our house is fine - palatial in fact by Chinese standards; substantial, concrete, semi-detached, with a flat roof, large shady balconies and verandahs, and a little garden with tussocky grass and neat low hedges – incongruously suburban. The other houses in this patch belong to professors and their families; the balconies are crammed with pots of flowers and the little gardens cultivated with flowers and vines. Ours is usually full of children and chickens.

We live upstairs, two other teachers live downstairs and we share a kitchen, an as yet empty room with a sink; and a bathroom, a small concrete room with a basin and a big enamel bath with taps that don't work. However, we are the proud possessors of a shower, a very precarious and potentially lethal plastic contraption that hangs on a coat-hook over the bath and emits yellow smoke at intervals. It is connected to a socket in the wall by an enormous plug and a lead that passes directly under the spray of water. It's a good job the weather has been too hot for anything but cold showers!

We've been here for just over two weeks now and have just finished our first week's teaching. China seems to get stranger and stranger. Our first impressions were not so much surprise as a kind of recognition – 'Well, it *is* like that after all'; there *are* a lot

3

of people and they *do* dress in blue, and, yes, there *are* hundreds of bicycles. I suppose what we were recognising were the clichés about China; what we are finding strange now are the subtler details. I think culture shock is not so much a shock as a kind of rising damp. There have been so many new experiences and sensations that I don't really know where to start. But to begin at the beginning. . . China really started when we boarded the Chinese Jumbo at Gatwick, feeling confused, excited, terrified. Inside was rather like a Chinese restaurant with patterned wallpaper, fans, and tea to drink, though food was, unfortunately, very English sandwiches and lumps of fruitcake. The highlight of the twenty-hour journey was waking at 5 am with a strange unearthly glow in the cabin and looking out of the window to find the sun rising and the wingtips nearly touching the Himalayas. We flew over the rosy snow-covered peaks for nearly an hour and in all that time only saw one little village deep down in a valley. As the mountains gave way to a muddy brown desert, one of our Chinese companions touched my arm and said, 'Now we are in Chinese air space.' And still five hours to go to Beijing!

Beijing was a confused, dreamlike experience. The airport was tiny, seemed much too small to be the airport of the capital city of the most populous nation on earth, and was curiously desolate, with dusty empty halls. No escalators, moving pavements, plush cafeterias or jostle of businessmen and holidaymakers here but a lot of bare tiles and concrete walls, dingily lit and looking rather abandoned.

We were met at the airport, our luggage was piled on the back of what looked like an old army truck and a minibus drove us to our hotel about an hour away on the other side of Beijing. Our first impressions, as I said above, were partly the reverse of surprise, a confirmation of expectations, but also our first taste of that very Chinese sensation of visual overload – so many people, so much happening. The road into Beijing from the airport is very straight and lined with plane trees, rather like a French road in the countryside, but unlike a French country road, it is jammed with traffic: rickety old buses bursting at the seams, mule carts with loads of hay, wood, or vegetables, minibuses, army trucks and antiquated lorries, people pushing or pulling heavy loads on

4

handcarts or carrying them in the age-old fashion on a pole over one shoulder. And bicycles! Bicycles with pannier baskets, bicycles with child seats, bicycles with trailers, two people on a bicycle, people riding two or three abreast, pedalling gently, talking. But all this traffic is moving very slowly, people seem in no hurry to get anywhere. And the whole effect is very drab: dusty grey-green trees, lorries, trucks, and jeeps all in the same colour of army green, and that same army green or blue worn by nearly all the cyclists and pedestrians. It is a crowded street unlike any other in the world – no bustle, no noise, no colour. It feels very unreal, like a slowed-up, monochrome dream sequence.

Perhaps jetlag had something to do with this feeling of unreality, but we were allowed no time to indulge it – jetlag, it seemed, was not on the schedule. At the hotel we were told, 'Please rest now. We are going to a banquet this evening. The bus will collect you in twenty minutes.' A quick wash, and then we were off again to *The Peking Duck* for an amazing meal, starting with 1000-year old eggs (pickled in lime – really only about two months old) and progressing through such delights as white ear fungus and sea slugs to the climax, which was duck – the whole duck and nothing but the duck including beak and feet (since then we've eaten a lot of strange things including eel stew, waterlily roots, lotus berries, and tortoise . . .). In front of each plate were four glasses, containing beer, *maotai* (a very strong spirit, a little like Schnapps, but not so smooth; its taste is unique, dry and grainy), a thick sweet red wine which tasted as if two sips would produce an instant hangover, and cigarettes. All consumed indiscriminately throughout the meal, though beer appeared to be the staple drink while toasts were drunk in wine or *maotai*. A lot of toasting went on, accompanied by speeches. Every ten minutes, approximately, someone made a speech and we all stood up and toasted the success of the project, the Four Modernizations, friendship between Britain and China, co-operation, hard work, and anything else we could think of. We couldn't work out if the speeches came in a special pre-arranged order or not, or if people had been assigned to certain speeches. It all seemed very random and people seemed to speak as the spirit moved them. There was a star-studded cast at the banquet, with Ministers of Agriculture and Education and various TV and radio personalities, but I was too tired to focus properly and saw everything through a haze of jetlag and red wine. Charlie, however, rose to the occasion with a splendidly platitudinous speech.

The banquet ended abruptly. After a while the stream of dishes ceased to flow, and someone got up and tapped on his glass with a knife for attention. Instead of making a speech though, he simply said, 'I think everybody tired now and need a rest.' And that was that.

We all went to bed in a rosy glow of alcohol, tiredness and noble sentiments and were all up at six the next day for a visit to the Great Wall and Ming Tombs. Up the Wall and down the Tombs.

We were all astounded by the Wall: the breathtaking rise and fall, curve and double-back over the steep green mountains; a huge stone snake writhing over a most improbable landscape, almost vertical in some places, and crowded with Chinese tourists in baggy blue trousers and white nylon open-necked shirts, wearing large-brimmed white sunhats, some with *Seagull* cameras: old-fashioned twin-lens reflexes with brown leather cases. Photo sessions along the Wall seemed to involve a lot of artistic posing and much fiddling with the camera. Most surprising to me was the lack of steps; the stone surface on the steep inclines was made slippery by countless feet and we had to cling to the parapet in places to avoid sliding back down. Beyond the watchtowers, ruins stretched into the distance, off to the Gobi Desert in one direction and to the Yellow Sea in the other, gigantic broken stones covered in grass and weeds.

We tottered up and slid down the steep slopes, almost swept off our feet by the strong wind and then were ushered back to the minibus and whisked off to the Ming Tombs, where we walked down the broad avenue between the two rows of giant stone animals that form the approach to the tombs, and then were escorted to lunch.

This took place in a little restaurant, behind a screen – Chinese diners on one side of the screen and us on the other. It appeared that this was the part of the restaurant reserved for 'foreign friends', and that, while the food was identical, prices were different on the two sides of the screen. Since then all our meals have taken place behind screens, even in the campus dining room, where we are not allowed to go and queue up at the main mess hall with staff and students, but have meals served to us in a small dining room separated from the main one by a folding hospital screen.

This image of The Screen has become a symbol in my mind for the elaborate measures taken to insulate the foreigner from ordinary Chinese life. This is partly courtesy – a desire to give the foreigner the best of everything and to shield him from the hardships of everyday life, but it also effectively prevents him from coming into close contact with Chinese people. I was amazed at the elaborate arrangements that had been made to take care of us: everything from minibuses to meals in restaurants to onward tickets to Wuhan had been prepared in advance and there seemed to be an endless supply of guides and interpreters from the Ministry of Agriculture to look after us. Our hosts appeared startled when we asked if there was a bus into Beijing from the hotel. They explained that we would never be able to find our way round Beijing by ourselves, the bus system was much too confusing and we couldn't speak Chinese. We might get lost, and as we were their responsibility, they couldn't allow that to happen. Why, when he was in London, Professor Zhang stated as conclusive proof, he wouldn't have dreamed of going out on his own to explore, he just waited in the hotel till someone came to collect him and show him round. Their alarm was genuine: never having travelled on their own abroad themselves, they could not imagine how a tourist can muddle through in a completely strange country, armed only with a map, common sense and sign language. I also began to realise the awful sense of responsibility that the Chinese have for us, much as parents have for children or teachers for pupils in their care. At a welcoming banquet in Wuhan, the college secretary informed us solemnly, 'If a hair of your head is harmed, I am responsible.' I am beginning to feel like an immensely valuable and very fragile piece of porcelain.

In the end, realising that our bid for individual exploration might well look like discourtesy, given the care with which our programme had been arranged, we gave up the bus expedition and settled for a walk around the hotel, which was in the fields on the edge of the city. We had not gone far, however, when we came upon huge signs saying NO FOREIGNERS BEYOND THIS POINT. So we gave up, succumbed to jetlag, and went to bed.

The next day brought a trip to Customs for Charlie and a visit to the Forbidden City for the rest of us. We were led into the back entrance of the Imperial Palace, having arranged to meet Charlie and Professor Zhang at midday at the Tiananmen entrance under the huge portrait of Mao. Once again, though, individual exploration was not on the cards, and our guide for that day was paranoiac about letting any of us out of her sight, fluttering around and clucking frantically like an apoplectic hen when any of us disappeared from view into an inner courtyard for so much as ten seconds. She was too busy counting heads to tell us anything about the history of the place, and there was scarcely any time to look at a guide book between being ushered out of one courtyard and herded into the next, but I still found time to appreciate the simple and elegant lines of the architecture, the brilliant colours of red walls and golden roofs against the bright blue sky, the felicitous names: the Hall of Supreme Harmony, The Palace of Heavenly Purity, The Palace of Earthly Tranquility and the elaborate and refined aestheticism of an age with such a detailed code of symbols: no decoration was accidental, everything had a meaning: sundials symbolize righteousness, the bronze cranes and tortoises on the terraces denote longevity, elephants mean peace, and the Dragon is, of course, the symbol of the Emperor.

There is little refinement or elegance left in modern Beijing though, as we found when we emerged into Tiananmen Square looking south to where the once unbroken vista across to the Qianmen gate is now crudely interrupted by the massive granite of the Mao Mausoleum, and east and west to the immense Stalinesque monoliths of the Great Hall of the People and the Museum of the Revolution that flank the square. Our guide looked so relieved to have got us all to the right place at the right time that I began to feel a little guilty at our irresponsible Western individuality, and to wonder what penalties she had been threatened with for losing one of us!

8

While the others were sightseeing, I had my first taste of Chinese bureaucracy. Boxes and boxes of books and teaching equipment had arrived with us on the plane and to get them all down to Wuhan without delay we had to sign for them at the Customs Office. We drove down there in a black *Shanghai* saloon, large and luxurious with curtained windows, along the wide dusty grey concrete of Beijing's eight-lane highways, built in antici-pation of some future century's traffic problems, but empty now and giving the city a curiously desolate air. The Customs Office was an old circular domed building in a dilapidated state, with peeling grey paintwork and shabby whitewashed walls. High wooden counters ran round the circumference of the echoing space and some weary clerks were at work behind them. Professor Zhang tried to attract the attention of first one and then another without success, and ended up by getting quite excitable, which surprised me as I had expected an inscrutable *sang froid* to pervade such dealings. While we were waiting, several of the clerks got up and wandered off, returning with tin lunch boxes or enamel bowls of rice and vegetables, which they ate sitting at their desks or perched on the counters. Another group dragged in a ping-pong table, which they set up in the middle of the room. The deafening echoing clack and rattle of the ping-pong balls made conversation virtually impossible, but Professor Zhang persisted valiantly, and eventually succeeded in getting the infor-mation that, before we received authorization to move the equipment from the office, we had to get permission from another customs office. Into the car again, and to a much smaller office in a run-down old mansion in a back street. As it was lunchtime, we had to wait. I stood on the porch and watched chickens pecking in the yard among the bicycles and pots of flowers. The office was small and littered with cardboard boxes and jam jars of green tea. Finally, a clerk materialized who said no, he couldn't put his seal on the document until he had had an official request from the first office. 'But they sent us here,' said Professor Zhang in anguish. 'Yes, but where is their official letter of request?' After nearly four hours we were back at square one. We gave up and went to meet the others for lunch.

9

That evening we boarded the train for Wuhan, sixteen hours away. We travelled soft class: four berths in a compartment, very genteel, with embroidered antimacassars, silk quilts, carpeted floor, lace tablecloth, potted plant on the table, and a huge thermos of hot water for making tea. (These thermoses are everywhere: in hotel rooms, station waiting rooms, restaurants. A girl brings two to our house every day, and a trolley of them is delivered to the staffroom and administrative offices every morning.)

Our hosts relaxed considerably now that there was no danger of our getting lost or straying off, and we had a wonderful journey across the central China plain. Mile after mile of wheat-fields, small red brick villages in walled compounds, and never a glimpse of countryside without a person in it – peasants working in the fields, children returning home from school, an old man fishing in a stream, a farmer washing down his water buffalo in a river. We woke the next morning to a more intricate, beautifully sculpted and terraced landscape, as wheat gave way to the rice paddies of southern China, and the golden fields were replaced by the lurid emerald green of young rice.

At Wuhan we were met by a delegation of fresh-faced young girls – the young teachers that we will be training. One of them introduced herself as 'Spring Daisy' and that's exactly what they all looked like. We spent the first week in a hotel, as our accommodation wasn't ready, and commuted in to the campus each day. The hotel was beautifully situated by the side of a large lake, described by Professor Zhang as 'very scenerous'. And it certainly was, with pagodas everywhere, arching bridges, teahouses and dragon boats.

We were amazed and very pleasantly surprised by our first sight of the campus, which is in a park-like setting at the edge of South Lake. Red brick apartment houses and student dormitories, concrete teaching blocks, some low single-storey, one or two-room houses and a patch of two-storey semis, one of which we're currently occupying. All the buildings look in a rather raw and unfinished state, though they have been operational for years, but are set among bamboo groves, gardens with exotic flowers, orchards, and surrounded by open countryside: paddy fields, rape fields, tea plantations and vegetable allotments

– every square inch minutely cultivated. Chickens everywhere, and herds of cows and buffalos regularly pass by the windows of our teaching block.

Everyone lives on campus: it's like a small town, inhabited not only by students and teachers but also by a vast service industry of cleaners, cooks, admin staff, shop assistants, nurses and doctors. There are three shops, a post office, a small free market at the gate, where you can buy eggs and vegetables, a clinic, a dentist, a carpenter and a campus tailor where I got a pair of sea-green trousers with a bright orange zip made for 60p. There are also three schools: kindergarten, primary and middle. All the primary children have been taught to say 'Hello' and 'How do you do?' to us and when we arrived there was a big red and white banner over the entrance to the campus saying A WARMLY WELCOME TO YOU.

But the campus is much more than just a place to live for all the people who work there, more even than a community in the Western sense of the word. It is their work unit, a phrase that has connotations that we are only just beginning to grasp. One of the first questions asked in China is *'Ni shi neige danwei ren?'* or 'What unit are you from?'. The work unit, or rather the unit leader, has what seems like complete power over all aspects of a person's life. Your unit leaders not only pay your salary and issue ration coupons. They allocate housing, decide if and when you can get married and if and when you can have children. If you already have the statutory one child, or if your pregnancy does not fit into their plans for your work schedule, you may be persuaded to have an abortion. If a young couple need married accommodation, or would like a bigger flat after their child is born, they must apply to the unit. If a couple are thinking of divorce, people from their unit or street committee, a neighbourhood social welfare organisation, will visit them and try and talk them out of it. There seems to be very little individual decision-making at any level.

The college is our work unit now and we have been issued with little red unit cards of which we are very proud! Of course, as privileged foreigners, we have more freedom to arrange our own lives, but an amusing incident last week gave us a taste of corporate decision-making. We had just moved all our luggage into the flat and discovered that we had been allocated not one but

11

three beds: one double and two singles. We were debating how to arrange the furniture when a delegation arrived, sent to help us move in, and suddenly the flat was full of people all earnestly discussing whether we should sleep in one bed or two singles, and where the best location for the bed would be!

Our teaching building is a long five-storey block with rooms connected by balconies that run the length of the building. It looks rather like a ship. It is, in fact, a converted student dormitory, with our students living on the first three and a half floors and the top one and a half floors cleared for classrooms. We make our way from room to room along the balconies, ducking under rows of student washing! The students live five to a small bare room with concrete floor and roughly whitewashed walls. There is just enough room for five beds and five desks end-to-end along the walls and a small space in the middle. At the ends of each balcony there are washrooms with (cold) showers and concrete washtroughs. There are also mass washtroughs outside. Each student was, on arrival, issued with a bed, a desk, a chair, a mosquito net, an enamel washing bowl, a thermos, a rice bowl and a spoon. They arrive with small bags of clothing and personal possessions, and large bundles of bed linen tied up with string. They come from all over China, and, despite the cramped and very basic living conditions, are delighted to be here, eager to learn, and a joy to teach.

The week before term started we spent unpacking 45 boxes of books, fixing whiteboards to the walls, unpacking and installing audio equipment, recording tapes, and cataloguing the library. There was literally nothing but fifteen empty rooms and a load of cardboard boxes when we arrived. Somehow it all got done in time for the 'Opening Ceremony': a splendidly pompous affair with two hours of speeches by various Deans and Vice-Deans (of which there seem to be quite a number) and visiting dignitaries, all recorded for posterity by China TV and *The People's Daily*! The ceremony became noticeably less pompous when we all adjourned to a restaurant for the inevitable banquet. More speeches – in fact almost everyone made a speech! The theme of a marriage between China and Britain was introduced and developed at length with every speaker embroidering on the subject and the suggestions got wilder and more risqué as the level of *maotai* in the bottles went down. As the evening wore on through twenty odd courses and innumerable bottles of beer, *maotai* and wine, people got up and wandered round the room, visiting other tables and, of course, making speeches – there would sometimes be as many as five or six speeches going on in addition to the main one!

Since we arrived we've made one trip into the centre of Wuhan, or Hankou, as the main part of town is called. Wuhan is a conglomeration of three cities grouped around the confluence of the Han and Yangtze rivers. Wuchang, where most of the colleges and universities are, is on the south bank of the Yangtze; Hanyang, a mainly industrial area, is in the triangle between the two rivers; and Hankou, the main commercial and shopping centre, is on the north bank of the Yangtze. The trip into town from the college takes up to an hour and half by car – we're very much out in the country, at the end of a long causeway across South Lake: a beautiful drive, the lake covered in lotus flowers, frogs croaking merrily, rice paddies all around and mountains in the distance.

We drive into Hankou across the immense Yangtze bridge; road above, rail below. The river is nearly a mile wide at this point: muddy red-brown swirling water, crowded with river traffic: ferry boats, big four-tier Yangtze steamers carrying people upstream to Chongqing or downstream to Shanghai, barges with loads of wood, coal, concrete, the occasional junk with huge sails, or little sampan chugging across the river. I get a tremendous thrill just from looking at the river and thinking, 'This is the Yangtze' – the magic of a name.

Hankou is a big brown and grey city, with huge pompous boulevards lined with plane trees – acres of tarmac separating the buildings, and little backstreets of low houses with wooden balconies festooned with washing. I've never seen so much washing in my life – it seems to be a national sport! The city centre is the area of the French, German, British and Japanese conces-sions, dating from the town's Treaty Port days, and the architecture is massive, colonial, with pillars and stone balconies and impressive flights of steps sweeping up to ornate entrances,

13

but all rather run-down, neglected and shabby.

Shops baffle me: huge gloomy cavernous interiors, dimly lit, surging with people, and a blur of noise rebounding and echoing off the roughly painted walls, the goods for sale tucked away in dusty rows on shelves behind the counters. The bank is an imposing Edwardian building with immense carved doors. Inside are marble floors, swishing ceiling fans and rows of wooden desks behind the counters with clerks immersed in enormous ledgers – all very Dickensian. There is a hand-painted notice on the wall saying CORDIAL, ACCURATE, SPEEDY, CONVENIENT. Service is certainly cordial, and, so far, accurate, but hardly speedy or convenient: cashing a travellers' cheque or taking out salaries can take up to an hour and a half, involving lengthy calculations on abacuses, and receipts handwritten in triplicate.

Off the main street is a wonderful street that we have christened 'Eel and Tortoise Street' – because that is mainly what is for sale there! It is a market street, narrow, cobbled, with wares spread out for sale on the cobblestones: baskets of eggs, big barrels of rice, sheepskins to sew inside winter coats, all kinds of dried fungus and mushrooms, green tea, hens in wire coops or a ruffled mass of feathers in wicker baskets, ginger, garlic, bundles of chives and scallion, a beancurd barrow with soft white squares of fresh beancurd or harder shrivelled orange cubes of dried or fermented beancurd, baskets of Yangtze fish, still jumping and thrashing around, slabs of meat laid out on the cobblestones or strung up on a wire, seasonal vegetables: chillies, peppers, onions, carrots. But the main part of the street is taken up with buckets of eels, writhing and squirming in a tangled mass; and tortoises, crawling over one another in wire cages. Buy one and it will be gutted for you there and then: eels nailed down by the head and slit – one quick knife stroke from head to tail; tortoise shell levered off, exposing the innards, legs and head still moving, guts and blood spilling red and slippery over the cobblestones. I also saw a snake for sale and three dead rats. I don't know whether the rats were a delicacy or just demonstrations of the efficacy of some patent rat poison, but the snake was definitely destined for someone's supper. On that appetizing note, I think I'll sign off and go to dinner!

14

Letter two

SOME SNAPSHOTS

Letter two
SOME SNAPSHOTS

14 June 1983
This letter is not really a letter, but more like a photo album – a sort of A–Z of snapshots of daily life and street scenes: things that have surprised or impressed us in the month we have been here so far.

A is for Abacus – to be found in all shops, offices, banks, and hotels. There are very few tills or even calculators, and the dingy, echoing shops are full of the click-clack of the wooden beads against the frame. They are beautiful objects: dark polished wooden beads on bamboo rods, brass trimmings on the oblong frame. Fifteen columns of beads, seven beads in each column. I can't work out how they function and stare, fascinated, at the shop assistant's fingers as they flutter across the frame, spinning beads, until she arrives at some improbably exact sounding total: 'Five *yuan*, eight *jiao*, and six *fen*.' Children have abacus classes in school; we stared through the window the other day at a class of eight or nine-year olds, each with an abacus on their knees, fingers fluttering in unison, as the teacher took them through the complexities of addition and subtraction.

B is, of course, for Bicycles. Where to start? Perhaps with the first bicycle imported into China years and years ago, which must have been copied immediately and which is now produced in the millions by dozens of different factories, over and over again. All bikes look the same, though there are scores of different brand names. Sober black machines, monsters with one gear, of all ages and in various states of decay. I have seen bicycles with huge gas bottles or televisions strapped to the back, bicycles being used to carry sick people to hospitals, bicycles transporting household furniture, bicycles with bunches of squawking ducks or chickens tied by their feet to the handlebars, a whole family on one bicycle: Mum side-saddle on the luggage-rack, and a couple of kids on the crossbar. People ride two or three abreast, chatting. Everyone rides very slowly. In a country with no private cars, the bike takes over as status symbol. Do you ride a rusty old worker's bike, designed for carrying heavy loads, with its reinforced stays and luggage rack, or do you spin past on a glossy new *Flying Pigeon*, hubs decorated with dayglo pipe-cleaners, a strip of lace along the crossbar and maybe brown paper or polythene wrapper fluttering in the breeze – proof that you have only just purchased it? The best bicycles come from Shanghai; there are three prestige names: *Forever, Phoenix,* and *Flying Pigeon.* The latter is reckoned to be the classiest, though they all look identical to me. I am surprised that in this country, where so many heavy loads are carried on two wheels, where so many bike miles are covered by so many millions of people, that bikes have only one gear. I am also surprised that they are so expensive: 150 *yuan*, or about £50, is not cheap when it represents about three months' salary for the average worker. No bikes have lights; at night you just ring your bell and hope for the best. The bell is very important, and the first thing the prospective Chinese buyer tries out – rather like an Italian and a car horn. A policeman came to give us a talk about traffic rules in preparation for our buying bikes. These included: 'Don't carry passengers', 'Don't ride on the left', and 'Don't cycle with an umbrella', but you frequently see people doing all three.

C is for Crowds clogging the pavement, spilling over into the street, blue and green in winter, a blend of washed-out pastels in summer. It is difficult to be in a hurry in a Chinese street, dodging round clumps of window shoppers, squirming through groups of slowly sauntering families. The Chinese themselves never seem to be in a hurry: drifting down the street, slowly, dreamily – a nation of somnambulists. Shopping is difficult too: a sea of blue backs between you and the counter; doubly difficult if you are foreign, since more crowds, attracted by your presence, swell the numbers of those already there. One advantage of being a foreigner though is that we never lose each other in a crowd – just look for the flash of brighter colour, the body that's head and shoulders above the other bodies, or the place where the crowd increases in density as a knot of onlookers gathers to stare at the foreigner. I admire the patience of the Chinese in crowds; also the ability they have to shut themselves off from the pressure of too much humanity, to remain small, self-contained islands in the swarming streets.

D is for Dogs, which are supper on four legs here. You don't see dogs in towns; they are not kept as pets, but sometimes in the country you will see a few – small mongrels usually. Guard dogs? Or being fattened up for the winter? Winter is the traditional time for dog stew. 'Nice and warming', say my students, smacking their lips appreciatively.

E is for Eating, which takes place anywhere. While banquets and formal dinners are elaborate, almost ritualistic occasions, ordinary eating is a very casual affair, not even requiring a table, just an enamel bowl and a pair of chopsticks or a spoon. On the campus, students and teachers wander off, bowl and spoon in hand, to fetch breakfast, lunch, or dinner from one of the communal mess halls, and then wander back, eating as they walk, or squat by the side of the path or under the trees to shovel down spoonfuls of rice. Our students eat outside, standing in rows along the five tiers of long balconies, gazing out over the lake and orchards. Waving to them as I pedal off home on my bike, I feel as if I'm waving goodbye to the passengers on some huge liner leaving port.

F is for Fans, ubiquitous in summer. Many older buildings have giant ceiling fans like aircraft propellors. Most modern buildings have fanless ceilings, but may have a small electric fan on a stand in a corner. The price of these also amazes me: about 150 *yuan* for a small one – two to three months' wages for a family. Best of all are the little hand-held fans of pleated paper with gaudy designs of flowers, birds, or animals. Men as well as women carry these, with no distinction as to subject matter and one of my favourite sights is to see a dignified cadre on a train or at a meeting solemnly fanning himself with a design of cuddly pandas or cute kittens.

19

G is for Greetings. Until we got used to them, we found Chinese greetings strange, abrupt, even a little rude. 'Have you eaten yet?' is probably the commonest: of the same order as 'Nice day, isn't it?'. At first I thought this was a prelude to a dinner invitation, as it would be in the West, and the Chinese must have found my elaborately polite replies very strange. 'How old are you?' and 'How much do you earn?' are questions that follow hard on introduction, and we were rather taken aback by these at first. Age seems particularly important as an indicator of social standing, and, as we like to know someone's job before we can properly 'place' them, so the Chinese like to know each other's ages. I was baffled when on asking my first class to introduce themselves to each other, they all went round asking each other's ages to find out who was the oldest and who was the youngest. That established, they settled back, obviously feeling more secure: they now knew whose opinions to respect and whose advice to value.

H is for Hairdressers. Most Chinese girls still wear their hair in plaits or bunches if it is long, and in a neat pudding basin if it is short, but curls are now 'In': it is chic to be waved or permed, and increasing numbers of Chinese women are visiting the beauty salons and coming back with their lovely sleek shiny black hair frizzed into a very 50s-style perm. Hairdresser's salons are terrifying places in China. Perhaps Chinese hair is especially reluctant to curl, but ordinary rollers aren't enough to persuade it. Instead, hanging from the ceiling are festoons of electrically heated curling tongs: a tangle of wires with metal clips at the ends. Women sit in rows in these salons, which are open to the street, clamped into these devices, with wires leading from their heads to the ceiling, looking as if they are victims of torture or undergoing some strange psychological experiment instead of beauty treatment.

I is for Ice Cream. Ice lollies really. These are sold on street corners and in parks for a few *fen*. The vendor usually has a big white-painted wooden box insulated with rags and padding, with ice inside to keep the temperature low. At the end of the day the box is simply strapped to the rear of her bike and she cycles home. Some vendors prefer to be mobile and wheel their bikes around, crying out their wares. Some do not aspire to the wooden box and simply store the ice-cream in a wide-necked thermos flask. The lollies look curiously home-made, come wrapped in a blue and white paper, and taste of nothing much but water, though flavours are described as banana, chocolate, and soya bean. There's a bright pink one too, which I suppose might be strawberry, though I haven't seen strawberries in China. The best thing about them is the Chinese word for ice-cream, which, when the vendors are yelling it out, sounds like 'Bing-Bang'.

J is for Jackets. These come in three colours: grey, army-green, and blue. There are two shades of blue: traditional worker's blue and a lighter blue-grey. There are subtle distinctions of style and cut. Some hang loose and baggy from the shoulders, some are shaped. Some have two pockets, some have four. A touch of style is to wear a fountain pen in the top pocket. Everyone was wearing jackets when we first arrived, but on June 1 these all disappeared and were replaced by loose white nylon shirts for the men and summer frocks for the women. Jackets reappear in the autumn, apparently: by National Day (October 1) everyone will be jacketed again, and, despite fluctuations in temperature, will stay jacketed throughout the winter and into the early summer. Once buttoned into your jacket, there is, it appears, no unbuttoning until June 1.

K is for Kitsch. There is a lot of this about, and the *Arts and Crafts* store has some extraordinary collector's items in among the exquisitely embroidered tablecloths and delicate brush paintings of bamboo or plum blossom. Here are a few of our favourites:

a green and brown plastic Tang Dynasty camel
a bright green table-lamp in the shape of a grand piano
a relief sculpture of pines and cranes in pink and black plastic
a quartz alarm clock with a tinted photo of a toothy Shanghai film star
a photo of a smiling Mao printed onto a cloth hanging with a surround of peonies

a *Double Happiness* spittoon with a design of dancing pandas
a white frilled china plate with a plastic bubble in the middle.
Inside the bubble: a cross-eyed, buck-toothed, fluffy white
kitten.

L is for Loudspeakers. There is a network of these all over the
campus: attached to telegraph poles, fixed under the eaves of
dormitory blocks, perched in the trees, and we found this rather
sinister and Orwellian at first. Every work unit and village in
China has a similar system. The distance between the speakers on
our campus means that the sound from different speakers reaches
your ears at different times, and this creates a curious echo-like
burbling effect. We find them hard to live with. I canvassed
opinions among our students. Attitudes varied. Some found
them stressful. Some relied on them for waking up in the
morning, some appreciated the news broadcasts, but by far the
majority seemed hardly to notice them: to have a happy ability to
shut out the announcements and the news and the music and to
live out their own lives unperturbed. I hope we develop this
ability soon. The daily programme is as follows:
6.30, wake up to the National Anthem, followed by some
announcements and then some cheery 'rise and shine' music.
Around seven o'clock or so, as we are cycling to work, there is
news and weather. Then the programme closes down until
9.45, when there is exercise music (the same all over China) and a
female voice chanting: '*Yi, er, san . . .*'. This lasts about twenty
minutes. Then at
11.30, there is music signalling the end of morning classes,
announcements, news, and more music. There are usually a
couple of uplifting stories too, such as the tale of a handicapped
student who had overcome her disabilities and become a teacher.
A quiet period for afternoon siesta follows until
2.15, when more music, this time soft and soothing, wakes you
from your nap and continues till
2.30, when you should be at work. Finally, at
5.00, a last burst of music and announcements signals the end of
afternoon classes and the start of suppertime.
    In winter the reveille is half-an-hour later, and the nap time is

shorter. On Saturdays, summer and winter alike, the wake-up music is half an hour early. This seemed terribly unfair to me, so I asked why: 'So that people can get up earlier to clean their houses.'

M is for Mosquito nets – an unavoidable feature of Chinese summertime. These either hang from a hook in the ceiling or are draped over bamboo poles, like a four-poster bed. We have been given two single ones and wonder if that is part of the One Child Family policy.

N is for Naps. The morning finishes at 11.30, and after lunch the whole campus goes to sleep. There is not a sound to be heard nor soul to be seen between 12 and 2.15, when soft slushy music is played to wake the slumberers. This summertime siesta continues through the winter too, though in an abridged version. Apparently, the right to the noontime nap is enshrined in China's constitution. You see people asleep at all times of day, though, and in all sorts of places: nodding off between sacks of flour on the back of a lorry, or sprawled out on a heap of sand on a tractor trailer; dozing off in staff meetings, or snoring their way through political study. We have seen a small boy having forty winks on the back of a water buffalo, and an old man asleep in charge of a donkey cart. People also frequently seem to sleep in the road, with scant regard for traffic, but the most dangerous snooze we have yet seen was at a railway siding when our train stopped at a station: two soldiers were comfortably curled up in an ammunition wagon, on top of a pile of hand grenades.

O is for One Child Families. The basic unit of Chinese society is now the threesome, and on Sundays in the park or out for the evening stroll you can see plenty of young parents: each couple with a single toddler or plump cherubic baby. Posters everywhere show smiling couples with their one child. The child is always a girl: the Chinese still cling to their traditional preference for boys, and there is a national 'Girls are OK' campaign going on. In spite of this, peasants in the countryside still prefer large families, preferably with a predominance of

23

males, to help out with the work and support them in their old age. The policy is not working as well in the countryside as in the towns, where more workers get state pensions and are not so dependent on their offspring for support. There are still many multi-child families in the countryside, and the practice of female infanticide reportedly continues. I asked my students, many of whom come from families of six or seven children, what they thought about the policy. They thought it was necessary, but were quite open about the social problems of a nation of only children. 'Parents pay too much attention to an only child', they said. 'They will get spoilt and then we will have a nation of selfish individuals.' They were also worried, as parents, at the thought of being a heavy burden to their children, with each young couple in the future having sole responsibility for two sets of parents. But they all, without exception, had signed or intended to sign the pledge, which, in return for the promise to have only one child, entitled them to certain benefits such as better education and free medical care for the child, better accommodation, and a family income supplement of about 8 *yuan* a month.

P is for Prices, which puzzle me. I understand the basic principle, which is that basic necessities: food, clothes, and accommodation are cheap, and consumer goods are expensive. A pound of carrots costs a *mao* – about 3p, and a pound of beancurd is not much more expensive. Meat is pricier: a chicken or a large fish bought in the free market will cost a couple of *yuan* – about 50–60 pence. Our students pay 1 *yuan* a day – about 30 pence – for all their meals. You can buy a pair of trousers or a shirt, or have them made by a street tailor, for a couple of *yuan* too, and the basic flat-soled cloth shoes are also about that price. Rent is a minimal *yuan* or so a month, and electricity and gas prices are also low. Anything that could be classed as a luxury item is, in contrast, astronomically expensive: cameras or cassette recorders cost around 200 *yuan*, and the price of a television represents something like a year's salary in a country where most workers earn between 50 and 100 *yuan* a month – about £20–£35. But it's the price of some perfectly ordinary everyday items – not as basic to survival as food, but which certainly couldn't be regarded as luxuries – that amazes me. A perfectly ordinary plastic washing-up bowl costs 5 *yuan*: nearly half a week's wages for a lower paid worker – the equivalent in our terms of £30 or so! Yet everyone seems to have one. Everyone seems to have a watch as well, and the cheapest of these cost about a month's wages. A metal bed that I saw in a department store the other day cost 39 *yuan*, and a wooden pushchair cost 30 *yuan*. No wonder so many people carry their babies in their arms. When a couple get married, the man is supposed to give his wife 'the three things that go round': a wristwatch, a sewing machine, and a bicycle. By my reckoning, that would eat up the best part of a year's salary for a young worker. And that's before they get started on the metal beds and plastic washing-up bowls, let alone tape-recorders or televisions! Late marriage is encouraged by the government as part of the One Child policy, but maybe it takes a young couple most of their twenties to save up for the basic essentials of housekeeping!

Q is for Queuing. There are some situations where you queue and others where you don't. I'm not quite sure of the rules. People queue up to buy train tickets, standing patiently in long barely moving lines. They begin queuing, too, hours before their train arrives: a line tailing back from the barrier and stretching right across the station yard. But when the train pulls in and the barriers are lifted, everyone runs forward and the line becomes a mass of pushing, elbowing, struggling bodies. People don't queue in shops, and you need a loud voice and determined elbow to get what you want there. But buses are the worst. Most buses are crowded, and everyone knows that the only way to get a place is simply to fight. I am surprised by the desperation with which people launch themselves at the doors before the bus has even stopped, and at the tangle of bodies, as those trying to get off are forced back into the bus by those trying to get on. I saw a baby on a woman's back being crushed between two young men who were pushing to get on. The baby screamed, the woman turned round to shout, almost wrenching the baby's head off, the two men grunted and cursed. Or another time, an old woman shoved aside by teenagers less than a quarter her age. Once on the bus, different rules apply, and I am amazed at the schizophrenic transformation that takes place there. Calm is established. Everyone settles into that self-possessed tranquility which is the hallmark of a Chinese crowd. People take care not to tread on each others' feet: they helpfully pass money from hand to hand down the bus to the conductor, who perches by the door, hands full of tickets and grubby banknotes. I have even been offered a seat by someone who nearly pushed me over in the effort to get there before I did. At the main bus station in Wuchang, uniformed officials with whistles keep passengers in line. But at every bus stop in town it's open warfare.

R has to be for Rice. This is the basis of three meals a day for the southern Chinese: rice porridge for breakfast, eaten with salt or sugar, peanuts or pickles; bowls of steamed rice with beancurd or vegetables and maybe a little pork, chicken, or fish, for lunch and supper. When protein is limited, you make up for it with bulk, and we both marvel at the quantities of rice – huge bowlfuls of it – that people consume here. Rice is always white, short-grained, and cooked in huge containers, so that it arrives in your bowl in sticky lumps. Easier to pick up with chopsticks though. Rice is just rice to me, and I never considered that there might be different flavours and textures. The students are very particular, and complain about the Wuhan rice. They say, 'It's hard and makes our stomachs uncomfortable.' The best rice comes from Suzhou: light and fluffy, creamy in colour, and soft in texture. May was rice-planting time, and the fields were full of peasants: men, women, and children, calf-deep in the water, coolie hats or white bonnets to keep off the sun, bent double, setting out the young plants in neat rows. The fields are a vivid green now with the sun glinting on the water between the rows, creating a wonderful luminosity. A lovely sight.

S is for Street-life. A walk down a Chinese street can be a bewildering and dizzying experience. There is too much stimulation, too many impressions coming at you from all angles; you get a sort of visual overload and after a few minutes exposure can find yourself craving the blander but more restful surroundings of your flat or hotel room. Here are some observations made in the course of one five-minute walk down a Wuhan street: a teashop full of old men drinking green leafy tea from cracked bowls, smoking, playing chess, cards, snoozing in bamboo chairs: a workshop where men are making woks, cutting out circles from sheet-metal and hammering them into shape round a mould; a shop full of safes; a stall selling bright plastic raincoats and umbrellas; ice-cream sellers, peanut-sellers, fruit-sellers; vendors of gilt badges and cheap plastic souvenirs; a man staggering under the weight of two huge baskets of vegetables suspended from a bamboo pole across his shoulder, peculiar swaying, half-running walk; children in bright orange and green frocks, plastic sandals, hair tied into bunches with gaudy ribbons; People's Liberation Army men and women in green uniform, red-starred caps; din of bicycle bells; khaki-green jeeps and lorries, horns blaring, scattering cyclists and pedestrians; battered buses bulging with passengers; a traffic policeman standing under his huge umbrella in the middle of the road, ineffectually waving his arms, shouting through a megaphone, no-one taking any notice; an old lady with bound feet, child's feet on an aged body, hobbling painfully, barely able to walk; a night-soil collector – everyone gives him a wide berth; glimpses into house interiors, dim and dark, bed with mosquito net, table, low bamboo chairs, a bright poster, maybe a faded picture of Mao, the occasional glimpse of a flickering TV in a back room; water porters, two wooden pails on a bamboo pole, swaying, slopping water, carrying it from the pump to the house; a bag shop, full of the ubiquitous black vinyl bags; a noodle house, dark smoky evil hell's kitchen interior, huge wok on a charcoal stove, great baskets of dumplings ready to be steamed, an old lady deftly cutting and flicking the dough into little boats around the meat filling, a man hacking roast duck into chopstick-size pieces with a huge hatchet, a queue of people waiting for meal tickets, others eating, sitting on low wooden stools around large tables, spitting out the bones and gristle; chickens in the street in bamboo cages built around the bases of trees, or wandering free; square wooden pushchairs: a platform on four wheels with a cage around it, the baby standing up, holding onto the sides; a tailor's workshop open to the street, four old men sit at treadle sewing machines, another cuts and measures cloth; rows of washing

27

strung between houses, bedding hung out to air; a tree, unbelievably, full of fish which have been strung up to dry; a tea-seller:
glasses of tea stand ready-poured on a cardboard box, a square of
glass over each to protect them from the flies; sunflower seeds for
sale done up in neat little cones of newspaper; an old woman with
a huge solid pudding of pasta, still steaming, from which she
pares noodles in a circular motion, using an instrument like a
potato peeler; pigeon fanciers: old men squat in huddles, the birds
are passed from hand to hand, wings spread out, examined and
discussed; a young girl, permed hair, high heels, skirt short for
China, minces along delicately, stops, hawks loudly, and spits; a
poster exhorts the people to use all their resources to develop
science and technology, another reads (in English), 'One couple,
one child: eugenical and well-bred'; a young couple carry a
suitcase together, their fingers just touching on the handle –
passion, Chinese style; two young men wander along, their arms
round each other; two policemen, hand-in-hand; a glimpse into a
dentist's, open to the street under the sign of a huge grinning
mouth, the dentist has a grubby white coat and a pedal power
drill; a clinic, red cross outside, sleazy interior, four or five
patients being examined at the same time; Chinese medicine
shop, rows of roots, leaves, herbs; next door *Coca-Cola* is for sale
in a juice bar. And everyone, everyone dressed alike: girls in
socks, skirts, loose blouses over the skirts, older women in baggy
grey or black trousers, men in the same unisex trousers and white
nylon shirt, or moth-eaten vest in the standard colours of green,
red, or blue.

T is for Tea. Teatime is all day. Every room contains cups or
mugs with lids, and a thermos flask or two: big, red or blue,
decorated with flowers, containing piping hot boiled water.
There is not always an accompanying tea caddy, as many Chinese
simply drink hot water: tea is a luxury. Tea is sipped or slurped
slowly. A pinch of the large green or brown leaves is put in the
bottom of the cup, hot water poured on, the lid replaced. This
ritual is repeated whenever visitors come, and at official recep-
tions. Tea is drunk as an *apéritif* before banquets and dinners.
Frequently as a tourist or official visitor, I have been offered tea,

and then after five or six minutes been invited to move on, not even having had a sip of the tea, which seemed to be purely symbolic. We found the large leaves floating in our teacups difficult to deal with at first, but have developed methods of slurping the tea through clenched teeth, using our teeth as tea-strainers. The best tea is *Long Jin* or *Dragon Well* tea from Hangzhou. It has a truly beautiful emerald green limpidity, and a subtle taste, full of harmonies and overtones. *Silver Needle* tea from Changsha tastes slightly peppery; the local green tea here is very refreshing. *Oolong* tea from Fujian Province tastes slightly smokey. *Jasmine* tea is a delicate red-brown. Hankou tea shop sells over sixty varieties. Most people seem to drink tea out of habit, like smoking, without seemingly taking much pleasure in it. Tea is brewed in all sorts of containers: porcelain cups, tin mugs, screw-top jars, thermos cups, bowls; and the same brew is topped up time and time again. On the train to Wuhan, a sixteen-hour journey, our travelling companion only changed the leaves once, but refilled his cup every half-hour or so. Bus drivers wedge their screw-top jars into a piece of rag on the dashboard and take furtive sips in between gear-grinding and horn-blowing. Chinese tourists on the Great Wall had jars of tea swinging in their net bags of provisions. It is always drunk pure: no milk or sugar, though in Tibet tea is mixed with yak butter. In teahouses all over China, old men sit the afternoons away, playing chess or cards, listening to storytellers, drinking from the same bottomless, miraculous bowl of tea. A big black kettle will circulate, topping up the fragrant brew every hour or so. No question of being moved on because your drink is finished, or being asked to buy another drink. Tea stops time still, you need time to drink in the sights and sounds, and there is no better place to observe street-life and what remains of 'old' China than in a teahouse. Tea is not drunk during meals, except by the Cantonese. It is an ongoing, daylong activity, and an essential part of travelling, as no-one seems to do anything on journeys but sip tea.

U is for Uniforms. In this country, everyone looks as if they're in uniform, and sometimes it's difficult to sort out those really wearing uniform from those just wearing normal clothes. Soldiers of the People's Liberation Army, for example, wear the same dull green jacket and trousers as anyone else, but have a red star on their cloth caps; and railway official's blue is indistinguishable from anyone else's blue until they put on their rather military style hats. My favourites are the policemen, who look like spruce milkmen in their blue trousers and white jacket with smart red trimming.

V is for Vendors and itinerant peddlars of all sorts of things. In Mao's China, these small-scale entrepreneurs would have been branded as 'capitalist roaders', but this kind of limited private enterprise is now permitted, and these purveyors of plastic toys, shoelaces, ribbons and other unconsidered trifles are making a comeback. There is always a small group of people near the campus gates, squatting by the roadside with what seems like a very random assortment of objects spread out for sale on a cloth in front of them: key rings, cheap sunglasses, plastic sandals, socks, buttons, zips, bike parts, hair ribbons, sunflower seeds, string bags . . . Other vendors wheel their bikes, or carry goods on shoulder-poles through the campus, crying out their wares. There is the Egg Lady ('*Ji-i da-a-n*'); the cobbler, with tools and a selection of metal toecaps and heelcaps stored in two wooden boxes, which he carries on a shoulder-pole: the key-cutter, recognisable long before you see him by the clink-clink of two pieces of metal which he shakes in one hand; and my favourite: the rice wine seller, who wheels his bike, big tub of fermented rice strapped to the back, around the campus, with a long melancholy cry of '*Mi-i-i jiu-u-u*'.

W is for *Waiguoren*, which means 'outside-country-person', or foreigner, which is what we are here – and we have little chance of forgetting it. Small children point at you everywhere you go, shouting triumphantly '*Waiguoren! Waiguoren!*'. I am amazed at just how young some of these small *waiguoren*-spotters are: tiny, chubby toddlers, and, it sometimes seems to me, even babes in arms will point a diminutive finger and pipe out '*Waiguoren!*'. It must be about the third word they learn, after Mummy and

Daddy. Children aren't the only ones to succumb to this foreigner-fascination: a young couple passes in the street, she grabs at his sleeve to get his attention, whispering '*Waiguoren!*', and they both turn to watch us walk past. An old woman stops dead in her tracks, her mouth falls open and she watches us in a mixture of curiosity and bewilderment. We stop to buy some fruit at a stall: within about ten seconds a crowd has gathered, eyes wide, mouths open in astonishment, silently staring. It can be quite dangerous to be riding a bicycle behind another foreigner – particularly Jill, hair blazing in the breeze – since people will turn their heads to watch your companion and walk straight into you. I have never felt any hostility in this silent staring, only curiosity and fascination, but it causes a range of emotions in me. Most days, I find I have become immune, and scarcely notice the crowds around me while I'm shopping. Often I try and strike up a conversation, which leads to gales of laughter at my funny Chinese. But sometimes I find myself oppressed and intimidated by the silent stares and long for anonymity – somewhere where I could blend in with the crowd, not be noticed. We must look very strange to people. Jill's long red hair, in particular, attracts a lot of attention, and small children, otherwise perfectly well-behaved, walking in crocodile, holding onto each others' apron strings, have been known to burst into tears and run away howling at the sight! Old ladies are interested in Jill's freckles, and sometimes come up and rub her arm with a finger to see if they will come off. Worried by this, she asked a group of students if we looked repulsive to them. Terribly tactful at first ('Oh no, beautiful golden hair.'), they eventually admitted that, well, yes, they did find one thing rather odd. What was that? 'Coloured eyes.'

X is for Xenophobia. The Chinese have a reputation for possessing a profound mistrust of foreigners, and, given what we have done to them in the past, that mistrust seems perfectly well-founded to me! Historically, China has seen itself as a highly civilised and cultured nation surrounded by barbarians. It has a long tradition of self-sufficiency, of self-absorption, of ignorance of the outside world; and the Chinese attitude to foreigners has traditionally been a compound of disdain and indifference, though anti-foreign feeling has at times been institutionalized: in the last century, for example, it was a capital offence to teach a foreigner the Chinese language. Anti-foreign feeling reached its height in the Cultural Revolution, when people could be severely criticized, even imprisoned for contact with foreigners. The present regime's Open Door economic policy attempts to reverse that tradition by opening China up more and more to outside influences. It also reverses the traditional superiority felt by the Chinese towards the rest of the world, and I sometimes find my students embarrassingly humble, as they talk about how far China has fallen behind, and how much they have to learn from the West. Indiscriminate and excessive contact with foreigners is still frowned on, however, and all contact with foreigners is controlled – much more than we realize, I think. If our students visit us, they have to clear their visit with the Foreign Affairs Bureau in the college first. Should Chinese friends wish to invite us to their house, the invitation must be officially approved by the Foreign Affairs Bureau before it can be given. We have never been treated with hostility, rather with elaborate politeness – the foreigner as 'Honoured Guest'. This isolates you just as effectively – but with infinite courtesy.

Y is for Yellow, which in China means pornographic. The adjective can be applied to books, films, or, very often, music: anything with a heavy beat is labelled 'yellow'. Our videos and tapes were censored by customs officials, checking for 'yellow' material, with one officer solemnly listening his way through a whole box of blank cassettes to make sure there was nothing offensive on them. The film *Fame* escaped the censor – though I would have thought there was quite a bit of 'yellow' footage on that – and we showed it last week. I could feel the ripples of shock passing through the room. We talked about it with the students afterwards. They were a little shocked, but, more than that, mystified: they found the exuberant behaviour of the young dancers quite inexplicable. Opinions on the music varied. One student assured me that it was a medically acknowledged fact that music with a strong beat could cause people to lose control of

32

their actions – and who knows where that could lead? The others rather liked it. 'Exciting, but rather noisy', was the general verdict, and a lively debate ensued on whether kissing or spitting in public was more disgusting.

Z is for Zoos, which I don't like in any country, but find particularly upsetting in China. The reason is that, as a foreigner, you are more fascinating to the Chinese than the animals, and the pandas and monkeys play on unnoticed in their cages while huge crowds gather to stare at you!

Letter three

A DAY AT THE DRAGON RACES AND
A NIGHT AT THE OPERA

Letter three
A DAY AT THE DRAGON RACES AND
A NIGHT AT THE OPERA

30 June 1983

Since last writing, we've had a wonderful two-day trip, all paid for by Hubei Provincial Education Authority. A 5 am start on Tuesday, bus to the station, where we met some of the other foreign experts in the Wuhan area, about 20 in all: Americans, Germans, Rumanians, British, mostly language teachers, some medics and computer experts. We boarded a special carriage, shunted onto the back of the Beijing – Guangzhou express by a gigantic old rusty red and black huffing and wheezing steam engine, and then were trundled at their maximum speed of 40 mph down through Hubei into Hunan Province. Paddy fields, a luminous green, the young rice plants being planted and replanted by stooping figures up to their calves in water, then through beautiful steep hills, past hamlets and towns. We stopped first at a delightful town of about 3000 people, a mere 2000 years old, called Yueyang. It's on the shores of the second largest lake in China: about 60 miles long in a huge U-shape. The Yangtze runs through it. We took a ferry across to a lovely little island in the middle, called Junshan. It was by now pouring with rain, and most people decided to stay on the boat. We slipped and slid our way round, looking at the Dragon Spit Well, and a temple on top of the hill called the Three Times Drunk Temple. The story is that a famous legendary character got drunk three times here and was able to fly across the lake to Yueyang, then wrote a poem about it. Given the incapacitating effects of the drinks we have tried so far, I don't really believe anyone here would be able to drink *and* fly. We then walked, or rather, slithered through a tea plantation (looks just like rows of thick privet hedges) of *Silver Needle* tea, to a Tomb of Two Imperial Concubines, about 2000 years old.

On the ferry back, we were given lunch out of army mess tins with huge rough wooden chopsticks (which are much easier to manipulate than the classier thin lacquered ones) and a bowl of special rice cakes, called *zhongzi*, wrapped in bamboo leaves and tied up with string, looking a bit like green ice-cream cones. Inside is a rather horrible wodge of cold gluey rice, rather like congealed wallpaper paste. We ate them, choking, until someone said that the real idea is to throw them into the water! It is Dragon Festival this week, and apparently everyone throws these cakes into lakes and rivers to feed the dragons, of which more later. With relief, we hurled three cakes into the muddy brown waters of Lake Dongting as we disembarked down a steep slippery gangplank.

We then had tea: delicious delicate flavour. *Silver needle* tea is much subtler than the campus-grown green tea we get in Wuhan. The tea-room was in the bottom of the Yueyang Tower, a mere 1000 years old or so. China's equivalent of Shakespeare and Co, the poets Du Fu and Li Bai, both came here and wrote poems in praise of Yueyang Tower in the 8th century AD.

The pagoda tower was encased in scaffolding. We were told it was 'under construction' – they meant reconstruction. Or did they? A lot of old buildings are being renovated, repaired, or simply built again from scratch, after years of neglect or damage during the Cultural Revolution, when, with the command 'Destroy the Four Olds', Mao sent bands of young Red Guards rampaging through the countryside to find and annihilate anything that smacked of old ideas, old habits, old customs, old culture. Most temples, belonging to all four categories, inevitably suffered, but other more innocent buildings also vanished in the enthusiasm for eradicating anything old. But now the pieces are slowly being put back together again; China is being rebuilt, bit by bit, in a vast act of national atonement for past excesses. It's now all right again for people to be proud of their past, to glory in their cultural heritage, to visit, and even to worship in temples. The only trouble is, you are never quite sure if the Ming temple or Tang pagoda you are visiting really is Ming or Tang and not a twentieth-century reconstruction. The fabulous Hall of Five Hundred Arhats near us in Hanyang, a huge, dusty, cobwebbed place full of life-size bronze statues of arhats, looks untouched. I asked our guide what happened to it in the Cultural Revolution. 'Nothing', she said, 'people liked it too much'. On a subsequent visit another companion was more cynical. 'In China', he said, 'we are very good at making things look old.'

Tea over, we returned to our special carriage, and were coupled to the back of another train for another two hours to Changsha, the capital of Hunan, about 220 miles south-west of Wuhan. We were immediately struck by how much calmer and less industrialized it is. Wuhan is a huge industrial complex, none the less interesting for that, but you can smell Hanyang for miles and a pall of smoke hangs over the city. Changsha is elegant in comparison. We were whisked to a fabulous hotel, set in a lush park with lotus pools, magnolia trees lining the avenue, and grotesque Yogi pandas and deer moulded out of concrete grazing among the bamboos!

We trooped down to supper, thinking of a hot bath and an early bed. Then: 'Please hurry. In ten minutes we go to the theatre.' We gobbled our dinner, got into a bus, and were rushed to the opera. My God, what a wonderful evening! We forgot our soaking feet (no spare socks) and tiredness. It was *The True Story of White Snake*, a traditional Chinese opera, in Hunan style. Opera is a ludicrous word to use. A lot of concepts are untransferable: 'opera' gives a completely false impression. It is more like pantomime, cum circus, cum musical, cum folk dance, cum high drama. The costumes are lurid. The music is loud and clashing, full of percussion and fabulous rhythms. Two-string fiddles, gongs, drums, shawms, cymbals, wood blocks, all hidden to one side of the stage by a gauze screen. The story was very complex, but no odder than, say, *The Magic Flute* which also involves the supernatural and fantastic happenings. A wonderful ghost, big black beard and rolling eyes; very sexy dancing by the two lead singers: White Snake and Black Snake; weird high nasal falsetto singing and dialogue. The girl who accompanied us was very good: she interpreted and explained the symbolism and told us the plot as it unravelled. I think she was probably bored – young people in China tend to think opera is for the oldies – but she didn't show it at all.

It actually turned out to be the original feminist opera, in which deceitful and wife-battering husbands are defeated by true sisterly solidarity. Add to this a dash of anti-religious feeling, with a wicked abbot, a few duplicitous monks, plus plenty of magic: medicinal herbs with strange properties, ghostly armies, pagodas vanishing in thunderclaps, and you have the main ingredients of the plot. Here is the story as we understood it: White Snake and Black Snake are two immortals who change into beautiful girls. White Snake is somehow higher up the social scale of immortality, so Black Snake is her maidservant. White Snake falls in love with a young man called Xu Xian and marries him. She uses her magic powers to set him up in business, providing him with a medicinal herb shop. As the herbs have magic properties, he does very nicely, thank you. But marital bliss is doomed to be short-lived: at this point, enter a wicked Buddhist abbot who warns Xu Xian that his wife is not all she seems to be, and gives him a potion to change her shape. When Xu sees her in her real form he dies of fright (this is where it begins to sound like a feminist parable!). White Snake gives him a potion to bring him back to life, but Xu is not at all grateful, and absconds to the Buddhist monastery where the wicked abbot shelters him. White Snake assembles an army of underwater ghosts to attack the monastery and bring him back. The abbot tries to capture White Snake. Neither side wins, and the abbot realizes he cannot capture White Snake because she is pregnant, which somehow makes her invulnerable. So he sends Xu to live with her again till the child is born. Black Snake realizes this is a trick and tries to kill Xu, but White Snake stops her. As soon as the child is born, the abbot and Xu capture White Snake and lock her up in a pagoda. Black Snake acquires a magic fan and waves it at the pagoda. It disappears in a clap of thunder and she rescues White Snake. The two ascend to heaven, giving up men for good.

It all seems like a wonderfully random concoction of colourful costumes, painted faces, clashing gongs, unbelievable characters and illogical plot. In fact, everything is very highly ritualized, with the characters drawn from a list of stock types, costumes from a few prescribed styles. Make-up is applied according to very strict rules and every stage gesture is part of a convention and has a symbolic meaning. Male characters can be old or young, military men or scholars and gentlemen. Old men wear beards. Young men have falsetto voices. Then there are the *jing* characters, warlike men with painted faces and long beards. The colour of their faces tells you about their character. Red is for courage. Black faces denote a fierce character. Blue faces are cruel and white faces are treacherous. Beards are similarly symbolic. Red or blue beards are worn by magicians. A full beard shows the wearer is wealthy and a tripartite beard shows he is cultured. Moustaches, on the other hand, mean that the wearer is crude and uncultured. Direction is important too! An upward-pointing moustache means a crafty man; a downward-pointing moustache means an uncouth man. Clowns can be male or female, but they always have white faces. There is quite a complex classification for women, as opposed to the simple young/old, civilian/military distinctions between men. Obviously the Chinese see women as having far more complicated characters! Interestingly, they correspond to Western archetypes of women as madonna, whore, witch, wise woman, or adventuress. *Qingyi* is the good girl: matron, obedient wife, or filial daughter. *Huadan* is sexy, flirtatious, with suggestive glances and much play with a red handkerchief. *Caidan* is a wicked lady who walks with long strides. *Laodan* is a wise old woman. Feminists would approve of *wudan*, who is a female adventurer with a mind of her own. All gestures are ritualized and associated with particular characters. Men may laugh openly, for example, but women must cover their mouths with their sleeve to show laughter – a gesture that my girl students still have. Men go in for a lot of tossing of beards, and women make a lot of play with the long sleeves of their robes, throwing them forward and then catching them up again. Even the way characters move across the stage is prescribed: the cultivated man has graceful movements but the military man takes long strides. The *jing* wears platform soles and has high kicking steps. Females take little mincing steps, apart from the *caidan*, who marches across the stage, and the *wudan*, who goes in for acrobatics.

Because of the tone system in Chinese, songs are incomprehensible unless you can see the words, so each line of the libretto was projected onto the wall at either side of the proscenium arch. There were two very short intervals. The dancer-singers were bathed in sweat. Most interesting was the audience which was full of 50–70-year olds, tapping their fingers, smiling in recognition of favourite bits of the story, craning their necks to look at the words, mouthing the words to themselves, getting up, scratching, walking around, talking to their neighbours, spitting, eating peanuts and sunflower seeds. At the end, no curtain call: just a short burst of clapping, the curtain shuts and everyone's off back home, no ceremony, no fuss, everyone in their day-to-day garb of dustman's jackets, baggy trousers, and sandals. Even the bigwigs with whom we banqueted in Beijing or Wuhan make no more pretence to dressing up than a clean shirt and a fountain pen in the top pocket.

The next day was Dragon Festival, and we went to see the Dragon Boat Races. But first to a strange and wonderful exhibition in the museum. The 2100-year old body of the wife of the Chancellor of Changsha was discovered in 1972 in a set of three tombs just east of Changsha. The body is near perfectly-preserved, because it was buried in sealed triple-layer coffins packed with charcoal. An exhibition of fabulous tomb artefacts and the body in a hermetically sealed case: a gruesome vision of death, doll-like, pop-eyed, mouth fixed open in a permanent scream. But it was fantastic to see 2000-year old chicken bones, fruit and vegetable seeds stored in jars, silk socks and undershirts, musical instruments and weapons, all accompanying the body on its journey to death.

Next, into the bus again and off to the races. The river about 100 yards wide at this point, a bridge covered with yellow, pink, red, and green flags and streamers, banks lined with people. Dragon boats, about thirty feet long, prow carved into a dragon's head, men on each side with Red Indian canoe-type paddles, with a drummer and gong beater in the middle, helmsman on a long tiller, and a long paddle as rudder. They row the boat to the beat of the drum 1-2, 1-2, 1-2, and the clash of a gong. The boats all rowed in front of the crowd as if to show their form, then made a big circle in the middle of the river, and then went back to the bridge. We learned that this was a symbolic act, to search for the body of Qu Yuan, a poet who drowned himself in the 3rd century BC. He is a national figure: an adviser to the King of Chu in the Warring States period, he was unfairly dismissed from office by the King who preferred the more flattering advice given by others and listened to malicious rumours about him. In protest against a society that did not know how to value a good man, he committed suicide. Legend has it he declared: 'The world is muddy and I alone am clear, all men are drunk and I alone am sober. I had rather cast myself into the everflowing waters and be buried in the bowels of fishes than hide my shining light in a murky world.' He has a 'Poetry Reciting Pavilion' dedicated to him on East Lake in Wuhan, and is commemorated annually in Changsha, where he drowned himself in the Mi-Luo river, but is remembered all over China, both as the father of Chinese poetry, and as an example of an incorruptible man who clung to his principles and refused to be a sycophant. The Dragon Boat Races seem to have got mixed up with his legend somehow, and the feeding of cakes of rice seems to be both to the dragons and the poet. Anyway, all the boats raced up and down, sometimes singly, sometimes in pairs, everyone yelling 'Jia You' ('Get a move on' or 'Go it'). It started to drizzle, and everyone pulled out umbrellas. A bit like Henley I suppose. Fascinating to see policemen in their white milkman's jackets munching ice-cream, or drinking coke, or strolling around arm-in-arm. Loads of terribly loud firecrackers cracked and spluttered on poles or were thrown at our feet. Kids rushing about, old women staring at us, cadres strutting around importantly, crowds, crowds, crowds of all these people on a Chinese Bank Holiday. I don't know when the actual race took place, if at all; no-one seemed to know what was going on, not even the organizers, who were in a launch with red flag flying and tannoys blaring. I think the whole spectacle was more important than any real race!

Lunchtime, and we boarded our bus back to the hotel, where a huge banquet for about 200 people had been laid on by Hunan Provincial Government. Luckily no speeches were required of any of us, but several were made, which no-one listened to. Our table concentrated on the food, the *maotai* and the other drinks. White wine is like muscatel: sweet and sickly. The red wine is like very bad port, or, in some cases, like neat camp coffee, mixed with liquorice. Very headachy. Beer is excellent, not too strong, lager-like (not surprising, as the first brewery was set up by the Germans in the early 20th century). Hunan food is very peppery, rather like Sichuan food, and quite unlike the bland and oily Hubei cuisine. Bloated, and more than a little tipsy, we staggered back onto the bus again for the station, via a high-speed shopping expedition in the centre of Changsha.

Back at the campus, life is much easier now that we have bikes. We can get to work in two minutes instead of twenty, and get fresh air blowing through our shirts as we swoop down the hill on the way home. We have big black monsters of bikes: *Yongjiu* or *Forever*, made in Shanghai. Comrade Zhao didn't want us to buy these heavy workers' bikes; she thought we should have gone for the lighter, more stylish *Flying Pigeon* models. We found it hard to see the difference. They all come equipped with locks and chain guards and cliplock stands, all to add to the weight, no gears, powerful brakes, big loud bell and lamp clip on the front. But you cannot find bicycle lamps anywhere! Cycling at night is a matter of luck and guesswork. Going out in the early evening we keep an eye on the other side of the road and try to memorise the exact location of all the piles of bricks, heaps of sand, and mounds of wheat that litter the tarmac, for the return journey in the dark. We tried fixing torches to the front of the bikes, but this was a mistake – they seemed to attract pedestrians, like moths, who would stray blindly across the road and stumble into the front wheels.

When we first got the bikes, it was with the proviso that we could only ride them inside the campus grounds: this college is very unused to foreigners and seems terribly scared that we will have an accident, or get lost, or do something we shouldn't, if we are allowed out unchaperoned. But we cheerfully ignored the ban, and they seem to be becoming reconciled to the fact that they have to let us out of their sight sometimes! There are some wonderful bike rides on paths and tracks through the little hamlets and farms around the campus: paddy fields and tea plantations, water buffalos and lotus ponds everywhere. We have taken to bike rides after work, in the lovely evening light.

Everyone sits out on these warm evenings on low benches and stools around the doorways, chatting, playing music on bamboo flutes or two-stringed fiddles, having a last game of chess before the light fades.

We often get invited to smoke a pipe or have a glass of tea, but our Chinese isn't good enough to sustain a conversation yet, though we are having lessons three times a week now. A lot of time is taken up with tone drills, which make me despair of ever being able to speak properly, as our teacher races up and down through the four tones like an opera singer doing voice exercises. One of my worst confusions is with the word *tang*, which spoken with a rising tone means 'sugar', and spoken with a flat tone means 'soup', so I am always baffling the kitchen staff with odd requests and they stare at me incredulously as I ask for some soup to put on my porridge. For all they know, it could be a strange Western custom. We manage quite well with day-to-day requests and a little light shopping, though we got into a ludicrous situation the other day, trying to buy toilet paper at the campus shop. The assistant didn't understand us and called all the other assistants to help. A crowd gathered. No-one understood. No-one understood our drawing of what we wanted either, though one assistant helpfully produced a light bulb and another tried an electric plug. With a crowd of about thirty people around us, we drew the line at miming, though this would have probably cleared up the misunderstanding, and we slunk off home to borrow some from the neighbours.

We have been given Chinese names now. I am Ji-Li, which means 'Good Luck', and Charlie is Cha-Li, with no particular meaning. The characters in his name mean 'Search' and 'Reason'. He translates it as 'Looking for Excuses'. We are having seals carved with our name in characters. I was born in the Year of the Rabbit, so have a seal carved in the shape of a rabbit. Charlie chose a fat and smiling Buddha, which is how he reckons he'll look after two years of Chinese food!

The food we get is consistently good. We have a nice old cook who comes from Shanghai and can do some Western dishes, since in pre-Liberation days he used to work for a British official at the Hong Kong and Shanghai Bank, whom he refers to as 'my master', which we find upsettingly colonial. So we are occasionally surprised by chicken pie or egg-custard, but mostly we have very good Shanghai cuisine, slightly sweet. Shrimps with green peas, stir-fried cucumber, beancurd in sauce, pork with garlic shoots. We get a lot of fish – river fish – cooked whole, with one eye staring up reproachfully out of the sauce. There's more fruit around now – there didn't seem to be any when we first arrived – and we've had some small hard peaches and lychees. We have tried various experiments with breakfast. Chinese breakfast of rice porridge with pickle or peanuts was too much culture shock too early in the morning, and we have opted out of the boiled egg, steamed bread, and sleepy teacher style breakfast on offer at the dining-room, in favour of tea, fruit and mooncakes (small pastry cakes stuffed with mincemeat and dates) back at home. The only thing wrong with our diet is too much protein! Most Chinese get very little protein: a daily diet of rice and vegetables and beancurd, with meat on special occasions. They have a vision of the Western diet as composed entirely of meat, and in their anxiety to provide us with Western-style luxury, they have neglected roughage almost altogether. They were amazed at our request for less meat and more vegetables. I hope it didn't look like ingratitude! We also had to request smaller helpings – it felt obscene in a country which is barely self-sufficient in food to be leaving meals uneaten. Westerners must look so large and overfed to the Chinese that they imagine we all have gargantuan appetites.

I'm not yet used to the rhythm of things in China. Decisions seem to get deferred for weeks and then things start happening with alarming rapidity. Take the teachers' hostel for example: the newly-built block where six of the other British teachers live. For about ten days, while we were in the hotel, not much seemed to be happening: a few workmen asleep outside, a couple of old ladies with paintpots . . . then suddenly the Dean of the college arrived back from a lecture tour, took stock of the situation and announced that we would be moving in the next day. We didn't believe him, since the place still looked like a building site, but the next morning a minibus arrived to transport our luggage to the campus — people had worked all night on the hostel! It's the same at every level from planning courses to requesting paper: protracted negotiations, stalling, then everything happens in a rush; the clash of our 'go get 'em' culture which wants things done by yesterday, and the slow but sure Chinese method which wants things done in their own good time and according to the rules, which seem to be partly subconscious social codes, partly a very creaking bureaucracy, mainly the fact that no-one seems prepared to take responsibility for anything in case they get it wrong. Much of our bewilderment must be due to the fact that we, of course, do not know how their system works. We do not understand their decision-making process, and will probably never learn much about it. So much is hidden from us: it's rather like being a child again in an adults' world, where things are mysterious and unexplained; you are fenced around with prohibitions you don't understand and decisions suddenly swoop down on you from above. One afternoon last week we were suddenly told: 'Dinner will be at five o'clock tonight instead of half past five.' 'Why?' 'Because you are going to the theatre in Hankou'. The Foreign Affairs Bureau had arranged a trip for us to see the Urumqi Regional Song and Dance Ensemble. The evening was a real treat, actually, despite the abruptness of the announcement. Very different from the Chinese opera, and more Russian in flavour: girls with long plaits and embroidered skirts worn over trousers, men with Russian style hats, everyone in boots. Wild music and whirling, flying dancing. A comic wrinkled-faced old man who did trick balalaika playing: upside-down, back to front, even behind his back. The whole evening had an exuberance and a flamboyance that seemed entirely un-Chinese, though the wholly Chinese audience lapped it up. One song was unmistakeably Chinese though – a catchy little number which went: 'We are proud and happy to make the grasslands so fertile, thanks to the Communist Party.' Most of the audience seemed to find this quite funny.

I'll end with a few snapshots and a quote from a student letter: Chickens everywhere, all over the campus, pecking and scratching in the bamboos. Early mornings: shuffle of sandalled feet in the darkness outside our house; runners everywhere in vest and shorts; people fetching breakfast from one of the communal mess halls, taking it back to their families, or eating as they go; women coming back from shopping at the free market, net bags full of vegetables; students wandering around, reading to themselves, mouthing the words. Several are teaching themselves English and memorizing long lists of what seems like completely random vocabulary. 'Dumpling', you will hear them mutter with great concentration as they stroll among the bamboos, 'Radar', 'Lampshade'. 10 am mid-morning break, and the paths and balconies are full of students and teachers doing exercises or *taiji* in time to the music on the loudspeakers.

Children, plump and round, like solemn-faced dolls, surprisingly brightly-dressed; the little girls with gaudy ribbons in their hair, the boys often wearing a miniature army general's or airforce cap. Toddlers wear split pants to save on nappies. Children have very few toys, and those they do have are very simple: a ball, a wooden push-cart, a metal hoop and stick.

Feet of all shapes and sizes. I want to take a film, scores of slides of nothing but feet. Kid's bare feet running through the dirt, old men's slow feet shuffling in cracked plastic sandals, feet in the traditional cloth shoes, black cord or velvet with a strap, flat cloth soles, fashionable in England, but out of vogue here. When I bought a pair, my class was disdainful. 'Oh, no-one wears those any more', they said, 'only really old people: people over thirty.' Old ladies feet, tiny, cramped, painfully hobbling, and you cringe at the thought of the little girl screaming as her parents forced her footbones into shape all those years ago. Some daring fashions: high heels, cuban heels, buckles, some lurid colours of purple and bright green, but mostly shoes are flat and sensible. Sandals are never worn without socks, which come in startling colours, transparent nylon, and sweaty in summer.

Sounds. The two really distinctive Chinese sounds are spitting and shuffling. The sound of feet in plastic sandals slopping along the pavement and the grating, then explosive noise of hawking and spitting, together with the squawking of chickens and the ring of bicycle bells are a constant background to our daily life on campus. Add to this the burbling tannoy; the sound track of the Saturday night film, audible all over the campus; the sound of children from the nearby primary school chanting their lessons in unison; mutterings of students memorizing their textbooks as they walk down the path; the metallic click of heel caps, fixed incongruously to sandals; the cries of the occasional peddlar, and the campus sound-picture is complete. In the cities, the spitting and shuffling still go on, but are drowned out by other sounds: the cacophony of bicycle bells and car horns, the constant cheap popular music blaring out from street corners and the cries of ice-cream sellers, knife-grinders, key-cutters, shoe-repairers advertising their wares.

Workers putting a roof on the building opposite; a wonderful system: sand and cement in two long piles, two workers turn them together with shovels, a third mixes in the water. Two more carry the mixture in buckets on bamboo poles over their shoulders to the pulley system – a long pole on a tall strut. A bucket is hooked to one end and a man presses down on the other. The bucket goes up to the men on the roof, who send down an empty bucket in return. There is just enough concrete in the bucket for the men to spread before another bucket comes up.

Finally, from a student sick-note: 'Dear Teachers, I am terrible sorry not to come to your useful and charming lessons, but I am still ribbed with illness and a dire headache is torturing my brain.'

Letter four

FLOODS AND HOT WEATHER

Letter four
FLOODS AND HOT WEATHER

20 July 1983

The main news these past week is the floods – you would be very impressed by the sight of the Yangtze in recent days. It is very high due to the heavy rain, and streams down the middle at about 12 knots. Last Saturday, Jill and I caught a ferry back to Wuchang across the mile-wide muddy brown stream. The ferry is like an old Isle of Wight ferry, crammed to bursting with people, shopping, bicycles, and chickens. In the middle it was making no headway at all, and was actually moving backwards at one point! Eventually it summoned up the strength to push against the flow and moved nearer inshore. The sides of the river are well banked up, after the disastrous floods when it burst its banks in 1954. That year, most of Hankou, Hanyang and Wuchang were under water, as Wuhan is the place where the Han, itself quite a big river, meets the Yangtze. The Yangtze is threatening to burst its banks again and the Han is already flooding; an army of about a million have been mobilized to cope with the floods. The college is on high ground some way outside the town, so we are not in danger, but the middle of Hankou was an amazing sight last week with hundreds of people, trousers rolled up, silently sloshing through almost knee-deep water, bicycles up to mid-wheel, buses and trucks splashing through. About nine or ten streets were transformed into rivers; all the ground floors of the houses and shops were flooded. People were busy moving all their furniture to the upstairs floors and, when a little weak sunshine appeared, hanging all their bedding out to dry – the centre of the city was festooned with quilts! But the most surprising thing is the apparent unconcern: people going about their normal daily business with stoical indifference, the rush hour taking place as usual despite the river-like streets. And the resourcefulness: flooding in the paddy fields near the college leading to a surfeit of fish, everyone comes along with acres of net, which they fix up on poles to trap the fish when the rain stops and the water drains away.

We have been to another opera since last writing and are fast becoming addicted. This was performed by the Wuhan Opera, and was more of a ballet really. A much more polished (but rather blander) performance than the last opera we saw, and in a very posh air-conditioned theatre with a statue of the Great Helmsman outside, and quotations from his writings engraved all round the foyer. The opera was about Qu Yuan, of Dragon Festival fame, and told the story of his fall from power due to the evil influence exerted on the king by a wizard and someone called Bad Person. Wizard cast a spell on Qu Yuan, while Bad Person got the ear of the king and persuaded him that he should ally himself with a large and powerful neighbouring state, disregarding Qu Yuan's advice. Bad Person eventually got power, ousted Qu Yuan, and deposed the king, who died in exile. Qu Yuan continued writing poems to the memory of the old king and reading them out to Bad Person in the hope that they would shame him into goodness, but Bad Person was irredeemably evil and took no notice. Qu Yuan therefore had no alternative but to drown himself in the river in a splendid final scene, where the shadows of swimming goldfish were projected onto the backdrop from an overhead projector full of water at the front of the auditorium. Some interesting instruments in the orchestra – we wandered over to have a look in the interval – two-stringed violins called *erhu*, and an instrument like a zither, very like one we saw in the 2000-year old tomb in Changsha museum. Moon-shaped lutes and mandolins, flutes and shawms, a percussion section with gongs, drums, sets of carved wooden blocks graduated in size, and an instrument with small pieces of stone hanging from a wooden frame. Most interesting was an enormous instrument that looked like a set of gigantic copper bagpipes. The base was a huge bowl with about a dozen pipes sticking up out of it, a copper tube for mouthpiece and accordion type buttons. A friend who accompanied us said it was called *sheng* and 'looks like a phoenix with its wings spreading out and also sounds like a phoenix'. Only one or two of the musicians had Western music notation with clefs and staves. Most had lines of numbers with some indication of rhythm: 654_812. All the music was transcribed by hand. All the musicians were in shorts and shirts or vests and had with them enamel mugs containing green tea – a quick slurp of tea or drag on a cigarette between bars!

Some snapshots: Saturday night cinema on campus. The film begins at 7.30 in the huge open air cinema and from about 7.00 there is a steady stream of people from all over the campus, each carrying a stool, and an umbrella if the weather looks bad, making their way to the cinema where admission is a couple of *fen* and the film is shown on two enormous screens. Rain doesn't deter people and neither, apparently, does the cold weather in winter, so we'll need our warm winter woollens then. We've been to two films: one was *Di Sange Ren* – 'The Third Man'! Incongruous to see the shots of old Vienna with the bats flitting across the sewers and to see Orson Welles dubbed in Chinese and hear everyone talking about 'Hally Rime'. The other film was Chinese – a mixture of slushy-romantic and politically educative. About a love-affair between a man and a woman in the same work brigade: idyllic scenes of moonlit rambles and bathing in mountain streams and picnics under the plum-blossom, but all very chaste and innocent – no kissing, not even an embrace! Then the political bit: the gallant young worker, the flower of Chinese manhood, was made the victim of a criticism-struggle session by bad elements under the evil influence of the Gang of Four and cast out from the People's Commune. Hard times followed and the film traced his wanderings in a country running riot under the crazy regime of the Gang of Four until finally he was reunited with his true love under a more correct ideology and the future began to look rosy again as they went forward hand-in-hand to work for progress and the Four Modernizations.

Telephones: these are not really a viable means of communication in China. At least, they may be in Beijing or Shanghai or Guangzhou, but in the provinces they certainly are not. There are no private telephones in China but work units or blocks of flats will have a communal one. Everyone shouts on the telephone. The phone rings, you pick it up and an unknown but deafening voice is shouting '*Wei! Wei!*'. The correct answer to this is '*Wei!*

Wei!'. This can go on for quite some time, until one of the people finally identifies himself. Even ringing other people in the same town is not easy, requiring several attempts and a lot of shouting. Phoning Beijing from Wuhan requires half a day's preparation, and the voice the other end is barely audible, as if coming from the other end of a long dark tunnel. We have only communicated with England by telephone once. When the news about the floods reached England, our employers phoned to see how we were. The only word either we or they could hear was 'floods', so the conversation went like this '. . . . . floods?' '. . . . . FLOODS!' They hung up, still wondering whether we were about to be submerged.

We've had some experience with Chinese medicine recently, as both of us have been ill. Only with colds and stomach upsets, but we were immediately whisked off by our unit leaders to the campus clinic – a fascinating experience. A rather sleazy, dingy building, several small rooms leading off from a central corridor, but all completely open, no doors, so you can stare in at the examinations, injections, blood tests taking place. In the main consulting room there are as many as four or five examinations going on at the same time. We were examined at the same time as an old lady with earache, a girl with toothache, and a small child with a sore throat. All examinations take place under the stare of at least a dozen pairs of curious eyes! Plus the student interpreter, who very helpfully did my flies up for me after I had had an enormous antibiotic injection. But the medicine certainly seems effective. Some antibiotics – tetracyclin – and two gigantic glucose and vitamin C injections (they seem very keen on injections here) and then a vast range of herbal remedies for every different symptom. For Jill's cold: sneeze pills twice a day; cold tea, sort of honey-tasting brown granules, four times a day; cough grains, very small black grains to be counted out carefully, twenty to be taken twice a day; and laryngitis pills, ten at a time. The laryngitis pills contain: 'Rhinoceros Horn, Pearls, Bear Gall, Cowbezoar, Musk, Toad Cake etc' (we've both been speculating about the 'etc'). The sneeze pills are advertised as being 'for the treatment of snivel and nostril clog.' For my stomach upset: several glass phials of red grains – 100 twice a day, and a diet of rice porridge, brought over by Comrade Zhao in mess tins. We dutifully took our grains and tea and were as right as rain in a couple of days.

We've been learning Chinese chess, and Jill's reputation has gone up no end with the students since she actually beat some of them the other day! A fascinating game: cannons take by jumping, chariots zoom around all over the board, king and bodyguards have to stay within the nine palaces, and ministers cannot cross the water. I am struggling with the complexities of *Go*. *Mah-jong* next. I'd like to learn some of these Chinese card games, played on long cards with a system of dots, like dominos.

A nice 'chat corner' with a group of students who told me about Chinese customs. Yunnan Province at Spring festival has 'a game which the girls like to play with the boys.' It involves throwing a parcel of rice, which the girls may catch with both hands, but the boys are only allowed to use one hand. If the boy drops the parcel, he has to pay a forfeit: give the girl a present of some sort. If he hasn't got a present, he has to take off some clothes (couldn't find out how many) and give them to her. He then comes round to her house a few days later to collect the clothes. If she loves him, she will have washed them. If he loves her, he will bring her some sugar. What happens, I wanted to know, if he brings the sugar and gets dirty clothes in exchange, or if she gets no sugar in return for the newly-laundered clothes? That's life, it seems! Other interesting anecdotes emerge, like the 45-year old student in my class who remembers having to kow-tow to his parents every morning.

From today's Chinese lesson: 'Old Wang very likes drink wine. Requests wife buy two bottles. Wife says money not enough, not willing buy. Old Wang says invite people eat food not buy wine not viable (succinctly put, my sentiments precisely). Asks wife buy half fish buy one bottle wine can not can? Wife says all right, but evening you not allowed eat fish.' Sounds OK to me say Old Wang.

30 July 1983
We are now officially half-way through the Great Heat, as this month used to be called. Names of the months in the old Chinese calendar (they sound like Red Indian names to me):

Beginning of Spring	4	February
Rain Water	19	February
Waking of Insects	6	March
Spring Equinox	21	March
Pure Brightness	5	April
Corn Rain	20	April
Beginning of Summer	6	May
Grain Full	21	May
Grain in the Ear	6	June
Summer Solstice	22	June
Slight Heat	7	July
Great Heat	23	July
Beginning of Autumn	8	August
Stopping of Heat	23	August
White Dew	8	September
Autumn Equinox	23	September
Cold Dew	9	October
Frost's Descent	24	October
Beginning of Winter	8	November
Slight Snow	23	November
Great Snow	7	December
Winter Solstice	22	December
Slight Cold	6	January
Great Cold	21	January

Gives you some idea of what to expect! I'm not looking forward to Great Cold. Back to the subject of Great Heat: the thermometer now reads 115 degrees in the midday sun! Out in Hankou, most people have their beds in the street, like low tables made of bamboo and straw. The sky is a brilliant cloudless blue, after all that rain, and it's really not too humid – certainly not as bad as a couple of weeks ago when our clothes and leather shoes started to turn mouldy. Teaching is bearable too, though by the middle of the morning (i.e. about 9.30!) you are drenched with sweat and get progressively less and less energetic as the day goes on. The students are flagging, and have been for a week or so, poor things – sleeping five to a small fanless room is no fun. 'We are like five ovens in there', one of them told me last week. One even went to sleep on the concrete floor of the classroom last night in an effort to get cooler. The others told me with delight in the morning, 'Look how clean the floor is – that's because Tao-Tao has been rolling round on it all night!'. The situation is made worse by the fact that the college term ended two weeks ago, all the other students have gone home, and we're the only department struggling on. This is because we didn't start teaching until May, and they wanted to make the term a decent length: next year we'll stop on July 15 with everyone else.

We have our first graduates this week, and there will be a mini graduation ceremony on Wednesday, followed by a Chinese knees-up on Wednesday evening. The students are all very excited about it and we are very curious to see what will happen. Dancing is officially frowned on and 'yellow' music is banned. The students, however, are very keen to have us teach them to dance, as they don't want to be at a social loss when they go abroad.

The young teachers that we are training leave for Britain in a couple of weeks. They will spend about six months on a training programme there, and then come back to work along with us. We gave them a farewell dinner this week, complete with *apéritifs*, Western food, darts match, and lessons in how to use a knife and fork. We had an English visitor last week: Sally, the woman in charge of the training programme in England, came over to liaise and get a better picture of what was happening. Her visit led to two strange incidents. She was supposed to arrive on the 12.36 train from Guangzhou. Professor Zhang and I got a car down to Wuchang Station. Of course, no 12.36 train existed and the next train from Guangzhou was anyway delayed. So I thought I'd take Zhang over for a drink and a snack at the Railwayman's Arms or something like that, but no institution like a pub exists here. There are dark, hot little noodle shops with strange smells and gigantic woks simmering over charcoal pits, with meals for a few *mao*, where Jill and I have enjoyed eating on weekend jaunts into Hankou or Wuchang. But Professor Zhang insisted that we could not go to one of those, he would have felt ashamed to take a distinguished foreign guest into such a place. He maintained that there was nowhere to eat near the station, though my eyes could plainly see queues of people waiting in line for their noodles (did you know that Marco Polo discovered the noodle and took the idea back to Italy in the thirteenth century?), I said I'd be very happy; he got more and more embarrassed. Eventually, I suggested that I wait for the next train at 14.25 and he could go back to the college for lunch; I'd bring Sally and her luggage back on the bus. No, no, he would wait, and I should go back for a proper lunch at college. 'But what about your lunch, Professor Zhang?' 'Oh, I can eat down here.' 'But why can't we both eat down here?' and so on, round and round in circles. In the end I had to agree to go back to college, while he waited at the station on his own. Then he asked to borrow something from the driver. I thought he needed money, and reached for my wallet. 'No, no, you see to eat here I have to have a rice ticket.' I think that was the real cause of the problem; he thought that I would be refused food without a ration ticket and this would be embarrassing. Either that, or he thought foreigners were too posh for noodles. Or another deeper reason or rule of etiquette that I can't fathom. There's so much we don't understand about Chinese etiquette, as we found out when we were told on the evening before Sally left: 'There's going to be a banquet, and we invite you to be the hosts.' 'No,' we said, 'don't you mean the guests?' But no, they meant the hosts: it was a sort of double-decker invitation: the college gave the banquet in Sally's honour, on our behalf: we were thus the hosts and she was our guest. Banquet highlights included red braised fish, eel, fish paté, and 'Mother and Child chicken': a chicken in bits, head, body and legs made up to look like a real hen, with chicks made of mashed potato! As kitsch as it sounds, but very skilful. Best was turtle stew – something like jugged hare, with a rich gamy taste. Throughout, constant *ganbei* competitions. *Ganbei* means 'empty glass'. This means that when drinking a toast, you *must* empty your glass in one go and point it at your drinking partner to prove you've drained it. This meant half-a-dozen beer races with the Dean and the Head of Basic Courses, a marvellous, wily old guy with pebble glasses and mouth full of black teeth, who, at the conclusion of a couple of *ganbei* bouts, said to me: 'I see, Mr Han Cha-Li, you can drink the sea. I am not a good drinker, but I think in this matter we will co-operate very well. *Ganbei*!'

We were proudest of the fact that we spent the whole two hours talking in Chinese! We managed to hold a reasonably interesting conversation and crack a few jokes. After a couple of months we are on Lesson 8 of course book plus cassette and have achieved lift-off at last. Suddenly, patterns emerge and the stream of meaningless noise surrounding us splits up into small chunks, bits of which you recognise as words. Wonderful! The same thing on a much smaller scale with the characters. I have been practising writing and altogether reckon I can recognise about fifty characters, write about twenty. Chinese grammar, reasonably simple at first, with its absence of articles, tenses, and verb endings, which leads to a very telegraphic style of communication, is getting more complicated with prepositions that sometimes change colour and behave like verbs. Even a little knowledge of the grammar does help to correct the students. For instance, the word 'afterwards' contains the same root as the word for 'behind', which means that all our belief in the future being ahead of us, and the traditional language teacher's gesture of pointing ahead to indicate tomorrow, may simply baffle the Chinese student. There must be many more snares hidden in the differences of grammar.

31 July 1983
While Charlie was wrestling with the finer points of social etiquette, I had an interesting week helping my students with applications for universities abroad: most of them have so little knowledge of the outside world that they are completely confused by the whole business. A Tale of Two Students: one didn't turn up to the lesson last Monday, and the others said, 'Oh, he's just heard that he may be going to Canada and he's phoning to see if it's true.' He came to find me at lunchtime and said yes, it was true, he had to leave for his unit the very next day, but had no idea where he was going or when, not even sure what course he was being sent on. He and I both agreed that he could do with a couple of months more English before studying abroad, but he was totally passive: 'It's for my unit to decide, I can do nothing.' So off he's gone, not really knowing where or why. Another

61

student sent off for details of some courses that interested him and came to me with the application form – completely baffled, overwhelmed by the element of choice more than anything. He couldn't make up his mind which course would be best, or when to go (there were four entry dates a year), and after a few minutes discussion I realised that it was not simply a matter of talking over priorities and reasons as it would be in the West; I actually had to provide him with the criteria or framework for making the choice. He was so unused to having to choose, so completely at sea, that he couldn't even formulate the bases for making the choice, and clutched at everything I said, like the proverbial straw. What he really wanted was to be told what to do.

We've had the same problem with the evening activities. We provide two or three alternative activities each evening, like university clubs and societies, on the assumption that the students will choose the one they're most interested in, but we ran into difficulties the first few weeks and were told: 'There are two activities this evening. The students can't do both. Which should they choose?' We show a film three nights a week, and the first couple of weeks were very problematic, as the students didn't seem to understand the concept of choosing which night they wanted to see the film, and all tried to get in on the first night!

A conversation with three students, cycling up to the centre: I asked why people cycled so slowly in China. 'Oh, everything is slow in China.' 'Except when you get orders. Then you have to move really fast!'

Some interesting conversations with students in 'chat corner', where we talk about everything from punk rock to the Cultural Revolution. From everyone the same story about the Cultural Revolution: people went crazy, no-one knew what was happening, or what they were meant to be doing, and the whole country was embroiled in what was practically a civil war. The idea, apparently, was to show who was most loyal to Mao Zedong thought, and warring factions developed, each claiming to be the Only True Interpreters of his thought. Quarrels arose, and often developed into armed conflict. Wuhan University even now bears the marks of machine gun bullets, where two armed factions, the 'Million Heroes', branded as reactionaries, and the

'Workers' General Headquarters', who claimed to be the true supporters of Mao, fought a pitched battle. In this and subsequent battles in Wuhan, thousands of people were killed, injured, crippled. And this all over China! Mao's theory was that revolution should be permanent, and to this end he mobilized the country's youth as the vanguard of struggle. Millions of idealistic young people from all over the country joined the 'Red Guards' to destroy 'The Four Olds' and root out the ideologically impure, but somehow the idealism went sour, and the crusade turned into a wild orgy of vandalism. Schools were closed, education totally neglected. To quote one student: 'My teacher said, 'There is no school today: please go to the revolution.' Cultural and historical relics all over China were destroyed, but worse than this was the cost in human terms: people were denounced, persecuted, made the target of struggle sessions, where they were publicly criticized and humiliated, paraded through the streets wearing dunce's caps. Friend betrayed friend and children denounced their parents.

There are some horrible stories: one student's father committed suicide to escape his persecutors. Intellectuals, whom Mao called 'the stinking ninth category' of bad elements, along with other undesirables such as counter-revolutionaries and landlords, bore the brunt of the attacks and were exiled to the countryside away from their homes and families to do manual labour. Everyone has a story to tell. One professor was sent to break stones on Hainan Island; the entire staff of the Forestry College in Beijing was exiled to Yunnan Province in south-west China. One student, a professor of landscape architecture, who, in his own words, 'teaches trees', was sent to build roads. It broke his heart to have to cut down so many trees! One girl had tears in her eyes as she told me her story: her parents, both cadres, were made the victims of a struggle session and sent away for re-education, leaving her, at the age of nine, in sole charge of her younger brother. No-one explained to her what had happened, but she was publicly dishonoured at school by having her red Young Pioneers' armband ripped from her arm in front of the whole school. Her parents sent her money, but it was never enough. She wasn't allowed to see them. On leaving school, she got the highest marks in the whole province in the examinations, but because of her parents' background, was refused permission to go to college and sent to work in the fields. She continued to study by herself in the evenings, and after the Cultural Revolution and the fall of the Gang of Four, obtained permission to go to university.

Teaching and research seem to have ground to a more or less complete halt, though many teachers exiled to the countryside seem to have done some unofficial teaching wherever and among whoever they found themselves. Among my students, the older ones are bitter about the loss of time: 'I lost the ten best years of my life, when I could have been doing scientific research', said one, and another, very bright girl said, 'For eight years I stayed at home, pretending I was an ignorant housewife, hardly daring to talk to anyone. Now I have to try and make up for lost time, and find myself competing with much younger people.' The younger students had their primary and secondary education interrupted by the Ten Years Turmoil. They are, in general, very highly specialised in very fine disciplines, but lack a broad educational base – we have found them appallingly ignorant about the outside world. Most of my class did not know where Mexico was, for example, and the other day, someone asked me what language people spoke in Australia. 'It's all right for you,' they said when I expressed surprise, 'your middle school education wasn't interrupted by a revolution.'

Television programmes are often full of Cultural Revolution reminiscences: a programme yesterday featured a ballet dancer and a pianist, complaining how the heavy farm work they had been forced to do had ruined their careers. There is a whole literary movement, called 'Literature of the Wounded', devoted to description of the personal suffering caused by the Cultural Revolution. Much of this is official Party policy – a national tendency to blame everything from the lack of technical progress to the decline in public morality on the Cultural Revolution, and, not Mao himself, but the Gang of Four, who are the national scapegoats for everything – but there's no doubt that the Cultural Revolution was a horrific and mindlessly destructive nightmare of violence, the psychological scars of which China still bears. I'd like to know the peasants' side of the story though: how did *they* react to the influx of townies into their homes and villages, and how do they feel when they hear intellectuals or artists complaining about the degrading work and terrible living conditions they had to endure in the countryside? There is a great divide, if not exactly a class system, in China, between the intellectuals and the peasants. Before we came I found it difficult to see why poor old intellectuals were in the same class as landlords and other wicked privileged people who must be eradicated from society – surely intellectualism wasn't a basis for class division, but there is – and this in a country where the President of the college turns up to meetings in his baggy blue worker's trousers and moth-eaten vest, and the Director of the whole project, down from the Ministry in Beijing, sleeps on a bamboo bed with mosquito net in a corner of the office and eats rice and beancurd with the students – a certain snobbism to be detected among educated people towards the uneducated. 'Uneducated' is quite a strong criticism in China.

Most students and teachers at college and university seem to come from the 'intellectual' class, though there are some who have arrived by a different route. One of my students wrote in an introduction: 'I worked in a factory for two years. Then I was a farmer for five years before starting my studies. The only pity is I have never been a soldier', a comment I found rather obscure at first, until I learned about the worker-peasant-soldier tradition. Worker-peasant-soldier students are people whose class backgound was impeccable by revolutionary standards. Most people got into university through competitive exams, but during the Cultural Revolution these were abolished and a large number of ideologically correct workers, peasants and soldiers were admitted. These people had great prestige during the Cultural Revolution, when intellectual was a dirty word, but now with the big rethink of values and the new emphasis on progress and achievement, these people are rather looked down on. I notice that, of the two people with this background in my class, one is shy and diffident about himself and the other is constantly trying to prove he is better than the others, so I detect something of a working-class complex there. Reactions among my students to their *xiafang* or rustification experiences were almost uniformly negative; they regarded it as a waste of their time and their talent. When I told them I had worked in a factory and as a hospital cleaner out of choice, they were astonished and uncomprehending. Only one girl had any positive feeling about the experience: starry-eyed with idealism, she spoke warmly of how kind the peasants had been to her, and said that it was direct knowledge of how hard the peasants had to work and how important agriculture was to the Motherland that made her decide to do agricultural research.

The students had interesting comments on the after-effects of the Cultural Revolution: a sort of backlash of indifference. They seemed to feel that people no longer trusted each other as they used to, that the whole country feels it has been sold or duped – conned into a ten-year long mass hysteria, and that the naive and idealistic excitement of the early revolutionary days has been replaced by a mood of national cynicism.

3 August 1983

Just back from the Chi-knees-up. The graduation ceremony this afternoon was in a huge dingy amphitheatre and consisted of the inevitable speeches. One by the Director, saying how proud he was of the new graduates, and urging the students on to greater efforts. One by a spokesman for the departing students, expressing gratitude and hopes for the future. One by a spokesman for the students who will be returning next term, saying how 'moved they were by the British teachers' hard work and kindness', and expressing the determination to work hard for progress and for the Motherland. All very stirring stuff. This evening, a charming celebration put on by the students, who had all put 50 *fen* in a kitty to buy plum juice and sunflower seeds and sweets and pears. Each class did a turn – a song, organised by the class monitor, and there were some individual turns too: songs, animal imitations, and music on the mouth-organ, flute and *erhu*. We did a sketch and a funny song in return. All introduced by community singing: 'Solidarity for ever (× 3) for the Party makes us strong', to the tune of 'John Brown's Body'. Then the students wanted to see us dancing. They all have an avid curiosity about

Western dancing, but were too timid to join in – some ran off and hid! We did eventually get some of them dancing, but they were overcome with embarrassment. They could not understand that there are no formal steps in disco, and thought we just didn't know them. A spokesman for my class said to me, with that delightful Chinese frankness that I am coming to love, 'If we had realised that you danced so badly, we would have never asked you to dance in front of everyone.' Sedater Chinese dancing eventually took over – waltz type, but with very complicated steps, men dancing with men and girls with girls.

It continues to be very hot – 124 degrees (in the sun) the other day. There are beds out all over the campus now, a couple cunningly rigged up on the basketball pitch with mosquito nets strung up to the goal posts. Students are tired in the morning after a sleepless, sweaty night, and by midday no-one has any energy. Exhausted and sweaty, Charlie and I too have taken to the custom of the midday nap. I am constantly surprised at how consistently good-humoured, affectionate, and full of fun the Chinese are, despite the living conditions – piled into the little rooms like sardines, the exhausting heat, and the food, which is awful when they get it, and sometimes non-existent (several times in the last weeks the cook hasn't provided enough, so that late-comers don't get any). Through it all they are charming, smiling, always pleasant, full of jokes, and despite the physical proximity they live in, very tender and respectful of each others' feelings. They seem to know how to manage their space very well. Other things that surprise me are their naivety, their romanticism, and their astonishing creativity. They are extraordinarly fresh and innocent: girls of 25 behave like 16-year olds, and in general they have a childlike spontaneity and enthusiasm. I have never been in such an uncorrupt nation. Charlie's image of China is like one gigantic kindergarten. (I think it's more like a cross between a kindergarten and an army camp.) There's a total absence of sexual self-consciousness as well. Some people hold the theory that the Chinese are repressed; I think it's more like a childlike state of innocence. Girls all wear the same unisex shapeless blouses and loose trousers as the men, and now in summer, little-girl skirts and ankle socks, or Sunday-school frocks with sashes and puffed sleeves. They all sit in class totally unselfconsciously with knees apart, displaying quite a large acreage of brightly coloured floral patterned bloomers. The men don't appear to notice.

Romanticism surprises me too in one way, but I suppose in another it's an obvious outlet in a society where so much is bleak and drab. In a society that seems so sexually innocent, romance is of the teenage magazine, holding hands, moon-in-June variety. Chinese films are unashamedly slushy, the country is full of sentimental chocolate box art and the Western films that have achieved the greatest popularity among our students are *Love Story* and *On Golden Pond*. *The Sound of Music* is also a big hit. Everywhere you go, you can hear tannoys broadcasting *The Hills are Alive* or people humming *These are a few of my Favourite Things*. Chinese romanticism always contains the same stock elements, as these two quotes from students writing about happiness will show:

> For me, it is impossible to imagine happiness now without her love. She has been my classmate now for the last three years. I have not words to describe her excellences. She works hard and constantly for the glory of her country and the good of the Party. In my class she was class monitor and I was social secretary, so we had many opportunities to meet and discuss. But she did not know my love. One night I determined to tell her. You cannot imagine how nervous I felt! I will never forget that night: the moon was bright, the air was sweet, the environment was exciting. She was very surprised when I confessed; she had not imagined anything. She did not share my feeling, but agreed to continue to meet me. We saw each other often and eventually she agreed to become my wife. We have known each other well for over two years now and although we cannot get married till the year after next, it is knowledge of her love that is the main reason for my living.

> I will never forget the night I fell in love with the girl who is now my wife. We were walking along the bank of a river, the waters made a sweet noise, the moon was full, there was a soft breeze blowing, the scent of flowers was on the air. Since then many years have passed but the feeling is still the same. We now have two children. We live a simple life, but full of happiness. On Sundays, my wife and I play football with our children in the park. My wife and son are one team,

my daughter and I are another team. The neighbour's daughter is the referee. We live in a small flat, we have no comforts, no TV, but we are happy.

But what is so striking about these pieces is their freshness! It is as if the clichés are still new in China, not yet worn out. The age of the students who wrote the pieces? 31 and 42! It is unimaginable that Western men of that age would write with the same innocence, freshness or lack of sophistication – or that they would put such things on paper for their tutor! Come to that, I can't imagine anyone in the West writing it – even 15-year olds are too sophisticated! Another student wrote me an (unsolicited) essay called *My Elder Brother – Love or Hate?*, a totally unselfconscious and uninhibited outpouring of his complex feelings of admiration, jealousy, resentment and bewilderment. I have never been in a society where feelings are expressed with so little self-consciousness. The Chinese don't seem to operate at any distance from themselves, as we do in the West. Affection is very openly expressed – though not between the sexes – and you often see men walking hand-in-hand, or girls with their arms round each other. My class often hold hands with each other while working. Quarrels and disagreements seem to be equally public – everyone joins in: a crowd of twenty or thirty people gather round, taking sides, shouting encouragement. The students say this isn't a common sight in the rest of China though, and that Wuhan has a reputation for quarrelsome people, particularly in the summer as the temperature rises and irritability increases. I suppose the openness of emotion is to be expected in a society where people live together in such proximity. As to the lack of self-consciousness, there just isn't room for distance from oneself or from other people. But the lack of self-control or self-censorship surprises me in a country where there is so much public control and censorship. I suppose that's in the realm of opinions though, and it's emotions that are freely expressed. In the West we express our opinions publicly, but are more guarded about our emotions.

We are off tomorrow! I can hardly believe it – it's been a tiring and sweaty end of term and we don't really feel prepared to go. But we're booked on the 8 pm boat down the Yangtze to Wuhu,

69

thence by bus to a mountain called Huang Shan, where we'll climb to the cooler heights and stay in monasteries on the way. After that we'll go to Hangzhou and Suzhou, and then either north via Xian and Luoyang to Chengdu and another mountain called Emei Shan, or south via Guilin to the same mountain. Either way, we plan to return via Chongqing and a three-day boat trip through the Yangtze Gorges back to Wuhan. The other teachers have similar plans, but everyone is going their own way: an individualism that our Chinese hosts found hard to understand. They imagined we would all go round China together, as an organised tour with guides and interpreters, and were amazed to find we had other plans. They were somewhat reluctant to let us go our separate ways, and wanted to arrange the whole tour for us, but we, horrified at the thought of spending all holiday in a big group, as well as every waking hour in term-time, insisted, and they gave in. They must find this Western need for personal space and individuality very anti-social! – they actually feel lonely if not part of a big group, and seem to have no desire to get out and 'do their own thing'. All this adventure is hard to visualize: we lead such a sheltered existence here, with people taking care of our every need – you never need to venture outside the campus really. It feels rather like the first step out of hospital or prison, although there has been enough adventure and experience within the campus walls to have kept us constantly entertained, diverted, stimulated, or just plain puzzled for the last two months.

Letter five

AROUND CHINA

Letter five
AROUND CHINA

16 September 1983

We've been in China four months today! In some ways it feels like yesterday that we stepped off the Chinese Jumbo at Beijing's tiny deserted airport, but in many ways it's all beginning to feel comfortably familiar, things have lost their novelty. I am no longer surprised by the split trousers, the bicycles, or the tortoise sellers; shopping, once a bewildering nightmare, is beginning to seem as routine as Sainsbury's on a Saturday morning, and coming back to Wuhan after our month-long holiday felt like coming home – it was pleasant and reassuring to see the chickens scratching around, the red brick houses, and the odd familiar face.

You can never completely relax though: China seems to have an inexhaustible supply of surprises, like the revelation yesterday that three Public Security men accompany us every time we go to the opera 'to make sure we don't get lost and that no-one steals our handbags.' I must say I had wondered who the extra bodies in the minibus were, but assumed they were just stray campus opera buffs. Or the not so pleasant news that the tannoy will be on all day today (Sunday) broadcasting live the public trial and sentencing of about eighty violent criminals, thieves, rapists, and murderers, a lot of whom will probably be executed. There is a steady procession of people from all over the campus, carrying stools, so presumably there is some central meeting place. We are mercifully out of full blast of the tannoys here, can just hear an echoing burble in the background through the bamboos. In one's day-to-day dealings with them, the Chinese have such humanity, subtlety and humour, that it's a rude shock to be confronted with something like this.

But what contrasts you see every minute in this vast country. Travelling round gives you a peculiar impression of uniformity:

the same clothes everywhere, the same items in the shops, the same black bicycles, khaki green lorries and jeeps, or big black-curtained limousines, the same exercise music at precisely the same time over the whole country, and, from Shanghai to Kunming, the same minutely tended countryside, like one vast kitchen garden. But there is also the shock of violent contrasts: a wayside stall selling Japanese cassette recorders for example, a brand new apartment building in the last stages of construction fenced about with swaying bamboo scaffolding, an old woman bent double pulling a wooden handcart laden with *Hitachi* TVs, the flicker of a colour TV set inside a tiny two-room house containing nothing else but bed, mosquito net, bamboo stool, and gas ring.

We started our travels on the Yangtze; caught a boat down-river to Wuhu, a 24-hour journey, and a very relaxing way to start the holiday. After two months in the Wuhan heat it was very pleasant to float down the river with a bit of a breeze and have nothing to do but read, eat, and snooze. We were constantly entertained by the choice of music over the ship's loudspeaker; most incongruously, the theme tune of the trip seemed to be the 'Blue Danube'. The lower Yangtze flows through a plain, so the scenery was not dramatic, but occasionally we would go through a series of steep limestone hills, rather like Guilin, of which more later. Small industrial towns line the river and old pagodas covered in grass and weeds would be next door to a smoking power station or brick works. The river was very full after recent floods and we zipped along; boats coming upstream really had to fight their way against the current. Wuhu we only saw in the dark, as we arrived late in the evening and left at 5 the next morning on a jolting unsprung local bus that stopped about every ten minutes on the eight-hour journey to pick up and set down peasants, with great baskets of vegetables, bunches of chickens tied together by their legs, or wooden barrels full of eggs packed in sawdust. Part of the bus journey retraced our route back along the Yangtze, and we saw how much damage had been done by the floods: fields submerged, whole villages under water. We stopped a couple of times in little towns (I suppose you'd call them one horse, but in China so many people are around to do the heavy work that it doesn't really fit), and had the most delicious snacks of deep-fried rice cakes with peppers and garlic, and spicy beancurd in their equivalent, I suppose, of a transport cafe. We were on the main road south from Wuhu, no wider than a country lane and much bumpier. Often lined with plane trees with white paint on the trunks, a bit like France, but for the fields behind: hills seemingly built up of layers of horizontal segments, every available piece terraced into paddy fields. Water everywhere, dribbling through channels to keep the level up under the rice. People everywhere too, carrying loads across their backs on poles, stooped over the rice, squatting, staring into space, even lying in the road asleep. When they lie in the road, they always seem to have their head towards the middle! And road sense is not something that has developed here. Our bus had three horns. One was a fairly normal honk-honk which was used almost continuously, providing a bass continuo to the rhythmic jolting of the vehicle, with the odd pause as the driver took his hand off to grind the gears painfully. The second was a high-pitched scream which was used to frighten old ladies, chickens, other vehicles (no-one took a blind bit of notice, but it kept the passengers awake, so maybe that's its main purpose). The third was truly horrendous, like some screech from a devil in a Chinese opera. This was in use in towns when no horn could do anything to unjam the milling crowds but a bus driver has to vent his frust-ration somehow at being stuck behind four handcarts and a posse of cyclists, and perhaps it's better he presses a button to do so than get out and fight. But bus travel is marvellous! You are in the heart of the country and you can stop every few hours for a stroll round villages and towns you can reach no other way. The disad-vantage is a numb bum after two hours but that is counterba-lanced by the relief when the bus breaks down unexpectedly (we had two breakdowns and one wait due to a lorry crash) and you can get out and stretch. And when you do eventually reach your destination, you feel you have worked to get there.

Huang Shan was full of tourists, but no other white ones – all Chinese or overseas Chinese. It reminded us very much of a spa town in the Alps or Pyrenees. Stone houses, trees, a gorge, a stream with healthy water, a bath-house and the delightful feeling that the whole place was dominated in everyone's mind by the thought of a big famous mountain waiting to be climbed. However, as we stayed longer we began to notice the subtle differences. First, the trees swaying in the breeze on the slopes opposite were not trees but big bamboos (they sway particularly gracefully and delicately) and the Chinese mountaineers were not loaded up with expensive rucksacks in gaudy colours, hiking boots, ice-axes, and all the other paraphernalia that people seem to need in Europe. A string bag with some tins of fruit, a screwtop jar of tea, a knobbly stick, a pair of plimsolls and they're off: people of all ages, shapes and sizes, puffing and panting up the steep stone staircases. Very hard work, moving your feet up steps: you bend your knees more than you would on a path, quite apart from having to go at a snail's pace because of all the other people. We're used to going to mountains for peace and solitude, but this is a mass pilgrimage.

Huang Shan is a very famous 'scenerous spot' because of the pines, weirdly shaped rocks and pinnacles, and swirling mists. In fact all the ingredients of a typical Chinese painting, which is actually called *shan shui huar* or mountain-water-painting. Motifs from Huang Shan are used all over China: on calendars, on biscuit tins, on this cup I'm drinking from. So everyone comes to admire what millions of people have admired before and called beautiful. So you must have a photo of yourself or your family lined up in front of the beauty spot. No-one seems to take photos simply of scenery, with no people in. We took a lot of pictures of Chinese tourists taking photos of each other. They adopt very coy and self-conscious poses, like in the 30s. But on top of all this, Huang Shan is indeed extremely beautiful. The pines are twisted in strange shapes above swirling clouds, rock pinnacles appear everwhere through the mists, and there are dizzy drops on all sides.

We could have stayed days at the top, but disaster struck and Charlie broke his foot! Up at four o'clock to see the dawn, in company with several hundred other people, we watched a watery pink sun emerge through a sea of clouds over serried ranks of shoulders in identical blue quilted jackets (standard monastery dawn-watching kit: we were wearing them too), and to the accompaniment of spitting, belching, and coughing. Charlie's accident happened incredibly quickly: he just turned his foot over going down a step in the dark, and within about half a minute it had swelled up to twice its usual size and become a lurid combination of colours. Rather more spectacular than the sunrise actually! The descent took eight and a half hours of painful hobbling, though offers of help came from all sides and he received no less than four bamboo sticks, several aspirins, sweets, apples, some evil-smelling green embrocation, plasters with 'ointment to reduce swelling', and a foot massage from a beautiful female barefoot doctor (wearing gymshoes). A charming old couple, an architect from Nanjing and his wife, waited for us near the bottom to show us a quick route to the hotel. Anyway, this meant that the rest of our holiday was devoted to a comparative study of medicine in different parts of China: the first aid post in Huang Shan where plasters and ointment were applied; a Red Cross hospital in Guilin, where we had an amazing trek through kitchens, back yards and people's living quarters to find the X-ray machine, 1940s, German, and where the Head Consultant was summoned in person to apply a cardboard splint to the foot; and a teaching hospital in Chengdu, where another ancient X-ray machine confirmed the fracture was mended and an elderly, very distinguished grey-haired consultant removed the splint and told us the story of his English friend who had worked with him in a Shanghai hospital for twenty years before Liberation, and had returned to China on holiday last year and died in Shanghai. He seemed rather pleased by the fact.

Anyway, the foot episode was added spice, rather than a serious hindrance, and didn't stop us doing anything we had planned, except climb Emei Shan. Our next stop after Huang Shan was Hangzhou, reached via a beautiful, but excruciatingly uncomfortable eleven-hour bus journey, for the most part along winding dirt tracks and unmetalled roads on a rickety old bus that freewheeled all the way down the mountains. We were thoroughly relieved to reach Hangzhou and sink into a bit of Western decadence – an imposingly monstrous piece of Soviet architecture called the Hangzhou Hotel, grim and forbidding from the outside, but inside full of such delights as baths, beds with real sheets, and cold beer – American: *Budweiser*! (One of the strangest things about China is the occasional Western luxuries that surface in unlikely places: Kunming yielded *Coca Cola* and Chianti; Chengdu, Cheddar and *Mars* bars!) And all this for 12 *yuan* a night. As 'foreign experts' we can stay anywhere for the same fixed price (tourists were paying 40 *yuan*), and get train, plane, and boat tickets at a reduced rate (tourists pay about double the Chinese price).

Hangzhou was bliss, and we spent three days strolling along willow lined causeways, taking slushy photos of Jill in romantic poses by the lake against a background of lotus flowers, drifting around idly in boats, spending whole afternoons drinking the delicious *Dragon Well* tea in the various tea-pavilions on the little island on the lake, observing the Chinese on holiday, and viewing the 'Ten Prospects', some of which were:

> Autumn Moon on the Still Lake
> Impressions of the Moon above Three Deep Pools
> Lotus Stirred by the Evening Breeze near the Distillery
> Watching the Orioles in the Waving Willows
> Sound of the Evening Bell at Thunder Peak Pagoda
> Observing the Fish at Flower Harbour

The Chinese seem to have a passion for labelling their landscape – every rock, pinnacle and pine-tree on Huang Shan is similarly labelled: Pinnacle for Viewing Clouds, The Pine Tree in Welcoming Posture, The Flower Blooming from a Poet's Pen-nib in a Dream – they have a propensity for making art out of nature and turning a country walk into an aesthetic experience.

Hangzhou was a lovely place to rest up after the descent of Huang Shan, though in fact we didn't discover the foot was broken until Guilin three days later when it started hurting properly. We hobbled around West Lake and to a beautiful monastery with cliff carvings of Buddhas (saved during the Cultural Revolution, apparently, by the personal intervention of Zhou Enlai, who also saved a huge Pagoda of the Six Harmonies near the river). The monastery is now working again and has a delicious vegetarian restaurant, where we got into a long beery

78

conversation with a family on a Sunday outing. The cliff carvings were in a wood opposite: overhanging trees, and slippery paths swarming with people.

From Hangzhou we took a 36-hour train ride to Guilin. Our comfortable night's sleep was wrecked by a man in the berth below us, who chainsmoked all night in the dark, despite our pleas and noisy coughing. It turned out in the morning that he was quite an amiable old buffer who was coach for a schoolkids' acrobatic team! The ten-year old kids would keep flocking in for a bit of English practice. As an English teacher in China you never actually stop work. Strangers always come up and say, 'Where you from?', launch into a self-criticism of their English, and end up by asking, 'What are my weak points?'. Often they are more interested in pulling out the phrases they have learned than in listening to your replies, and this can lead to conversations which sound as if they come straight from the Theatre of the Absurd. Even on the top of Huang Shan we held a mini-English lesson. In the Alps everyone would have been ignoring each other and concentrating on the view. Here they flock round to peer at the exotic fauna – foreigners!

Guilin is in all the guide books, and photos of the area abound on Chinese calendars. It has 'limestone karst scenery' – though don't ask me what karst is. The limestone hills are indescribably strangely-shaped, about three hundred feet high, mostly covered with shrubs and trees, and they rise almost vertically out of an otherwise flat plain. The most spectacular bit, a three-hour boat trip down the Li River to a little town called Yangshuo, is an incredible journey through prehistoric scenery – I almost expected to see dinosaurs emerging from the bamboos. The river was full of small craft made of three or four bamboo poles joined together, slightly curved at the ends into a gentle scoop shape, carrying great loads of vegetables up and downstream, ferrying people from one side of the river to the other, or used by cormorant fishers: old men with their black birds, each with a ring around its neck to prevent it swallowing the fish. There were also hordes of small boys, swimming in the river and waving to the boat. No girls, which the French couple next to us took as conclusive proof of female infanticide. Despite government policy and education campaigns, many peasants still regard girls as not only inferior but a positive misfortune, and suspiciously high boy–girl ratios have been reported in parts of the countryside. Anyway we saw no girls in the river, but we did see a few on the bank, which made me think that the reason for the lack of girl swimmers might simply be that swimming is a macho activity.

Guilin itself was the least pleasant town we visited in China – ruined by a too rapid Westernization and too many tourists. It was the only place where we felt commercially exploited: hordes of street vendors, pestering and insistent, and bands of small children offering to change money: Foreign Exchange Coupons (FEC), the tourists' funny money, which is convertible, for *Renminbi* (RMB), the Chinese currency, which is non-convertible, at a rate of 100 FEC for 120 RMB – officially illegal of course but taking place quite openly on the streets of Guilin. The only place, too, where people have tried to take advantage of my Western gullibility to charge inflated prices, something the Chinese would ordinarily never do: normally they are scrupulously honest in shops and there are at least fifteen people watching to make sure you get the right change. Though I suppose state-owned restaurants and hotels don't set a very good example with their two-tier price system for Chinese and foreigners! Guilin actually felt more like Morocco than China – everyone on the make. Maybe China is beginning to lose its innocence – too many tourists too quickly perhaps.

Guilin is also a victim of the uglification that affects most Chinese cities. Gradually, the maze of low, one-storey houses built around courtyards that forms the centre of a traditional Chinese town is being pulled down and replaced by rows of faceless concrete apartment blocks – a pattern we saw repeated everywhere from Hangzhou to Chengdu. One of the strongest impressions left in the mind by a trip round China is . . . bricks! It seems as if everything is being either pulled down or put up and the whole country is one enormous building site. It is one aspect of the modernization programme that is worrying us. China is very proud of its rehousing policy, and there are endless programmes on television showing architects working late into the night for the good of the country and the benefit of the people, and shots of model families in bright new apartments with three piece suites and colour televisions. Certainly, living conditions in the old ramshackle wooden houses in the city centres do seem, to Western eyes, appalling: most families live in a couple of rooms at most, no running water, public toilets and a communal pump or stand-pipe in the street. But the impression one gets wandering round in the streets is not of squalor or misery, but of a wonderful sense of companionship and warmth. A lot of living goes on in the street – people spill out of their houses onto the pavements, and everywhere there are groups of people eating, talking, women sewing or knitting together, small children laboriously copying characters, or chanting lessons in groups, a few people gathered together to sing songs to the accompaniment of flute or *erhu*, old men playing cards, shouting, slapping down the cards, babies and toddlers being passed around for a cuddle, a group of neighbours admiring an old man's new canary. One of the great strengths of Chinese society seems to be their solidarity, the warmth of their relationships, and this is, in part, due to the communal living style – nothing is secret, nothing is private. This is sometimes hard for Westerners to cope with, but what we see as irritating nosiness and an intrusion into our privacy, they see as a way of caring.

Anyway, I just hope that these sterile new apartment blocks don't do for China what they've done for the West and lead to the fragmentation of society and the alienation of the people that live in them. Fragmentation of communities began in the Cultural Revolution anyway, with the policy of sending urban youth to the countryside to work, and continues now to some extent with the policy of job assignments, which often separate people from their parents and even husbands, wives, or children. Alienation and disillusion also seem to be an aftermath of the Cultural Revolution, particularly among young people. A social problem much talked about at the moment is 'Hooligans'. This is how the Chinese translate *liu-mang*. We would probably say toughs, or wide boys. *Liu-mang* are a new problem in China. Their emergence is blamed on the Cultural Revolution, which, it is felt, created such moral turmoil that today's youth, born in the 60s and brought up in that turbulent period, have become disaffected, alienated, with no secure values to hold on to. They have been christened 'The Lost Generation'. 'Born in famine, brought up in chaos', people say. Most young people in China today say they are not interested in politics; they have had enough ideology. But what is left in China if you take away the ideology? What do these young people, whose parents idealistically called them Li Love-China, or Wang Serve-the People, believe in now? Televisions? Tape-recorders? Refrigerators? Will they call their children *Toshiba* or *Sony*? Actually, China's problems of disaffection seem mild compared to those in Britain, and their *liu-mang* are not nearly as frightening as ours. But you don't have to step very far out of line to be noticeable in China. *Liu-mang* are recognisable in the streets by their swaggering walk and their clothes: Hong Kong imports or copies of imports, jeans, cord denim or gaberdine jackets, cap worn at an angle, fag in mouth. It's considered cool to wear sunglasses, preferably with the label still on. But although they look positively innocent compared to Hell's Angels or Skinheads, China's crime rate is creeping up: signs of the West's malaise are beginning to show here too. China seems to be in a very sensitive state at the moment. What happens to a naive, idealistic and essentially religious nation when they are told that the religion they followed so passionately for the last couple of decades was a sham and a con-trick and are given no new religion to replace the old but the god of material prosperity and economic progress? That the Cultural Revolution was a big mistake and that the Gang of Four were very bad elements indeed has been official Party policy for a long time. What is new seems to be a gradual reassessment of Mao. Very careful, delicate, veiled criticism in the papers is becoming more common. Statues have been removed from public places. One of my students was laughed at by the whole class when she said her favourite poet was Mao, and another student referred to the Great Helmsman as 'our so-called great leader'. But there could be a switch in attitude at any time. When Charlie went to Wuhan Airport to pick up some boxes of equipment, he was surprised to see, behind a pile of crates in a warehouse a huge, cobwebbed statue of Mao, gathering dust. 'Is that for import or export?' he asked Professor

Zhang, who looked worried and said 'Sshh'. It seemed that the statue had been removed from public display outside the terminal building, but fearing a shift in policy, it had been thought prudent to save it in case of future rehabilitation . . .

Anyway, after Guilin, another 36-hour train journey took us to Kunming – a complete contrast, and in my opinion, one of the pleasantest cities in China. 6000 feet up for a start, so wonderfully cool. Called 'The City of Eternal Spring', Kunming is 60–70 degrees all year round, with trees continually in blossom. And so far has escaped too much modernization, in its far-off south-western corner. In fact life there has a distinctly pre-Liberation flavour: the city is full of wonderful teahouses, crammed to overflowing with old men, chatting, playing games (the only place where we saw *mah-jong*, banned for many years), snoozing, smoking huge hubble-bubble pipes, or listening to storytellers. The parks too were full of storytellers: every pavilion had a rapt audience listening to an old man telling a tale with dramatic pauses and gestures, or to a musician playing the *erhu*, or to two old ladies singing a verse drama in parts. A society of grandparents and grandchildren: parents are out at work, so young and old make their own entertainment in the park. Kunming had many specialized street markets too: one whole street would be full of chicken-sellers, another of aubergines, another of flapping fish and squirming eels. Best of all was the pigeon-fanciers' market: old men eagerly examining, discussing and haggling over different varieties of pigeon in bamboo cages. But what we appreciated most was the colour! Most of China's 55 minority nationalities live in Yunnan Province, so the town was full of people in brightly coloured and richly embroidered national costumes. It made us realize that we have been suffering from visual starvation and were hungry for colour after three months of drab green, blue, and grey.

We were somewhat trapped in Kunming actually, as there was a five-day waiting list for a train out! (Only one train a day in either direction.) One of the hazards of travel in China is that you cannot always do exactly what you planned. Our plans to return to Wuhan via the Yangtze were similarly frustrated, owing to the shortage of tickets, and many of the students returned late this term for the same reason. Still, Kunming was a pleasant enough place to be trapped in, and we ran into several other travellers while we were there (most of whom were complaining bitterly about the difficulties of travel in China), including a charming pair of gay San Francisco psychologists, with whom we had many intense and earnest breakfast-time conversations about guilt hang-ups. Beats the *Times* crossword any day!

One day we went down to the Xilin Stone Forest, about 70 miles by bus, with an interesting party of French Canadians who were 'roughing it' round China. Amazing how much people will pay to 'rough' it; though actually their trip only seemed to be rough insofar as it was appallingly badly organized. The Stone Forest is extraordinary, like a limestone cave with the lid taken off; seemingly a network of stalagmites with no companion stalactites. These rock pinnacles twist and turn upwards for 50 or 100 feet from a high heathland, and cover an area of several hundred square miles. There are little ponds and pools in between, and parts of it really do look like tangled petrified forest. It was drizzling and the rocks seemed to change colour and shape under the rain as we walked. As we rounded a corner we saw a bear . . . jumped back, froze, and then realized it was just another lump of rock!

From Kunming to Chengdu the train goes through (literally!) some very impressive mountain country, but it was a bit like a trip on the underground much of the time, as a good half of it is through tunnels. The work, which took many years, was only completed in the mid-seventies, so some work must have gone on during the Cultural Revolution. This summer when it was so wet, many stretches were washed away in landslides. For much of its length, it's single track. I now understand why we got stuck in Kunming.

Chengdu we found oppressive from the moment we stepped out of the train. The station was fantastically crowded. It took us twenty minutes even to find where the exit was and another thirty to get out. We knew the hotel was miles down through the city and we'd need a taxi, but couldn't find any. There were scores of pedicabs: passenger tricycles which must date from the twenties, so old and rusty and heavy. We swore we'd walk rather than take one of those; it seemed so colonial and exploitative to be pulled by another human being, but they were so insistent and wanted our fare, it was late and we were tired after the journey . . . Culture shock and moral dilemma! At the last moment we suddenly spotted a little scooter cab, like a Vespa. We chugged down the wide city streets, past a huge statue of Mao, the biggest we've seen yet, fountains playing and flowerbeds full of bright red flowers, and were very relieved a) not to have taken a pedicab and b) not to have had to walk!

Chengdu had had a big build-up. Everyone we met had said how nice it was, but after Kunming we found it disappointing. We both got headaches and sore throats from the pollution, and spent most of the time trying to escape the town. One day we went north by bus to Dujianguan, where the river was diverted into a vast complex of irrigation channels in 271 BC by one Li Bing and his son. It is in use to this day and now regulates the water supply for a vast area of agricultural land. A typical Chinese thing is to have temples dedicated to such useful people as engineers or soldiers. The temple by the dam had maps of Li Bing's project, statues etc. Is there an English church dedicated to Jethro Tull or Brunel? Because of The Foot we couldn't ford the river at one point, so instead went uphill and through the old city walls, where there was a village spread out under the trees. Old women spinning and two men operating a strange device that looked like two huge violins, to fluff up cotton to make quilts. There was a violently swaying bamboo bridge over the torrent, and in the temple the finest grotesque animal carvings on the roof beams that we've yet seen.

For two days we made another sortie, to Leshan, that really was the high spot of the trip for both of us. This small town is about 150 miles south of Chengdu, near Emei Shan, the Buddhist mountain that we couldn't climb because of The Foot. Facing the town, on the other side of the river is the *Da Fo*, or Big Buddha. He is seated, facing out over the confluence of two big rivers, staring out to Emei Shan. He is 220 feet high, carved out of the red sandstone cliff, 1200 years old. His hair is bushes, ferns grow out of his ears, rain has created tear streaks down his cheeks, his eyes seem to wink knowingly at you. You get a boat across the river. Stairs mount the cliff through woods, past many carved, eroded statues in the sandstone. Suddenly you come face to face with him, on a level with his eyes. We managed to get a sampan along to his feet. Two boys poled us along against the current to a cave in the rocks. We clambered over the rocks and into the cave, crawled through the cave to a hole in the rock at the other end, and then suddenly we were staring up from by his toes. Each toenail over a metre long! It was like a mixture of the Famous Five, Rider Haggard, Gulliver, and Ozymandias. He really is an incredible sight, but since Leshan is rather out of the way, there were very few tourists there; in fact to get there we had to take train, bus, horse and.cart, plus some walking. It was worth it!

Nearing the end of our holiday, we returned to Chengdu and spent a suitably autumnal afternoon to suit our mood, at Du Fu's house, just outside Chengdu. Du Fu lived there in the early 760s and wrote some of his best poems there. His house also serves some of the best tea we tasted, and we sat in the teahouse for a whole afternoon, with our bowls constantly refilled from an old black kettle. Last moment of peace, as the journey out to Chengdu airport (!), hotel(!!) and the grim evening we spent there with a vile meal under the whine of mosquitos and the glimmer of 40-watt bulbs are best forgotten. Aerodrome is perhaps a better word for Chengdu, with its flyblown handpainted posters advertising radar equipment, and crowds of people with string bags of bananas and oranges, and cardboard boxes of household equipment, queuing for the flight to Lhasa. Chinese air travel really is unique in the world – I hope! Inside the small ancient Russian built propellor planes, Ilyushins and Antonovs, the hostess serves green tea from a kettle and hands out boiled sweets to suck for the pressure. At the end of the journey you get a souvenir: paper fan, puzzle, or plastic key-ring. It must be like air travel in the twenties was, with the same anxiety about weather and basic safety.

Letter six

A WARMLY WELCOME TO
OUR WATERWORKS

Letter six
A WARMLY WELCOME TO OUR WATERWORKS

30 November 1983

By the time you get this it will be very nearly Christmas, a fact which seems hard to believe as I sit here typing on the balcony in the late afternoon sunshine, cocks crowing in the bamboos, sound of children singing from the nearby primary school. Autumn seems to be the pleasantest season in China: brilliant blue skies, sunny days, crisp mornings and clear cold nights; always a knife-edge of cold beneath the sunshine, though. We are trying to last as long as possible in summery clothes to harden ourselves up for a winter of teaching in unheated classrooms. Not so our students who are up to two and sometimes three pairs of long-johns already – we are placing bets on what the winter record will be. (Digression on underwear, which is voluminous and brightly-coloured: huge baggy bloomers for the girls, technicolour vests for the men, and in winter, long-johns for both sexes. In general, the drabber and more dreary the outer garments, the brighter the underwear, and the unrelieved monotony of blue jackets and trousers in the winter, or the insipidity of the summer pastels, is enlivened by the bright green vests visible under the white nylon shirts, or a glimpse of brilliant crimson long-johns flapping around the ankles below the trouser bottoms. The lurid vests and long-johns also double as tracksuits and sportswear, and the campus in the early morning or at four o'clock is full of bright crimson joggers or electric blue volley ball teams. We are all intimately acquainted with our classes' underwear in all seasons, but particularly in summer, when most clothes are transparent – a fact which is neither exciting nor particularly revealing due to the adequacy of the underwear.)

We've been on a few trips since last writing, the first of which was a five-day trip to Shashi and Jinzhou in northern Hubei, courtesy of Hubei Provincial Government in honour of National

Day. National Day is October 1 and it closely follows the Autumn Moon Festival. On both occasions we were invited, or rather, summoned by Hubei Government to banquets along with all the other foreign experts in Wuhan.

Moon Festival is an occasion for feeling nostalgic, missing your family, staring at the moon, eating mooncakes (*yuebing*) which are heavy mincepie structures based on solid sugar mixed with fig, walnut, chocolate, or dried meat. Not good for the teeth! While we were at a rather dull banquet (or are we simply getting used to them?), our students were having a Chi-knees-up in the vast neon-lit cement-floor dining hall, eating mooncakes, missing their families, going out to stare at the moon, and getting quite drunk. When we arrived back, also quite merry, we cycled up and actually into the dining hall, and were met by merry moon-festive students. Two teachers had a bagful of firecrackers, which we lit and threw around, and then everyone wandered romantically down to the lake to eat more mooncakes, stare at the moon and miss their families again. I think the same thing happens at the Spring Festival. They are very good at mooning around missing their families, and this is in fact an age-old tradition; civil servants, those who had time to write poetry in the old days, were often sent to posts miles away from their loved one. Many poems by Li Bai, Du Fu, Wang Wei and others could serve as examples, but this one by Li Bai is particularly famous:

QUIET NIGHT THOUGHTS

Before my bed
there is bright moonlight
So that it seems
like frost on the ground:

Lifting my head
I watch the bright moon,
Lowering my head
I dream that I'm home.

The second occasion was to celebrate the 34th anniversary of Liberation. A Western-style buffet, though it included some very un-Western items such as roast sparrow, and a speech by the Governor of Hubei, very elegant in a grey silk Mao jacket. The cadre next to him had a stylish black jacket, which, with its stand-up collar, made him look as if he was Bishop of Hubei, but I suppose there's no such person. Still, the next day at Jinzhou museum, we were introduced to a 'Mr Wang, curate', so maybe there's some Anglican conspiracy among the cadres.

To get to Jinzhou, we had a bumpy and monotonous ride across the Yangtze plain, in Japanese minibuses designed for midgets: cramped seats and no leg-room. Fields of cotton bushes, covered with cotton wool balls ready for harvest, alternated with the usual procession of paddies, hamlets and water-buffalos. Whenever we stopped for a leg-stretch, a crowd would materialize out of nowhere. We stare at them, they stare back; the mutual fascination could be no greater if we were little green men just stepped out of our *Toyota* space craft. After ten minutes or so we jump back in and soar skywards leaving a group of baffled villagers. It's quite probable that many of the people in the countryside where we stopped had never seen a foreigner before. One of Jill's students comes from a little village in Hubei, where no-one had ever set eyes on a foreigner. When he went back during the summer holiday, the villagers all eagerly crowded round to know what his foreign teachers were like. When he told them that his teacher had red hair, they were frankly sceptical. 'Come off it,' they said 'you can't fool us. *No-one* has hair that colour!'

On arrival in Jinzhou, we were taken to a half-finished hotel and then to the museum, where, apart from the 'curate', we met a 2145-year old man, the one-time county Governor. A polite notice on the stairs says, 'Now go downstairs and see a man corpse please'. He was buried in some sort of pickle, which kept him in a nearly alive state: flexible skin, elastic joints etc, until 1975 when they unearthed him. For all its interest, the museum was in a terrible state: dusty battered cabinets, flyblown glass, condensation, mildewed labels. Like the forgotten cases of moths in Natural History rooms at school.

Next day we drove miles and miles up into the hills where we visited 'a household raising snakes'. Silver Circle and Golden

Circle snakes, deadly poisonous, bred for their medicinal qualities. They extract the venom, then pickle the body in *maotai* for some weeks. The resultant brew is apparently good for cardiac trouble and rheumatism. The snakes were in a pit, coiling round trees like tropical plants. They are like some fungi: beautiful but deadly.

The reason for our visit? Hubei Government aren't going to take you on a five-day tour of farms and factories for nothing! This was a good example of the success of the 'Individual Responsibility System'. As from two years ago the commune system began to be dissolved. Each peasant household is assigned land and makes a contract with the government to produce a certain amount of whatever staple crop is farmed in that area. This is then sold in state shops, and is purchased with ration tickets. Any surplus may be sold by the peasants, either to the state, in the case of cotton, for example, for which there is no private market, or on the free market. Each peasant household also has a private plot, where they can grow what they like and dispose of it as they wish. The Snake Farm was an example of one family's use of their private plot. Land can be sub-contracted, or rented out, but all land belongs to the state. This system replaces the 'Eating from One Big Pot' policy of the Mao years, when all land was collectively farmed in accordance with production quotas determined by the state. At the height of the Cultural Revolution, any sort of private property was frowned on, and families could be denounced as 'capitalist roaders' for keeping so much as a pig or a couple of chickens of their own. The defect of that system was, according to the present government, that, since proceeds as well as labour were communal, and everyone received the same, no matter how hard they worked, there was no incentive to increase productivity. The new system is designed to raise both productivity and the standard of living of the peasants, by encouraging private enterprise, personal initiative, and the profit motive.

Our next visit was also a good example of the success of the Responsibility System. We went to a work brigade with one household which has, on its own initiative, raised 500 chickens. Compared with three or four years ago, this is something really new, and all were justifiably proud of their work. Of course the whole village turns out for the benefit of us sixty *waiguoren*; they gape silently, bemused, as we tour politely, admiring this and that, take photos, and ask questions. The whole village has been swept clean and tidy for our visit, and everyone is wearing Sunday best.

After this serious morning, we had lunch at a hydroelectric plant by a big earth dam, and then boarded four small motorboats which chugged gently through the hot afternoon, as we dozed and chatted and sunbathed, and two hours later arrived at a tangerine orchard. An idyllic situation: red earth, dark green tangerines on the glossy-leaved trees, pines on the hills around, the only means of access by boat along the reservoir. We made our way up the steep hill, through the tangerine trees, and arrived at the village at the top. Again, the whole village, scrubbed squeaky-clean, turned out to welcome us, paths had been swept, and new latrines, screened by a rattan fence, had been thoughtfully dug for the convenience of the foreign visitors. We were served tea and tangerines, and the leader of the village made a speech. He seemed principally upset by the fact that the tangerines weren't really ripe enough to eat, and kept on apologising for it, as if he could be held personally responsible. We ate them anyway, and then scrambled down the slope to chug off across the reservoir again, leaving teacups and tangerine peel as the evidence of our visit. Once again I felt like an intruder from outer space.

The next day we went to an Old People's Home in Jinzhou, which houses 97 old people 'whose family can't take care of them'. It is considered to be the duty of children to support and care for their parents in old age, but these were all old people with no families. They were housed in low one-storey blocks built round a central courtyard with a lake and garden, two or three people to a room, spartan, but neat and clean. The old people were sitting out on the verandahs, chatting, the women knitting, the men playing cards or chess: 'very suitable games for old people', said the guide. Each inhabitant gets 22 *yuan* a month, free food, and clothes twice a year, in winter and summer.

But we spent most of the day in a commune just outside

Shashi. After the usual speeches from which we emerged glassy-eyed, mind boggling with statistics, we were able to spend some time just wandering round the village and talking to the inhabitants. This really was a model commune! 13 families, 67 people, of whom 30 are active working the land, the rest old people or children. The main product is cotton, with sugar cane as a sideline for profit. In 1978–80 the average annual income was 95 *yuan* per head; now it has increased to 272 *yuan*. Yields of cotton have increased from 38 kg per *mu* (6.6 *mu* = 1 acre) to 176 kg. It is a rich commune: 30 bikes, 5 TVs, 6 sewing machines and 6 rotavators. It surprised me that, with the new emphasis on individual initiative, they still reckoned up the sum total of possessions in this way. But they were proudest of the fact that 'every peasant has built his own house with the money he has made from sideline products.' From a distance the row of two-storey houses looked like a *Span* or *Bovis* housing estate; closer up, the brickwork is uneven, floors are made of trodden earth and walls are bare, the kitchen is in a shed out at the back. Water is still brought from the river, half a mile away, but they have plans to pipe it. I wanted to know less quantifiable facts like what did people do for entertainment, what did they eat, how often did they go to the town, what would their children grow up to do, and what were their ambitions for them. The woman we talked to had shoulder-length hair, a round and innocent, but battered and careworn face: a strange mixture of youth and age, naivety and experience. She lived well, she said: no rent to pay, since they built the house themselves, and they were self-sufficient in vegetables, eggs, chickens. Sometimes they bought pork. She went to Shashi quite frequently to shop – a journey of about 25 miles. For entertainment, they watched television in a neighbour's house; they were saving to buy their own. Her children went to school in a nearby commune; tuition cost 3.50 *yuan* a semester. The community had its own 'barefoot doctor' for everyday illnesses; more serious cases went to the hospital in Shashi. Most children would stay in the commune and carry on the farm work when they grew up: there were government regulations prohibiting the movement of labour from country to town. The only way out was to get a university place. She was hoping for this for her own children.

But most people, she said, wanted their children to stay with them, help them with work on the land, and support them in their old age.

During the next two days we visited a waterworks, a power station, a thermos factory, and, best of all . . . THE MANDARIN DUCK BIRD SHIT FACTORY. 'Where are we going next?' we wanted to know. 'The Mandarin Duck Bird Shit Factory, very famous in all of China.' 'Ummm, what do you mean exactly?' 'You know, the kind of shit you put on birds.' We were none the wiser till we reached the factory, which turned out to be the very famous Shashi Sheet Factory, turning out by the millions pairs of floral patterned Mandarin Duck bed sheets. It's wonderful what you hear if you keep your ears open! In fact it was a rather dull factory, but the Chinese guides loved it and bought three or four pairs of bird shit each, presumably for their friends and relations.

The workers were all women ('very suitable for this work' we were told) in the textile mill. Conditions here were Victorian: deafening clatter and air full of cotton dust. One huge weaving shop, fifty looms across and fifty up and down: two thousand five hundred looms clattering away twenty four hours a day. The women work eight-hour shifts, thirty minutes for lunch, two days mornings, two days afternoons, two days nights, two days free, a regular repeated pattern weaving across the year, year in year out, with a few days holiday at Spring Festival, and three more at National Day, May Day and New Year as the only respite. The girls are kept on the same job, not moved around for variety. We asked why, and why no ear muffs, and why were the workers women and the management men, and a lot of other awkward questions, and were told that a) the girls became very expert in one job, so it would be unproductive to move them, b) the noise level did not exceed the regulations, and c) 'that is a characteristic of our country.'

The thermos factory was enormous, gloomy, dusty, Dickensian: glowing red-hot glass through the gloom, workers stripped to the waist crouching to heat the molten glass in the furnace, rusty fans circulating the air. We saw every stage from glassblowing through to decorating the outsides with stencils of peonies or fluffy kittens. How are these for statistics? The factory produces seven million flasks each year and there are fifty such plants in China. That's three hundred and fifty million thermoses a year. Even with a population of a billion, I find it hard to believe that they are all needed. Still, every Chinese room I've seen contains at least two thermoses, and people do drink a lot of tea. But to make those seven million flasks, they must produce at least fourteen million bits of blown glass. We stood at the quality control end of a conveyor belt, where three girls stood throwing the imperfect flasks into huge baskets, and counted. About six out of every ten flasks ended up as a heap of shards in the reject basket. The din of smashing glass was everywhere. There seemed to be a tremendous imbalance in production rates of glass flasks and outer casings – about twice as many of the latter produced, so great barrowfuls stood around everywhere.

The waterworks was a surreal experience. A banner across the entrance proclaimed 'A WARMLY WELCOME TO OUR WATERWORKS' and a poster assured us that 'We do our best to prettify our premises'. Inside the gate were Stalinesque grey square functional buildings, surrounded by an extraordinary Disneyland of a garden laid out round and about and above the treatment tanks and pipes. Dolphins spouted water from one stage to another, lotus plants grew in one tank, ornamental walkways led from stage one pure brown Yangtze water, to stage two and three chemical treatment. Rose gardens surrounded the pipes, little bridges and mazes led across some of the ponds and tanks. As a further contrast, magnificent posters in Socialist Realism style decorated the factory walls: determined-looking workers gazing at the bright skies of the future. We were introduced to the water-works manager ('This man understands better than anyone else in China how to make a factory look beautiful'), and had a statistic-packed speech which ended, surprisingly, with the words 'I wish good health to everyone.'

The visit to the power station involved five minutes in the generating plant and about an hour touring the gardens and ponds laid out by the workers, with a twenty minute speech during which the word electricity was not mentioned once! Instead, the manager concentrated on the sideline efforts of the workers: fruit orchards, a rose garden, a fish reservoir, pig breeding. Each worker gets 10 *jin* (about 10 lb.) of pork and 30 *jin* of fish a year with extra at Spring Festival to 'enrich our living and make the festival more pleasure'. We toured the rose gardens, orchards, fish farm and pigsties, and drank tea in the workers' social club: a pleasant pavilion with tables for cards and chess. Everywhere huge posters exhorted us to 'Love Socialism, Love The People, Love Physical Labour', and beautifully drawn and lettered blackboards celebrated National Day. 'The workers get very happy working in this factory', concluded the manager.

The trip ended with an operatic performance given by opera students and primary school children. The best number was a song and dance routine by 5-year olds called 'Sanitation', whose refrain went 'Love cleanliness, love cleanliness, wash yourself, wash yourself', involving a flock of clean little birds who taught a pig to clip his nails, brush his hair and teeth and wear clean clothes. Then, the following day, a hair-raising drive home, during which we just avoided (I counted carefully) no less than eight head-on collisions. As we got out, shakily, glad to be alive, I said to Xiao Fan, our interpreter, 'What a driver!', 'Yes,' she agreed, 'very skilful.'

Since then, we have been invited to a Chinese family for the first time: for a gargantuan multi-course Sunday lunch with an ex-student and his family. He and his wife and two children live in two small rooms on the third floor of a bleak concrete apartment block, cabbages drying on the stairs and in the corridors, bicycles and kids' toys everywhere. One room on each side of a long dreary corridor, with a little gas burner, the kitchen, in the corridor. No bathroom, but communal washrooms at the end of the corridor. Most of the other inhabitants of the corridor had turned out to help with the lunch preparations. 'You are the first foreign guests in our building', they said. The room where we ate was mostly taken up with a vast bed, but also contained his and hers bookshelves, two desks, two armchairs, and a circular folding picnic table where we ate. When the table was unfolded, the room was completely filled with furniture. What a meal! It meandered on very pleasantly through about ten courses, a good deal of Chinese wine, and about three and a half hours. It reminded me of those long French meals where the wife keeps bobbing up and down to get the next course, except that here everyone was involved and there was a fluctuating population at table with family, friends, and neighbours all popping in to see the strange visitors and add their contribution to the meal. Our feelings were complex: we were delighted and honoured and moved to be invited into a Chinese family, but at the same time felt guilty and embarrassed at the amount of preparation and effort involved on our behalf. And the money! The meal must have cost quite a large proportion of a month's salary. The attitude to the foreigner as honoured guest is really one and the same with the foreigner as curiosity – we can never be quite accepted in this country, but are either treated like royalty, or stared at like animals in a zoo.

Several weeks later, at the halfway point of this 23-week term, we decided to take off for the weekend, and visit the nearest mountain called Lushan, or Green Mountain. It is about twelve hours boatride away downstream, and has always been a favourite summer residence for the rich, or powerful, or foreign. This means that in the late 19th century, indeed up until the forties, it was colonized by the Europeans, and the resort is a late Victorian relic, reminiscent of a decaying European spa town. The massif is about one hour's drive from the river and rises steeply from the valley, with impressive views over the haze of the Yangtze valley and south over Lake Poyang, the largest in China. It is indeed very green, clad with pine forests and harbouring many waterfalls and pavilions and dragons' caves and elfin grots. Being out of season, it was also practically deserted. This caused us some anxiety at first, as we couldn't find a bed for the night, the only hotel open November through April being full of Americans who were on a Nostalgia Trip, all having been born in China before Liberation. One of these came up and introduced us not only to himself and his family, but also, more usefully to the head of the local branch of China Travel Service. Now this organisation is usually very much less than helpful, but this chap was, after a couple of beers, struck by a brainwave. 'You can stay in the Chairman's house.' 'What's that?' 'The house where the Chairman stays.' 'Who he?' 'The Chairman.' Dumbfounded, we piled into an ancient Russian-made *Volga* limousine and were driven to a decaying mansion in the middle of the pine forest. A late Victorian-style granite residence with magnificent front door, ornamental staircase, mahogany everywhere, deep royal blue armchairs, thick carpets. 'You like big bed or two small one?' 'We like big bed (otherwise we'll freeze separately).' It may have been the Chairman's residence whenever he came to stay in Lushan, but I hope he brought his hot water bottle! We were frozen. And mice came and nibbled through the bag and ate the mooncakes we were saving for breakfast, waking us at 3 am. Extremely odd to arrive in an out-of-season resort in the mountains, to sleep in what were very probably Mao's old sheets, in a house which could very well be some Victorian parsonage, even down to the door-handles and tiles in the bathroom. By the time we were installed in the Chairman's bedroom, there wasn't a lot of time left for exploring, but we still managed to see Dragon Head Cliff, The Fairy Cave, and Three Ancient Trees. As at Huang Shan, every beauty spot is named; in fact the name is carved into the rocks in huge characters a foot high, so that you won't miss it, and often accompanied by some apt quotation from Du Fu or Li Bai. These famous mountains were visited by all, and must have the same place in the Chinese literary imagination as the Lake District does in the English, albeit some 1100 years earlier.

The boat back from Jiujiang on the Sunday night was much more comfortable and warmer than the one downstream on the Friday, and the moonlit landscape of mountains by the Yangtze was really romantic. At times we really feel that we *are* in a strange exotic country with a much longer history than Europe's, and to sail up the Yangtze by moonlight with sampans chugging beneath the mountains was one of those times.

1 December 1983
Last week's weekend away was not obtained without difficulty actually. The first attempt made by teachers to get away for the weekend was met with incredulity and some hostility. Charlie was asked: 'Please forbid the teachers to go away for the weekend'. When he explained that he couldn't do that, even if he had wanted to, they asked that all tickets be bought through the

unit. The next time two teachers requested tickets, they were told that unfortunately, no tickets were available that weekend. So they went into town and bought them themselves. Crisis. However all has been resolved, and not only did the unit buy our tickets for us, but even smilingly wished us a good trip. These restrictions on privacy, independence, and freedom of movement are the hardest thing for Westerners to accept in China, as, I suppose, Western individuality and self-will must be to the Chinese. Nothing is secret here. People wander into our house without knocking at all hours of the day and night, the most personal questions are asked without embarrassment, and any decision, however private and personal is subject to group discussion and analysis. A few anecdotes:

A colleague went to the campus tailor to get a money bag made for his summer trip, and was immediately the centre of a large crowd, all discussing how big the bag should be, whether it was better to wear it round the neck or the waist, and how long the cord should be. Word has probably now got round that if you mug him, his money is under his left armpit! My purchase of apples in the campus free market was the subject of an earnest discussion about whether I really wanted so many apples and whether they would all fit into the bag.

A few weeks ago, we were given a fridge – a real luxury in China. One of the teachers who lives downstairs, spending the day ill in bed, heard a constant procession of feet through the hall and into the kitchen. An investigation of the contents of the fridge that evening revealed a large number of bottles and an enormous, sad-eyed fish that none of us could lay claim to: we have a People's Fridge!

In the middle of the hottest period of the summer, one of our team became mysteriously ill. We all decided he must be suffering from heat exhaustion and went to buy a *jin* (about 1lb.) of salt in the campus shop, brought it back and forced the unhappy patient to drink a glass of salt and water. Ten minutes later, I cycled up to the teaching block, to be met in the corridor by Comrade Zhao, who immediately demanded: 'Why were you buying so much salt in the campus shop?'

A similar incident occurred a few weeks ago. There has been a national campaign to eradicate crime, culminating in a series of executions in all the major cities in China. The trial and sentencing was broadcast over the campus tannoys and the day after the shootings, large notices, bearing the names of the offenders and details of their crimes, were prominently displayed in all public places. There was one outside the campus shop, where I met a group of students who translated for me: seventy-nine people had been shot in Wuhan for crime ranging from murder and rape to theft and embezzlement. I was horrified, and said so; the students, of course, were much more guarded – no way of telling what they felt. A few minutes after this conversation, I cycled up to the centre to show the evening film. This time it was Professor Zhang who met me in the corridor: 'Hello Jill. I hear you were very upset about the executions.' The next morning, my class gave me almost exactly the same greeting: 'Hello Jill. It is said that you were very upset about the executions.'

A more annoying incident occurred when two of our male colleagues were invited to dinner by two British girls in a neighbouring college. Cycling out of the campus, they met the college minibus returning from the station with a guest lecturer and a college official. In reply to the greeting 'Where are you going?', they replied, in unison, 'Out!', and continued cycling. A few minutes later, the minibus, empty now except for the driver, passed them, waited for them at the end of the causeway, and tailed them to the other college. About half past ten, there was a knock on the door: a student whom the teachers knew only slightly had come with a query – a plausible enough excuse, except that the query was very trivial and half past ten is an unthinkably late hour to be calling in China. The visit was a reminder that the college knew of their presence and thought that it was time they were on their way home.

I'm sure our post is sometimes opened. Letters often arrive stuck down with sellotape, but of course we can't be sure if it's British sellotape or Chinese. A parcel from an ex-student was handed to me with the words, 'Do you remember Li? His wife has sent you some slippers.' A fat packet was handed to me by one of the admin staff, an ardent stamp collector, with the words

'Open it, open it, I want to see what's inside'. So I opened it, and of course had to give her some of the stamps it contained, but I'm convinced she knew all along what was inside. But best of all was the envelope handed to Charlie with the words, 'You've got six thousa . . . er I think this must be your bank statement.'

These small incidents, of which there have been many more, have caused a range of reactions in us, from indignation through mild annoyance to, on better days, amusement. I refuse to see anything sinister in them (though I don't like the thought that my post might be opened). I think the Chinese interest in our activities is made up in equal parts of a genuine concern for our welfare, a desire to be in control, and natural nosiness. Add to this a very different concept of privacy and a rather drab and monotonous daily life, and it is not surprising that the affairs and actions of ten Westerners in a college in the heart of China are seen as public property. What we see as an unwarrantable intrusion into our private lives, they see as a form of caring. Adjustments have been made on both sides. We have learned to become more detached about these incursions into our privacy and they, for their part, have made fewer of them – in the first weeks, the failure of one of us to appear at breakfast or the decision not to accompany the others on a trip into town would provoke a stream of visitors, anxiously demanding if we were ill, had forgotten the arrangements, or had overslept, but after the first month or so, such, to them, inexplicably individualistic decisions were allowed to pass without investigation and even without comment.

Maybe, as foreigners, our personal affairs are the subject of more curiosity, but the Chinese themselves draw different boundary lines between what is private and what is not. At the end of last term, I was having an interview with a student about what, in Western terms, would be a sensitive subject: he had fallen behind the rest of his group and I was advising him to go down a level. In the middle of our conversation, another student walked into the room. I explained that I was talking to Chen about his work, thinking that he would apologize and go out again, but he just drew up a chair and got involved in the discussion. A couple more of Chen's friends came along and joined in too. What in Western terms was a private matter, was, to them, a matter for group discussion and analysis – and, finally, a group decision: his friends, having considered the matter from all angles, came to the conclusion that he would be better off in a lower group, and he went, forthwith.

This lack of personal privacy does have a more positive side in the intimacy between people. I am constantly amazed at how well the students get on, living in conditions that would have a group of Westerners snapping and snarling within days. The other day I passed a dormitory block, whose inhabitants had hung out large red and white banners from the windows. I asked what they said. 'Oh,' was the reply, 'the room-mates are celebrating four years of living together in the same dormitory room.' 'Four years!', I said, 'I would have thought that they'd all be at each others' throats.' My student stared at me in astonishment. 'Oh no,' he said, 'very friendly.' I am always touched by the warm and natural affection that the students seem to have for one another and by the supportive nature of a close community where you never have to struggle with a task on your own; there are always several pairs of willing hands to help you carry luggage or move furniture or mend a bike.

In Guilin, though, we saw an old lady totter under the weight of the baskets she was carrying and fall, cabbages and beans spilling out of the baskets all over the pavement. From the other side of the road, cut off by the stream of traffic, we watched as no less than ten passers-by stepped over the old woman and picked their way carefully through the scattered vegetables. As we crossed the road, a woman on a cycle stopped, bent over the old lady, and flagged down a lorry to take her to hospital. But it had taken a few minutes before anyone stopped. I found it difficult to reconcile this image with the other, daily images of care and affection around us. Perhaps it's that human life is cheap in a country where there's so much of it, but I think it's that the sense of responsibility has different boundaries here: drawn round those you know and to whom you belong and excluding strangers – a kind of exclusive family loyalty.

In some ways, you never leave the family in China: you go straight from the security of your own family to the security of the larger family of your work unit: family, school, work, authority, counselling service, correction centre, and political education machine all in one; the single body responsible for all aspects of an individual's life: moral, social, political, physical. A trip to the teaching centre on a Sunday will reveal the students sitting around in little groups under the trees: political study. Our students have to measure up to strict moral and political, as well as academic criteria before they are allowed abroad. Where and when they go is not a matter for them; it's for their 'home' work units to decide. At the end of the summer term I helped a student with an application to an American universtity. The course was ideal for him and he was desperately keen to go. When I saw him again after the summer break, I enquired after his application. His face fell. He explained that his unit had refused to support his application, but sent in an application for him to attend a university in Canada – he wasn't so keen on the course there. Some weeks later, he handed me a letter to correct. I was handing it back to him when I suddenly notice that it was addressed to the American university. 'What's all this?' I said. 'Have you been given permission to apply now?' Well no, it turned out that he had applied secretly. 'I am just hoping that if the Canadians refuse me I can show my unit an acceptance from this university and then maybe they will agree to my going there.' 'But how did you get the reference letters?' I asked. 'Oh, that was easy. I just told my unit that they needed two copies, and then I sent one to Canada and one to the States.' But that was a rare case of student initiative. Most students are totally passive, if not always happy, about decisions taken on their behalf, though several of them were complaining the other day about the defects of the cadre system and work units in general. As scientists, they were unhappy that decisions about the subject of their research were often taken by Party cadres who were bureaucrats rather than scientists.

Jobs in China are not a matter of choice: you are allocated to your work unit, and, since jobs, under the 'Iron Rice Bowl' system, are permanent, that work unit is yours for life. At the end of the summer term the students all complained of lack of sleep. When I asked why, they told me that the loudspeakers had been

104

on since the early morning, announcing the job assignments for the newly-graduated students. Many families are split up, by separate job assignments. I have one student who teaches in Beijing, while his wife works in Yunnan, in south-west China, about 2000 kilometres away. They see each other once a year, at Spring Festival.

Allocation of housing is the unit's responsibility. Some of our students are waiting to get married, and have their names on a waiting list for rooms or flats. Until their name comes up, they have to go on living in separate dormitories. Space is at a premium, and it can be a year or so before a room becomes available.

We asked the students about divorce in China. 'Well, it's possible,' they said, 'but rarely necessary, because if a couple are having difficulties, everyone will know, and people from the work unit or street committee will come and give them advice and help.'

Your unit is a kind of intermediary between you and the outside world. It is not necessary often to step outside the walls of your unit – and most units are in a compound. If you need food, you can buy it at the shop, or at the free market in the mornings, or from one of the mess halls. If you need clothes, the tailor will run them up for you. Furniture is made by the college carpenter. There is a college electrician and maintenance service. Your teeth will be filled by the college dentist and your health checked by the college doctor: the unit will even see to it that you go at regular intervals. Any dealings with the bureaucratic public offices can be done by the unit: there is a man whose sole job it is to buy rail tickets for the campus. Some of my students, here for two months now, haven't been into Hankou yet!

Some final illustrations of the range of problems dealt with by the unit: yesterday the pedal came off Charlie's bike (so much for *Forever* bikes!). He did not tell anyone, but when he got to the centre, Comrade Zhao said, 'I hear your bike needs repairing. Please meet Xiao Yue here at 2.30 and she will arrange for it to be repaired.' (Our bikes are well looked after by the unit: on several occasions I have left mine outside while I popped in to visit someone, and returned to find it moved into the shade, or even

105

moved inside for safety.) On a completely different level: one of our students mysteriously left last term. The reason: his unit discovered he was having an extra-marital affair and expelled him. And a few weeks ago one of our students asked permission to be absent for a few days. 'You see, I am in family way and must be aborted.' Her unit had decided that it was not convenient for her to have a child at this point.

All this gives you a certain emotional security and peace of mind: life seems free from the countless minute – and major – decisions that are the fabric of life in the West. You are released from many of the anxieties and much of the stress, since you know your unit will take care of your material needs and welfare. And the lack of personal responsibility for your own life means a curious kind of freedom – freedom from agonizing choices and from a lot of the guilt and worry that goes with decision making. In a lot of ways you never grow up in China – which explains the innocence and naivety of many of our students. We oscillate between extreme reactions to this: much of the time I feel lulled into a soporific acceptance of whatever happens: I think on our return to Britain, we will just arrive at the airport and wait for someone to take care of us, organise transport, a job, somewhere to stay . . . But we do have outbursts of rebellion where we kick against the restrictions and the cosiness.

It's the weekend tomorrow, and there's a real sense of liberation in getting out of the college gates: cycling to East Lake or driving into Hankou. Last weekend, a friend discovered a wonderful place – a sort of Cultural Fun Palace with three operas, wrestling and acrobatics all going on simultaneously in different theatres. Wuhan's answer to the South Bank. We described it to Comrade Zhao. 'Oh yes, I know', she said. 'Why didn't you tell us about it?', we asked. 'Well, we didn't think that the people that go there are the kind of people you ought to mix with!' So we've made plans to go there this weekend!

106

CHRISTMAS, COLD WEATHER AND
A CULTURAL CLAMPDOWN

Letter seven
CHRISTMAS, COLD WEATHER AND A CULTURAL CLAMPDOWN

15 January 1984

We ended our last letter about to visit the Fun Palace in Hankou for the first time. We did that, then went through about two months of very cold weather, paralleled by a somewhat harsher political climate, had Christmas and New Year, visited Guangzhou, and are now looking forward to our Spring Festival holiday in a couple of weeks' time. So this letter will be about Cold weather, Christmas and Clampdowns. But first:

CULTURE: The Fun Palace (or, more properly, the People's Cultural Centre) on Zhongshan Road in Central Hankou is the South Bank, the Mikado, the Palladium and everyone's dream of circuses rolled into one, and it only costs 1 *mao* (about 3p) to get in. It is open every day in the afternoon and evening and is quite simply the best value night out in the world. We have been about six times now, and have made tape-recordings and taken photos, but none of that could show you what it's like. It's like entering a fairy castle, or returning to the middle ages, or suddenly finding yourself in the middle of a dream. The construction alone is quite strange, featuring a number of levels, balconies running round all sides and across gangways to a central hall. The place looks like an optical illusion. The central hall can seat about two thousand, in the pit and on two galleries. This is where the musicians and acrobats perform. Above them, on the roof, is a teahouse, full of spivs and tarts sitting around their thermoses of green tea, spitting sunflower seeds, cigarettes nonchalantly dangling from their lips, caps set at a rakish angle, listening to *Auld Lang Syne* or other cool modern music. Follow one of the walkways across: you come to a set of stairs up to another roof, where there are performing bears, monkeys, goats and other grotesque sights under the sky when the weather is good. Back down the stairs and along another walkway there is a large unraked 'opera house' with rows of wooden seats. It holds about 700 at a rough guess and is one of six such halls. You can wander in at the back, peer in through a window, or wriggle into a place on a bench. Or, as we did the other night, push open the stage door, wander in, talk to the actors and actresses, go and sit with the band bashing out frantic percussion, flash away photos for an hour or so. Next door is usually a Chinese Morecambe and Wise act, with the audience in stitches. Strange how stand-up comics have the same routine the world over. The main difference is that even our local-born colleague could not understand a lot of the Wuhan dialect they were talking, and the two comics were wearing the standard Mao jacket uniform. Wander along, and next door, in a hall on its own is, incongruously, a digital display weighing machine. Further on is a hall of mirrors. Next to that a sleazy pool hall with more lads with caps askew and fags in face, hunched over green baize under a pall of smoke, something like a scene from a Chicago gangster movie. Move on, in the next hall, a sugary sweet couple are singing in sickly harmony, romantic songs with a backdrop of lakeside scenery; they break into a selection from *The Sound of Music* after a while. The band, drums, sax, cornet, bass, look just like a 50s backing group: suits, slicked back hair, rather hearty expressions. Next door another opera, probably from a different part of China, as touring groups come here for a few weeks, and then move on, to be replaced by another group. Downstairs again, and in the courtyard there is a huge spherical metal cage, where a lady in pink with a long trailing white scarf on a *Yamaha* does Wall of Death motorbike stunts. Visitors from Beijing go green with envy when they visit, and we have twice stayed in a hotel in Hankou on Saturday nights in order to be able to stay there late at night. Last Saturday we went in and stayed an hour and a half behind the scenes of one of the operas. We were beckoned in by the leading actor, tall, heavily made up with a sickly grin, long pink robes, and funny long lobed hat, and there were the whole company in various stages of undress, plus the stage hands and make-up artists in everyday blue and green Mao jackets. Some of the actresses had their children with them backstage too. The contrast between the dull everyday colours and these fabulous costumes! We sat down and were given large mugs of green tea and sticky peanut brittle and bombarded with questions. It was a case of mutual fascination. They loved our curiosity and we loved their welcome. They move on in a month or so, and I just hope we can get the photos developed somewhere in time to give them. They work terribly hard: six days a week, two performances a day, and on Sunday 'just' an evening performance. A long training from an early age. Some of them were sitting around, going over their lines, others were applying the finishing touches to their make-up, some were getting into their elaborate robes and head-dresses, like any backstage anywhere, but a cosy down-to-earth family atmosphere, in this communal dressing-room with tea and chat, women knitting and children underfoot. We plan many more visits. Coupled with a meal of three or four dishes and a bowl of beer in a local restaurant, two people can have a wonderful evening out for the grand total of £1.25.

CHRISTMAS was very strange, as all the plans we had made to invite our Chinese colleagues for a traditional Christmas dinner, having got hold of two geese through Lao Su, our excellent cook, who said he knew how to roast them, were turned upside down when the Foreign Affairs Bureau invited us to a special banquet the evening before ours. Pipped to the post! Perhaps they felt embarrassed at the thought of accepting our hospitality, didn't want to be outdone. Well, we all got very merry at their banquet, which included our geese chopped up and cooked Chinese style, and received presents of calendars and fans from the Foreign Affairs Bureau, and then all suffered a sleepless night of vivid dreams, which we put down to the high level of monosodium glutamate in the banquet. It is called 'gourmet powder' in Chinese cookbooks, and they add it to any preparation because it 'makes it taste very delicious'. Next day, pretty much the same company assembled round the same groaning tables for a traditional English Christmas dinner. We were all too bloated to care very much, but we ended up with two Christmas puddings, thoughtfully sent by friends. Everyone tucked in (custard too!) and we asked Comrade Zhao if she liked it. 'Yes,' she said politely, 'I like . . . but NOT VERY MUCH!' They all seem very unsympathetic to Western tastes. Slabs of red raw meat!

Stinking dairy products! Milk! Butter! Cheese! In fact, there is a government campaign to get everyone to drink more milk, and this college does have a herd of Friesians, so we can now buy pasteurized milk in plastic bottles, but traditionally, as far as most Chinese are concerned, milk is for babies and old folk only.

We had a four-day weekend at Christmas, and hankering after peace and quiet and, above all, warmth, we two went south to Guangzhou, or Canton.

CANTON is very different from Wuhan. Getting out of the train, having travelled seventeen hours overnight, is like arriving in a different country. The weather is much warmer for a start: we were able to shed, thankfully, several layers of Wuhan woollies. And there are adverts everywhere, people look sophisticated, have permed hair, more colourful clothes, the shops are full of new cassette recorders, colour TVs, fridges. People don't stare as you walk by. We saw men in jeans and girls in high heels and couples walking hand-in-hand. Some girls were wearing make-up, and a few had jewellery. Men had smart jackets with zips and a lot of pockets. Some had flashy white shoes. People even walked differently, more briskly, with a slight swagger. The traffic was faster. It was all a little seamy: people on the make, a hint of corruption in the air. You could smell the West; after all it is only seventy miles down the Pearl River to Hong Kong. Traditional China is still very much present though, as we found when we explored the backstreets and came upon what we christened 'The Owl and the Pussycat Market'. Pangolins for sale, tree rats, snakes, turtles, cats mewing plaintively from wicker baskets, mongooses, dogs, large furry animals that looked a bit like badgers, owls staring mournfully out of wire cages – all destined to end up on the dinner table. The Chinese say of the Cantonese that they will eat 'anything with four legs that isn't a table, anything that flies that isn't an aeroplane.' We didn't sample any of this exotica, but ordinary Cantonese food, the real home-cooked version of what you eat in Chinese restaurants in the West, is delicious. Dishes are often steamed rather than fried, so are very clear-tasting and simple. Wuhan food tends to be rather oily.

But the best part of our Christmas trip was to meet an old

friend, who studied with us in London, to chat and reminisce, and to realise that it *is* possible to make a real Chinese friend. We went round an orchid garden, and a couple of parks, well into the dusk, chatting and strolling, and eventually to a beautiful little restaurant, the *Beiyuan* (North Garden) which is about eighty years old: old China, lacquer screens, stained glass windows to the eating rooms, and a little brook flowing through the middle. We paid and sent our guest home in a taxi, which made us feel very grand. She, of course, selected the dishes: steamed crab with ginger, *dim sun*, fish steamed in onion, tea. Simple and good. None of your monosodium glutamate to make it 'very delicious'.

COLD WEATHER: If we're honest, it's not *that* cold . . . but we're soft. The trouble is, that although the air temperature is not that much below zero, there are only two places in the whole of Wuhan which are adequately heated. One is in bed, with jumpers, tracksuit, mittens and hot water bottles, and the other is under the shower. But everywhere else, like nose sticking out, or elbow not under the stream of water, is freezing! Everywhere has bare cold cement floors, so the heat you have generated under your six or seven layers of long-john, vest, tracksuit, jumpers, overcoat, mittens, and ski-socks by cycling frantically to work, drains out through the soles of your feet within ten minutes. To sit down for more than about five minutes is agony, so it is very difficult to do any office work, and we all find ourselves fidgeting about irritably in a vain effort to keep warm. But think of the poor students, or any families south of the Yangtze who have no source of heating. Families will probably rig up a stove to burn 'lotus briquets': round cakes of coal dust with concentric rings of holes. You can see people making a supply all through the summer months: mixing the dust up into a paste, and spreading it out onto the pavement to dry, then cutting round or square blocks. Chinese cities in the winter are full of the acrid smell of coal dust from numberless family stoves. Our students had no heating, except the warmth generated by five bodies in a dormitory, and would retire to bed as soon as possible after the evening meal. So, for a while, did we, until life at home was made bearable by the New Year's gift of a pair of black cast-iron stoves. Teaching, however, remains a very chilly activity, and so does

113

eating, as the dining-room is heated only by a wokful of glowing embers placed under the table, and we all gobble down our food in an effort to finish it before it gets cold. Most of our students have horrible chilblains on feet, hands and face, but are resigned to this as a regular winter occurrence.

CLAMPDOWNS: The Crackdown on Crime continues. Reports have come in of lorryloads of criminals, placards round their necks describing their crimes, being paraded around town before being driven to public execution grounds for sentencing and execution by firing squad. The crackdown is nationwide, and in all the major cities, lists of names are posted up in public places, sealed with a big red tick to indicate execution. Often photos of the executed criminals are pinned on public notice-boards in a gruesome rogues' gallery. This highly-publicised campaign is an attempt to bring down China's crime rate. An article in *China Daily* reports that: 'in the past few years some serious crimes rarely seen since the founding of the People's Republic of China have appeared, together with the return of some vicious social phenomena that were eliminated decades ago . . . Some people attribute the crime rate increase to the mishandling of contradictions by some units and comrades. But this is not the case . . . People commit crimes out of unrestrained individualism . . . they must be treated as enemies of socialism. Severe punishment of felony is the main effective means of maintaining social order.' Most people I've talked to put the increase in the crime rate down to the Cultural Revolution, saying that all sense of law and order was lost in that period, and is only slowly being recovered. They see young people as particularly affected by the lack of any coherent system of law and justice during their formative years. Others I've talked to attribute a lot of the crime to the unemployment among young people. China is having trouble finding enough work to keep a billion pairs of hands busy. Most workplaces are overmanned, but there are still a lot of young people 'waiting for work'. There seem to be two sorts of crime involved in the wave: street crime such as theft, rape, murder, illegal money changing and procuring of goods, prostitution, mainly attributable to young people; and larger scale economic crimes such as misallocation of funds, bribery, embezzlement,

114

nepotism, attributable to 'corruption among the cadres'.

Reaction among the students has been mainly non-committal. A couple perhaps hinted at their feeling in the details they selected to translate for me: 'This one was only nineteen . . . unemployed . . . committed a robbery.' Some approved of the crackdown: 'China has a population problem,' said one, 'we have no room for these bad elements.' This seems to have been the general reaction according to an editorial in *China Daily* reprinted from *Fortnightly Chats*, which declares that the crackdown has been so successful that the crime rate has been cut by half, and in many places 'the people have set off firecrackers to celebrate and sent inscribed boards to Public Security departments to show their gratitude.'

Along with the Crackdown on Crime is another movement which started about the same time, in the autumn. It is called 'The Campaign Against Spiritual Pollution'. This cultural clampdown has been the cause of some weeks of paranoia among the foreign community here: a lot of people saw it as specifically aimed at foreign influences and felt very threatened by it. It made very little difference to our daily lives here, though measures taken varied from college to college. One college had all their videos confiscated, another group of 'foreign experts' were lined up and lectured on the evils of Western permissiveness. Our imported video films were subject to a vetting procedure by the college authorities (they had already been overhauled by customs some months earlier) who objected to two: *Lady Hamilton*, on the grounds that it 'condoned adultery', and *Storm over the Nile*, which seemed inexplicable to us, so we asked why. 'Oh, because it shows the British as a colonial power.' 'Well,' we said, 'we don't agree with that either.' So a compromise was reached: we wrote a worksheet with a disclaimer: 'The views expressed in this film are not necessarily those . . . etc, etc', saying we didn't agree with the sentiments portrayed in the film. They allowed us to show it.

Student reaction to all this was very interesting. Accustomed to and totally passive about the idea of customs vetting their films, they reacted with violent indignation to the thought that college officials whose rank was actually inferior to their own in their own colleges, were deciding what was and what was not

115

suitable for them to see. The conversation went like this: 'Jill, why are you showing an old film again this week – there are some we haven't seen in the store cupboard?' 'Well, since the Cultural Pollution Campaign, it has been decided that those are unsuitable for you to see.' An outcry: 'Why? Who decided? What's in the films that we can't see?' When I explained, they were furious: 'We're not children! Why should they decide for us? What right have they got to tell us what's suitable? I'm a Senior Lecturer, and Lao Wang over there is a Vice-Dean. We're senior to them, how can they tell us what to do?' It was status that seemed to rankle most! Then, as if a new light was dawning: 'Anyway, if they've seen them, how come they're not spiritually polluted themselves?'. It was as if they were discovering all the old chestnuts about censorship for the first time. The next morning when I arrived in class, they shut the door behind me, and, in a conspiratorial whisper: 'Jill, how about showing us one of those films – no-one would ever know.' Forbidden fruit!

Dancing seems to have disappeared since the campaign began: there are no more waltzes and quicksteps with couples carefully rehearsing the steps, man with man and girl with girl, and the students don't mention disco any more.

Students seem reluctant to visit us individually, though I don't know if this is college policy or national policy. They still come in groups though, when invited round for a drink or evening chat. Safety in numbers! I asked one ex-student with whom I was quite friendly if she would give me Chinese cookery lessons. She seemed quite enthusiastic about the idea, but when she came round on the appointed evening, she slunk in through the door like a scared rabbit. She taught me to make a simple dish, 'Eggs with Crab Taste', but would not stay to eat it with us, and crept out as furtively as she had come in. Since then, she has countered invitations to return with protestations of being busy, or not wanting to bother us.

There seems to be quite a bit of mistrust of foreigners around at the moment, though I don't know if this is connected to the Cultural Pollution campaign. Attitudes vary so much from town to town, and from college to college: it seems to be very much up to unit leaders to interpret rules as leniently or strictly as they

116

choose. However, an American at the university who fell in love with one of his students had a lot of trouble. It took them about four months to get a marriage permit, and they met with all sorts of obstacles and difficulties. Surprising, really, as, since the Cultural Revolution, marriage to foreigners has become much easier, and is even favourably regarded in such avant-garde places as Shanghai and Guangzhou. But Wuhan is terribly provincial and suspicious of foreigners, and the young lady in question was a Party member. So the couple met with opposition from every quarter, and even now that they're married and she has an American residence permit, she is having trouble getting a Chinese passport. And Public Security are investigating how they got to know each other in the first place: questioning his room-mate about how they met: 'How well did he know her?', 'Where did he and she meet?', 'Did she come to his room?', 'Did he ever go to hers?'. A friend, going to Public Security for a purely routine affair, an exit visa to Hong Kong, had a curious experience; the stamp on his passport took half an hour to put on and meanwhile, an official dropped in for a friendly chat: did he like Wuhan, what was he doing here, which college was he at, didn't he get homesick sometimes, did he see any other foreign experts, did he know anyone at the university for example . . . and, getting more probing: did he know any Chinese, did they ever come to see him, did he ever go to their houses . . .

An article in *Beijing Review* recently tried to allay foreign fears that the spiritual pollution campaign signalled the end of the Deng policy of opening up to the West, by using the image of a mosquito net. 'Our country,' it said, 'is badly in need of fresh air, and therefore we have opened our windows to the West, and are very grateful for the breeze that is blowing in from these countries. However, a lot of unwelcome and harmful influences may also enter with these good ones, and it is necessary to protect our country from these. We are therefore putting up a fly-screen to prevent the flies from entering, while allowing the fresh air to blow in.'

Our friend in Guangzhou was of the opinion that the campaign was directed as much against tendencies in China's own litera-ture, as against foreign literature and films, though she conceded there was a strong anti-pornography element. In the new wave of literature born out of the Cultural Revolution, people gave vent to their bitterness about the events of the Ten Years Turmoil, expressing themselves openly and critically for the first time since the 'Hundred Flowers' period of the fifties. A new kind of novel and short story emerged, which focussed on individual emotions and reactions. The government apparently feels that this bitterness has gone on long enough and that it is time for socialist literature to return to its proper job of bolstering national morale and painting a rosy picture of the future. Also that so much emphasis on the individual is unhealthy. A recent article endorses our friend's view: 'Certain literary and artistic works deny the existence of class struggle and replace it with an emphasis on human nature and love, some theoretical works neglect Marxism, replacing it with abstract humanism, and talking in abstractions about the value of what is human, although class struggle still exists in a socialist society. Some people also refer to 'alienation', referring to 'the problem of alienation in our socialist society' and some works encourage bourgeois liberalism, individualism, anarchy, pessimism and nihilism. All this encourages people to remain passive, to relax their efforts, to become corrupt, degenerate, greedy for personal gain, and to begin to lose their faith in socialism.'

So it seems as if the two clean-up campaigns go together: a twin attack on unhealthy individualist tendencies, and an attempt to eliminate the last influences of the legacy of the Cultural Revolution. There is another campaign going on in the papers, against 'Corruption in high places', and for 'Party Rectification' – a sort of 'Clean Up the Cadres' campaign. The papers list such crimes as misallocation of housing, misappropriation of funds, the securing of advantages for children and relatives, accepting of bribes and selling of services, dealing on the black market, favouritism in job appointments. A lot of bending – or just plain breaking – of the rules goes on; not too difficult when officials and cadres seem to be able to make up their own rules a lot of the time, and Chinese society is apparently not as cosy or as disciplined as it seems at first. Influence, connections, pressure, persuasion, and bribery are all used to ensure that some end up more equal than others.

We have become aware over the last few months of the more competitive aspects of Chinese society, and of how much pressure is put on students to succeed by their work units: a lot of them are under a good deal of strain and some of them come to see the teachers privately to convince them they have 'special circumstances' and therefore deserve special treatment. I have the top class this term, which is where a lot of them want to be, as they think they have a better chance of graduating more quickly from there, so some of them have come to me and the other teachers to persuade us that's where they should be. One engaging chap had a particularly smooth line: 'Ji-Li, what is your Chinese surname?' 'Han.' 'Well, that's the same as mine.' 'So?' 'Well, in China, when two men have the same surname, they can call each other brother.' 'So?' 'So Charlie is my brother and you are my sister-in-law.' 'So?' 'Well, in China, relatives can open back doors for each other.' 'SO?' 'Well, I'd like to be in your group next term.'

He was joking, but given the enormously complicated and ossified bureaucracy of most public institutions in China, the only way of getting anything done is via the 'Back Door': the Chinese equivalent of 'pulling strings'. Train tickets for example. Every station has a fixed quota of tickets, but these aren't always available over the counter, because the ticket clerk may be saving some for relatives, or relatives' friends, or friends of friends – just in case they want any. In fact, if you turn up just as the train leaves, there are nearly always seats and berths available, though they have officially been 'sold out' for days. I had enormous difficulty over a ticket to Beijing a couple of months ago, and it wasn't until about an hour before departure that I knew I was going for certain. This despite repeated efforts over at least five days to get a ticket, involving people from the admin office queuing at the station at all hours of the day and night, and phone calls to relatives and other influential people all over Wuhan. Two of my students arrived late from Shanghai at the beginning of term. Their explanation was succinct: 'Shortage of tickets, no back doors.' Another student promised us a ticket from Chongqing to Wuhan any time we needed one, because he had a back door to the ticket office. Another student in a discussion on what would be the perfect job: 'A cadre, because then everyone would give me presents to get in my back door.' I have read a few modern short stories on the difficulties of acquiring accommodation or obtaining other essential services if you are not prepared to go round with gifts of fruit or meat. At the end of last term, a student who has the looks of a Shanghai film star and the bearing of a princess, gave me a present of some coffee from her home town on Hainan Island. 'I think you will understand,' she said with dignity, 'why I did not give you this gift *before* I took the examination.' 'Tell me, Xiao Ming,' I said, 'would you have given me the coffee if you hadn't passed?' She drew herself up to her full height, bristling with dignity. 'But of course!', she said icily.

But there are other, more sinister aspects of the power wielded by cadres in their little kingdoms. There are some horrible stories of intrigue, backbiting and jealousy in these small closed communities: the reverse side of the coin of care and affection, I suppose. The structure of Chinese society means that it can be caring and supportive; it can also be terribly claustrophobic. One poor girl has been in trouble since her Head of Department took it into his head to arrange a marriage between her and a relative of his who works in the same department (go-betweens and introductions are still quite common in China). She refused the offer, since when her career began to take a downward turn. People were promoted over her, and she is worried that while she is away the Head of Department may take advantage of her absence to send his relative abroad instead of her. Stories like this are a glimpse into the abyss of insecurity, mistrust and paranoia that must underlie the cheerful friendliness of many of our students. Paranoia seems to be a condition of life here. Another legacy of the Cultural Revolution: no wonder that after years when policies could swing through an angle of 180 degrees overnight, and yesterday's friend was tomorrow's deadly enemy, many people are cynical about politics, afraid to commit themselves to an idea or opinion, fearing that the comparative freedom and security of the present regime is just a temporary phenomenon and that an over-passionate commitment to today's correct viewpoint could land them back in the fields tomorrow. The disturbing thing about living here is that you never know how much is paranoia, how much you are reading into things, what is reality and what is imagination. So much of living here is guesswork, for the Chinese themselves too: will what is correct today also be policy tomorrow? What consequences will this or that action, approved of or applauded now, have for me in the future? One of our students invited us to his home with these words: 'Come and visit me when you are in Nanjing. I am not afraid of another Cultural Revolution.' Do you accept such an invitation?

Letter eight

A TOUCH OF CULTURE SHOCK

Letter eight
A TOUCH OF CULTURE SHOCK

2 March 1984

Welcome to the Year of the Rat!

Judging from your letters and remarks about gilt and ginger-bread, I think we must have sounded a little disillusioned in our last newsletter! In fact, most of the time we oscillate between love and hate, admiration and anger, amusement and irritation, but we did indeed have a winter of discontent. Besides a growing awareness of the seamier sides of Chinese reality and the vague sense of a political climate of increased austerity, there were other, more direct, personal pressures: the difficulties of living in a culture so alien to one's own in general, and of living in China in particular.

It's difficult to explain the cumulative effect of the *drabness* of Chinese life, particularly in winter, when the only colours you see are the dark blue or green of people's clothes and the endless grey of the cement apartment blocks, the dusty streets and the bare trees. The dim lighting, the dreary shop windows and the cheap junk in the shops do nothing to relieve the monotony. The only colourful spots are the children, dressed in bright primary colours, with ribbons in their hair and long silk cloaks with rabbit fur hoods for the babies, as if people sublimate their need for colour, expressing it in the clothes they choose for their children. (By the way, we solved the mystery, which puzzled us all summer, of what happens to the bare-bum-babies in winter: they simply wear a small patchwork quilt tied with a piece of string around their waists, covering their rear.)

Chinese cities are visually very unattractive. I cannot understand how a nation with such an ancient civilisation and such a highly developed and refined aesthetic sense has managed to create so much ugliness in the last thirty years. China is a poor country, and poverty isn't beautiful (though sometimes, appallingly it is picturesque. We feel pretty immoral actually, as visitors in a Third World country: a line from *Middlemarch*, re-read recently, sticks in my mind, about 'the softening influence of the fine arts which makes other people's hardships appear picturesque'). But it's the new prosperity which has created the new ugliness: the giant raw unfinished-looking slab-concrete blocks, the monolithic public buildings, the wide empty roads, the new factories mushrooming up haphazardly all over the countryside. That, and the worst excesses of the Cultural Revolution, when many of the most beautiful buildings in China were destroyed.

Besides the visual monotony, there's the crushing weight of routine. Not one's own routine, which is self-imposed, and therefore usually bearable, but an unvarying pattern imposed from the outside. I sometimes thought that if I woke up once more to the 6.30 tannoy with its blaring morning messages and rousing music, I would scream! And the thought that all over this huge country, people in colleges, on factory estates and in communes are getting up to the sound of cheery announcements and then doing their exercises to the sound of the same music and the same female voice chanting '*yi, er, san . . .*', before going off rice bowl and spoon in hand to join the queue at canteen or mess hall . . .. Walking in the country the other day, we even came on a tannoy in the middle of nowhere, rice paddies all around, broadcasting out its messages to the fields. It's the repetitive sameness that is so claustrophobic, and the fact that people's lives are organized for them into this regular round of work, exercise, food, sleep, and the same few simple pleasures: chess, cards, the Saturday night film, the evening stroll.

Our inner resources were wearing very thin by the time our vacation came round. It was partly exhaustion, after a twenty-three week term of insatiable Chinese students, but everyone seems to have their own China breaking-point. I think many Westerners come to China with such enormously inflated expectations – of either an egalitarian utopia, or an exquisitely refined culture – that no country could possibly live up to them, and their disillusionment is as great as their expectations were high. I have never been in a country to which people reacted with quite such extremes of emotion. Our breaking-point was caused mainly by the sameness of daily life here, the monotony, the enforced routine, and by the sheer physical discomfort of being cold all the time and not being able to get warm. And, I suppose, though I'm not very proud of this, by the absence of easy pleasures, the fact that everything is so *difficult* in China: from having a wash, which entails going down a flight of cold stone steps to boil a kettle in a chilly kitchen to fill a basin to wash in a freezing cement bathroom; to buying a rail ticket, which entails at least three visits and endless haggling at both ends (you can't buy returns); to using the telephone – virtually impossible to get through and anyway inaudible if you do; to simply going into town to shop: an hour and a half on two buses and the ferry. And also that China is such an impenetrable country, especially as we don't speak the language well, and it's so difficult to get more than a stock response from people, that once the initial shock of the new has worn off, it's hard to get any further, and there is a feeling of endlessly circling again and again over the same ground, doing and seeing the same things and coming up against the same barriers.

Many others find the restrictions hard to bear. 'I didn't know a country could be like a prison', someone said to us the other day. One American student said that her image of the 'foreign expert' in China was that of a panda in a zoo: the keepers are so anxious to preserve this rare and exotic animal that they give it everything they can think of: food, light, comfort, an attractive cage, but can't imagine (or can't give it) what it really wants: a more normal life outside the cage.

So for various reasons, we were feeling rather jaundiced with China as the train approached Hong Kong. I actually felt rather nervous. The West again. Decisions to make. Things to buy. Bright lights. Cars. And when we got off the train and wandered down the street, Hong Kong looked like Fairyland to me. I felt like a country cousin come to the big city for the first time. People had hairstyles and coloured clothes. Cars moved fast. The shop windows were bulging with goods, dazzled you with chrome and steel. Nobody stared as you walked down the street. The things in the shops forced themselves on you with slogans, proclaimed what they were in large letters, instead of hiding away in brown paper packages. I was dazed by the colours, the clothes, the lights, the adverts. The glittering skyscrapers on Hong Kong Island looked like a magic city. I rediscovered words like fashion, style, smart, expensive, luxury. And luxury was what we found we wanted. When we got to the hotel (cheap by Hong Kong standards, wildly expensive by ours), what we found we wanted more than anything else was physical comfort, pleasures of the flesh. I have never before been delighted by the fact that hot water comes out of a tap when you turn it. Or contented merely because a room was warm enough to sit and read a book in. Or enjoyed a coffee so much. Anyway, it was good that pleasures of the flesh were what we were looking for, because Hong Kong is about very little else. Not much food for the mind in that city. However, we spent a couple of very pleasant days wandering round, reminding ourselves of things we'd forgotten, like the taste of cheese or orange juice or red wine, or how to use a knife and fork. It felt a bit like convalescence after a long and seedy illness. Our childlike excitement began to wear off a bit though, and Hong Kong seemed a little less like Paradise, when we tried to shop around for a camera lens and found shop after shop trying to cheat us. We began to miss the hordes of people who gather round whenever you make a purchase in Wuhan, eagle-eyed to make sure the shopkeeeper doesn't short-change you.

The next day we boarded the plane to Australia, stunned by the service, with hot towels, French cooking, and free champagne flowing all the way to Sydney – the contrast with peanuts and green tea on CAAC's battered old Ilyushins could hardly be greater. But it was in Sydney that the culture shock really hit us. Hong Kong is, after all, rather more Chinese than British: an odd combination of double-decker buses and rickshaws, street stall and supermarket, pub and teahouse, apothecary and Watson's the Chemist. I will never forget disembarking at Sydney Airport at seven in the morning (4 am Chinese time) and being over-whelmed by the sight of so many large white people. It was a rather horrific vision, as if the scale of things had gone wrong. I felt a bit like Gulliver. And so much exposed white flesh. Disgusting!

The sense of dream continued throughout our stay. On that early morning drive across Sydney to my uncle and aunt's house, everything seemed unnaturally vivid, too highly-coloured. The deep blue of the sea and sky! The little red-brick bungalows, each surrounded by a square of emerald green grass! The place looked like Toytown. The sense of unreality was heightened when we stopped off for coffee at my aunt's daughter's. They had just moved into a new house and were redecorating, so we were plunged into an earnest discussion of wallpaper and carpet and curtain patterns: a world we had completely forgotten and which seemed rather frivolous after the austerity and earnestness of China. But one of the nicest things about Australia was being in real homes again. So much of our life here is institutional, and we'd forgotten the sense of belonging to a society, of being able to take its normal everyday workings for granted, and of having an emotional support system of family and friends: a network of love and trust. So much of living in a foreign culture is exploration and discovery, you are always making an effort, and there are times in China when I could do with a pair of emotional and cultural carpet slippers.

Other startling first impressions: people on the beach and the shock of realizing that they had bodies under their clothes, after months of being surrounded by well-padded Michelin men; seeing people looking not just healthy but bursting with health; dogs everywhere; the ease of communications and efficiency with which arrangements are made – just pick up a phone to hire a car, repair your roof, deliver your washing-machine; people in the streets walking briskly and with a sense of purpose, shop windows; fast traffic; being plunged once more into the bewildering world of consumer decisions (I rediscovered the feeling, so much a part of daily life in the West, of making the *wrong* consumer choice); superfluity – too many facts, too many choices, and above all, so much ostentatious waste: shocking when you come from a country where all waste from beer cans and cardboard boxes to pig manure and human waste is put to use.

One thing we realized we had missed in China was the sense of space. It was wonderful to look out over nothing but miles of golden grass and blue-green gum trees, with only an occasional kangaroo for company. In China, the landscape is always plotted and pieced, every available inch intricately sculpted into patterns of paddy and vegetable allotment, and you are always aware of the pressure of too much humanity: you rarely see a landscape without a figure in it.

Bookshops too. We are both addicted, and of course in China we're illiterate, and can't even bark at print. The Chinese bookshops are like the stacks in a university library, full of worthy tomes in dull colours. How boring a library is to the uneducated! So much paper, so much dust, so many bespectacled intellectuals standing leafing through, not talking. In China, I feel like a small child, bored, waiting while its parents choose books to take home. In major towns there are foreign language bookshops. What a depressing sight! Row on row of the same dusty books reprinted in English, German, French: bad translations of Chinese classics, bad translations of modern stories, occasionally a more attractively produced picture book. The selection of foreign books to be found is extremely limited, some Dickens maybe, or a selection of short stories by venerable American authors. Not so in the third type of bookshop, for us much the most interesting, but to which we are forbidden access. FOREIGN LANGUAGE BOOKSTORE says the sign. And underneath: FOREIGN FRIENDS NOT ADMITTED. This is where the pirated books are sold. Our bank clerk, a gent with a literary bent, always has an English book on the go, a textbook or novel, selling for a few *mao*, printed on cheap paper, stapled together or flimsily bound, a direct photocopy of an expensive Western import. China is not signatory to the International Copyright Agreement, so anything can be copied and sold for a fraction of its original price, for the benefit of the masses. I suppose we are prohibited from going into these bookshops to prevent us from witnessing the full extent of the piracy. We did once manage to get into one such shop, and found a treasure house of what appeared to be completely random delights. *The Oxford Companion to Music* stood next to *The Elements of Style* by William J Strunk Junior, and near a shelf of pirated Graham Greene stood an Isaac Singer novel – what did the Chinese make of that, I wondered: both its Jewishness and its Americanness? A tableful of photocopied English language textbooks were selling like hot cakes, and strangest of all was a reprinted pamphlet on *Metal Fatigue in Cruise Missiles*. I wondered where that came on the bestseller list. It seemed as if any book or document that strayed into the country by accident had been reprinted in millions to be pounced on by a nation hungry for foreign prose, regardless of content or style.

The effect of Australia after China was like coming into a brightly lit room after a cold and dingy hallway. The shock of being in a country full of bright colours, in the middle of summer after months of drab winter, in a country which zips along with a delight in its prosperity after the slow pace of a country where most people barely have what we call essentials. It was really like being turned upside down. There were plenty of things we did *not* like particularly, and I wonder if we'll react the same way on our return to England. I missed my bowl of rice and chopsticks, and found the enormous slabs of meat rather hard to take. Driving was fun for the first hour or so, but the thrill quickly wore off, and after a day I ceased to be interested in the commercial radio stations. We had some disgusting junk food, pizzas and hamburgers, and it was alarming to realize that everything is based on money. In China, we rarely carry money around from day to day, as we rarely want to buy anything; in Australia, it seemed we needed money all the time.

We flew back via Singapore: a superb view over Hong Kong Island and the harbour as we circled in to land, heartstopping moment as we came in fast and low over Kowloon, wings almost touching the skyscrapers. Drizzle, cold after Australia. And that sinking uncomfortable feeling that we were only there because we had to head north, back into winter and work. After two days in Hongapore (the two places run together in my mind, like one vast airport duty-free shopping centre), we rolled up to Kowloon station, with our winter clothes on, our rucksacks and shoulder bags full of goodies unobtainable in Wuhan: slide film, red wine, good razor blades, cheese, new books – the Best of the West! The deep hot baths and central heating we could not fit in the cases.

Crossing the border on the train to Canton was fascinating, as we suddenly rediscovered many of the sights and impressions we remembered from our arrival in Beijing nearly a year ago now. After a couple of days of dread of going back as we hung around in Hong Kong, it was actually a relief to get back! Do people doing military service go through this I wonder? All the time we were in Hong Kong we were thinking, 'Next opportunity to leave is in July,' but suddenly it was all interesting again: the food, the way people walk and dress, the sounds in the street, the tannoy announcements, the jars of tea, the smells were all new again.

Since our return, the winter of our discontent is now made glorious Chinese spring. Oh what a difference the weather makes! We have peeled off our multi-layers of vest and long-john, it is no longer a punishment to have a shower, there is a hint of green in the paddies, there are buffalos ploughing the muddy lotus fields, farmers standing on the ploughs like very slow water-skiers, and rushing water can be heard everywhere as the paddies are filled through the complicated irrigation channels. There is blossom on the plum trees, some birds have come back, hens are fussing over new chicks and our photocopier assistant and one of the young technicians have fallen in love and walk, badminton rackets in hand, a discreet distance apart, through the trees after work.

Spiritual Pollution has disappeared without trace since our return, so the political climate, too, is milder. The Crackdown on Crime continues, though, but at a slower pace and without the publicity that surrounded it in the autumn. Now the papers are full not of fulminations against selfish individualism and decadent Western permissiveness, but of tributes to peasants who have had the initiative to set up businesses, and exhortations to get rich quick! Various theories have been advanced for the mysterious disappearance of Spiritual Pollution. Some say that the concept was so nebulous that cadres at grass-roots level had trouble inter-preting it – which would account for the difference in treatment in different units. Others say that the campaign was instigated through pressure from 'leftists' in the Politburo, unhappy at the decline they see in 'spiritual civilization' and revolutionary fervour, and at the growth of individualism, by-products of the

Responsibility System and policy of opening up to the West; and that these leftists have now yielded to pressure to liberalize still further. There seems to be an upsurge in the 'Party Rectification' campaign, Deng's strategy of replacing veteran revolutionaries in the party with younger, better educated cadres, who not incidentally are more sympathetic to his views. As always in China, a lot of speculation and little hard fact!

Letter nine

WOMEN'S DAY AND OTHER EXCURSIONS

Letter nine
WOMEN'S DAY AND OTHER EXCURSIONS

5 May 1984

Spring has now arrived in earnest. The famous cherry blossom at Wuhan University has come and gone, the paddies are full of water, the fields are full of bright yellow rape flowers, and bodies are beginning to reappear after months hidden beneath layers of padding. I've never looked forward to or enjoyed Spring so much!

Since our return, Jill and I and the others have been very busy: the trainee teachers have now returned from a six-month course in Britain and we are supervising their teaching practice, and last month I went up to Beijing for a week of meetings and report writing. On the whole, I'm glad we live in Wuhan. Beijing strikes me as a big dusty bleak city, whose guts have been ripped out and replaced by mile after mile of concrete blocks and wide roads, with the odd forlorn looking pagoda or temple poking through the polluted dusty haze. It does have top class international hotels, a Friendship Store where you can buy cheese and other Western products, and you can get films developed there. But you can't wander out of the front gate of the college and go for a country walk by the shores of a lake and see water buffalo, rice planting and steam trains all in the space of two minutes.

One afternoon I visited the Children's Hospital in Beijing. About four months ago, I was asked by our Chinese Director if I would make a tape for a friend of his. I said yes, of course, little realizing that it would involve me in five solid mornings in our recording studio, with a pile of medical case histories from an American textbook, trying to get my tongue round sentences and sentences of medical language, none of which I could pronounce or understand. I often had hysterics, had to stop, go away, come back again. Anyway, after five days, I got the tapes ready, and off they went to Beijing. The Director of the Children's Hospital, an old classmate of our Director (they studied together at Chongqing High School in the 30s: the equivalent, it seems of Manchester Grammar), wanted the tapes to help her with her English class at the hospital. I was invited over there to be thanked publicly. About fifty doctors and nurses were packed into a reception room and I was given three presents, which, in the polite Chinese way, you only open afterwards. They asked me lots of questions, some in English, some in Chinglish and then put on a little show for me. They brought in a plastic dummy baby, rigged up to a box with coloured lights. The sketch was about how to resuscitate a baby, and was performed by about seven doctors and nurses, who wear white caps that make them look more like kitchen staff than medical staff. The sketch was composed of many of the involved, tongue-twisting sentences that I had recorded months before. The baby was dying: 'Oh nurse, the infant seems to have stopped breathing.' They pressed on its chest: 'Oh look nurse, the red light is twinkling: the heart is no longer in function.' They inspected its throat: 'Nurse can you see the tonsils?' 'No I cannot see the tonsils, but I can see the vocal chords.' They resuscitated the baby: 'Oh the green light is twinkling: congratulation nurse.' After about twenty minutes, they bowed, we applauded and they then said, 'Thank you for coming to our show. Now please tell us our weak points in English.' As a memento of that visit, I now have a pottery Tang Dynasty camel in green and brown, a jade-green glass elephant and a tape of Chinese classical music, which sounds rather like Vaughan Williams in a strange way.

Some time ago now, we were taken round the three schools which serve this college, or unit of some 10000 souls. They are: a nursery, which they translate as 'kindergarten', a primary school, and a 'middle school', or, in our terms, secondary school. The nursery takes in children from the age of 56 days, the official end of maternity leave, to 6 years, the primary school deals with the 6–12 age range, and the secondary school is for 12–18-year olds.

The nursery is to look after the children of working mothers, but since in China that covers all women, the state has care of all its children from a very early age. The nursery buildings are like all others in China: dingy, dirty, unpainted and crumbling. But the chubby children, bundled up for the cold, with aprons and pinafores over their layers of padding, and the bright sun streaming in through the classroom windows made a very pretty picture. The principal, a kindly lady in her fifties, grey hair, white coat like a nurse, twinkling smile, took us round, and we sat in various classes at the start of the morning. All the classes were doing morning musical exercise to the moan of a harmonium in each classroom. Three women teachers per class of 35. While Miss Li pumped the harmonium, Miss Ding stood at the back and watched the children. One would be brought to the front to act as leader, and would shout numbers 'yi, er, san, si . . .' in time with the music and the others would follow the lead in a variety of mini-gongfu movements and Chinese operatic dance movements. Quite a lot of martial stamping and yelling, all in strict time. I asked what the words were to one song and it was about hygiene and cleanliness and developing their bodies to serve the Mother-land. All a lot more disciplined and ordered than in a British nursery school, no creative waterplay or sandboxes or building bricks. Even the children we saw in another classroom, dressed in doctors' and nurses' uniforms, bandaging patients' wounds and sending them off to the apothecary with prescriptions, were doing so in a very directed way: not free play, but a role play to learn about the health service. But the smiles on the faces, the bemused look of those at the back who didn't really know what they were supposed to be doing, and the warmth of the teachers were the same as any school in any country.

Next we went to the middle school, just outside the gates, and were rather hurriedly ushered into three different classrooms. I opted for a maths lesson, Jill for an English lesson, the others to the biology room. The contrast with the infants hits you, just as it does in Britain! From innocent enthusiasm, and loving smiles on teachers' faces, to authoritarian dinginess. I sat at the back of the maths class, quite understanding how I had managed to hate maths lessons all the way through school. The teacher was doing some elaborate explanations on the board, and whenever he asked a question, some brave fourteen-year old would stand up and mumble an incoherent reply. A colleague next to me said that they were doing advanced A-level standard algebraic operations.

So maybe I should have been impressed. Red star on the teacher's dais, squeaky blackboard, windows wide open to the wintry air, silent serious class. Not a touch of decoration or fun in the whole place. After twenty long minutes of maths we were taken up to the common room, and the headmaster, a rather nervous chap, talked to us in halting English and asked us to tell them their weak points. He said the purpose of the school was to teach the students to serve the Motherland, to understand the Party's thoughts, and to develop their minds. Knowledge had to be force-fed into the students' heads so that results would be better and intelligence developed, so the lesson content had to be aimed high and the pace kept up for the brighter ones even if not all the students understood. We asked what happened to children with learning problems. There didn't seem to be a formal system of remedial education, but he said that the dedicated teachers would give the children some extra coaching in their own free time.

The whole education system seems very competitive. Children leave school at 18, and go to college on the basis of a stiff national exam, which they take in eight subjects. Learning is very much by rote. In all eighteen subjects are taught at school, of which politics is one. English is the only foreign language. The students go home to eat lunch, and games are organized in the afternoons. Although there is great stress on obedience in class – everyone in strict rows of desks, sitting upright, standing to answer teachers' questions – there was a cheerfully disorganized atmosphere in the break, with children pushing, shoving, fighting, as in any British secondary school.

The third visit was to the primary school, built in 1957, with cheerful slogans on the walls: 'Study Well', 'Progress a little every day' etc. We sat at the back of a first year class of seven-year olds, and I was whisked back to lovely lessons at that age with lovely teachers. This lady was teaching Chinese characters. It was wonderful to watch: a very military style of teaching, but she had a presence which commanded instant devotion. We were spell-bound, and so it seemed were her class. Each Chinese character has several strokes in it, which must be memorized, and each character must be learned separately. There are said to be 50000 characters in the Chinese language, though the vast majority of

these are rarely used. You need about 2000 characters to read a
newspaper. To be able to read competently you need about 3000
characters. An educated person may have 4 or 5000. These seven-
year olds had a reading ability of 250 characters (we know about
600). The aim is for every child to have a reading ability of 3000
characters by the time they reach secondary school. To learn to
write is even more arduous. Each stroke has a name and the
strokes for each character must be written in a certain prescribed
order. We watched the children learn to write *didi*, which means
younger brother. It consists of the same two characters repeated.
Each has seven strokes. This is how they learned it: teacher draws
it on the board, asks what it is, the children reply '*Di di di*' 'Yes,
good, what is it, Xiao Wang?' '*Di di di*' 'Good.' She then draws it
on the board, naming the strokes in order as she does so '*Dian,
pie, hengzhe, heng, shuzhezhegou, shu, pie*,' using a different colour
chalk for each stroke. The children then chant the strokes in
unison, drawing them in the air with their fingers, as she
conducts the class. They finish by clapping their hands and
chanting, '*Di di di*'. Then a line of girls repeat the strokes, then a
line of boys. Then she gives an order, and the whole class turn to
the left, sitting sideways in their seats and repeat the strokes from
memory. Another order, and they all turn to the right and repeat
the strokes again. Then the character is erased from the board,
and she chooses a child to come and draw it on the board, using
the chalks. The class have to say if he's right. Here are the strokes
if you want to try for yourself:

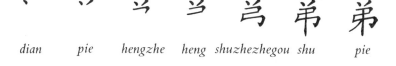

dian   pie   hengzhe   heng   shuzhezhegou shu   pie

I watched one boy as his exercise book dropped off the desk.
He was scared to pick it up, terrified that anyone would notice.
He waited till the teacher's back was turned and made a hurried
dive for it. Absolute discipline in class, everyone sitting up
straight facing the front, and no whispering, even of an answer to
a question. Of course they relaxed a bit at break, when they were

shy, then eager to ask questions about Britain. I asked about discipline and punishment. At first, a child will be criticized by his classmates and asked to apologize to them all for a minor breaches of discipline. Quite effective, I should think. The same system of peer group surveillance, and public criticism and self-criticism is used to keep people in line throughout their adult life too. Our students, for example, have class monitors, who have to keep a check on everyone's behaviour. At the end of the course, students have to write a 'self-evaluation', and the monitor has to write a report on everyone in the class. Both the student's evaluation, and the monitor's report are then sent back to the student's work unit. More serious breaches of school discipline would be reported up the school hierarchy to the head, who would inform the parents, and a note would be put on the child's record form. The child might be punished by work: cleaning the school windows etc. I asked about physical punishment and they were shocked. Young Pioneers and later the Communist Youth League play an important part in a child's life. Young Pioneers are from 7–12, the Youth League from 12–18. You can join the Party from 18 onwards. Apparently nearly all children belong to the Young Pioneers. Maybe three or four in a class would not be allowed to join, because of laziness or 'incorrect thoughts'. This social ostracism supposedly pushes them into line and they work harder to catch up with their peers. It seems to be a bit like scouts with politics thrown in. School is six days a week, and holidays are quite short, so they lead a busy life. On Saturday afternoons, everyone is supposed to volunteer to help clean the school, with the Young Pioneers setting a good example, and on Sundays, children are encouraged to help their parents. Everyone organized, like a big Butlins camp. I find myself alternately moved and appalled by this. The rigid routine can be very oppressive, as we found during the winter, but there is something about the sheer vastness of the country, the endurance of its people, and the commonness of purpose that is very moving.

20 May 1984
Charlie and I are slowly discovering more about Wuhan: two good restaurants, one of which serves Sichuan food and the other

a game restaurant which serves such things as hare, pheasant, wild duck and twenty different varieties of snake. We have found an interesting village-like area of Hanyang, with steep streets, white-washed houses and flights of steps: rather Mediterranean in atmosphere. Another interesting area is down by the Yangtze in Hankou, where each street has a specialized market: one is full of pot plants and flowers, another is full of exotic goldfish, and another full of canaries, goldfinches and small songbirds. This street and the last, are mainly full of old men, squatting round the cages or bowls, comparing the merits of one bird or fish with another, taking all morning to make their choice. There are crickets for sale too, in tiny wicker baskets. Old men or women keep one for company and take pleasure in the shrill rasping song. It's amazing to see – or rather hear – a cricket seller going down the street, carrying a shoulder-pole with fifty or sixty cricket cages on each end: the noise is deafening!

One nice thing about Chinese streets is street libraries. These consist of a wooden rack displaying various comic books and picture-stories, and several wooden stools or benches scattered around on the pavement. At any time of day, whatever the weather, as long as there is enough daylight, there will be people sitting around immersed in the books, having paid a few *fen* to rent a read. As in the teahouses, street-library society is almost exclusively male. I speculate on the reasons for this. Are women less literate? Or do they prefer more highbrow literature? Do they simply have less leisure time than men, with the precious hours before or after work filled with cooking, shopping and house-work? Or is the librarian's choice of adventure tales and war stories just not to their taste?

Wuhan has a new mayor, and the city centre is getting a face-lift: neon signs have appeared in the main street, and a rash of small coffee-shops have sprung up, serving thick sweet coffee, lotus soup, buns and cakes. The smoothest of these, called 'The Western-style Pastry House', has plastic seats and formica tables in booths just like a hamburger joint, serves pseudo-doughnuts and cream buns and plays smoochy music.

One of our best discoveries is a silk-tailor, who is used to making up Western fashions and will work from a drawing, or copy a dress, shirt or blouse. A lovely old man, very slow, very gentle, very precise. We went in there last week with a pile of silk and the garments we wanted copying. A curious crowd immediately gathered, attracted by the strange Western fashions and commented noisily on all our clothes. One little number, an Indian cotton frock with shoulder-straps and a low neck, drew horrified gasps and tut-tutting from the crowd. Regulations governing the cut of dresses and blouses were laid down by the government: they should not reveal the collar-bone or the hair under the armpit. It's considered loose to leave the top button undone. Things are changing though: last time I went to the tailor's, I saw that some of his girl assistants had copied one of my patterns for themselves, and I saw my skirt reduplicated in various patterns and colours and materials! I am waiting for it to appear in department stores in Wuhan.

Some weeks ago was a festival known as International Women's Day, though none of us had heard of it before coming to China. Women all over China were entitled to the afternoon off work, and a treat of some sort. Our girl students came to class with sweets and peanuts and sunflower seeds, which they distributed to everyone (men as well). (These 'Happy Sweets' – boiled sweets in wrappers bearing the double happiness symbol – are traditional in China. They are bought on festive occasions and offered to all by those who have something to celebrate. Sometimes we come into the staffroom in the morning to find a small packet of sweets on each desk, and then have to guess who got married or had a new baby.) The girls then all trooped off on a trip to the Botanic Gardens, the married ones returning to a meal cooked by their husbands. The female members of staff were taken to a reception organized by Hubei Government for its 'foreign experts' at one of the hotels in town.

We assembled in a rooftop theatre, where tables were laid out in a large rectangle, as if for a wedding, and spread with what looked like a children's tea-party: sweets, peanuts, fruit, cakes – the only thing missing was the jelly! A very impressive line-up of women at the top table: the Deputy Governor of Hubei province, the Vice-Mayor of Wuhan, some top cadres, plus a selection of Wuhanese women who had achieved some distinction in their chosen field: the ping-pong champion of China for example. I couldn't help noticing, though, that all the women were vice-this and deputy-that. However, when you consider the position of women in China not forty years ago . . .

A selection of speeches about the liberation of women, women's place in a socialist society, the progress made since Liberation in emancipating women from a feudal society, and the work that still remained to be done, while we munched cake and spat sunflower seeds. Then they invited speeches or songs from us, and a rather surreal part of the afternoon began. A woman who had introduced herself to us the week before as a 'radical lesbian feminist' was the first to stand up, and we all wondered anxiously what she was going to say. She made a speech about the joy of being a woman, and sang a song called, 'I'm glad to be a woman.' The Chinese nodded approvingly and clapped. An American girl stood up next, and made a speech about how absurd it was to exclude men from a gathering like this, since they were the ones who should be listening to the speeches, and how stupid it was to have a feminist movement excluding men. This was translated by the interpreter into something like 'Congratulations to women all over the world on their special day. I am so pleased to be with the women of China and take part in their celebrations today.' Again the women on the top table nodded and clapped. Finally, someone asked the deputy-mayors and vice-governors and higher cadres to tell us about their families, which they did, at length, one after the other, recounting the exploits of this son or that daughter, all translated first into English and then into French. They all seemed to have about five children each. After the speeches, we had our 'treat', a special performance by the Wuhan Acrobats (male), and then trooped off down to the dining-room for a banquet, served, I was disappointed to note, by waitresses. The festival was a curious combination of Women's Liberation, children's treat, Mother's Day, and cosy women's-get-together.

Another interesting day was our visit to the Hanyang cotton mill last Saturday. This, like the factories in Shashi, had a distinctly 19th century feel. After our tour, we were given an opportunity to talk to some of the women from the shopfloor, and I was very impressed with their seriousness, their earnestness (though presumably they had been selected as representatives for precisely those reasons). We asked them what they did in their spare time. Oh, read, did exercise, spent time with family and friends, but mostly studied, to improve themselves and give food to their minds. What jobs, we enquired, were considered to be the best in the factory. In general, the workers preferred those jobs where they could use their brains and not their hands. They then asked us some very penetrating questions, which we found hard to answer: what did the British workers expect from life? What were our expectations of the future? If their unit leaders organized some activity, did the British workers go willingly?

It's this combination of high-mindedness and naivety that is such an appealing (though dangerous, and occasionally irritating) characteristic. An announcement on the Hong Kong-Guangzhou train requests all passengers carrying 'explosives, firearms and other forbidden items' to 'please inform the guard immediately.' This innocent and idealistic earnestness of the people is one of the reasons I love China, and probably one of the reasons why Communism in China has always had a relatively good press in the West: you do get a genuine sense of self-sacrifice, lack of selfishness and personal greed, devotion to work for a common cause, and desire for self-improvement. It's just this quality though that has made people accept totalitarianism with such docility. That and their patience, their tolerance and uncomplaining, long-suffering nature. When a Western visitor praised this quality as one of the strengths of the Chinese people to the great writer, Lu Xun, earlier this century, he replied that it was precisely that quality that was their weakness.

Though now, there is a cynicism that the government's trying hard to suppress, together with a new interest in personal gain and profit, that it is actually encouraging. This is called 'fostering a spirit of initiative' and 'paving the way towards making the country prosperous.' An article in this week's *China Daily* praises Peasant Dong, who did nothing but sleep all day in the Cultural Revolution because, under the 'Eating from One Big Pot' system, his efforts in the fields were going unrewarded and he earned the same no matter how much work he put in. But now that he has been allocated a strip of personal land, under the Responsibility System, he is working day and night and has made more than 10000 *yuan* for himself in 'sideline' goods. Peasant Dong has done very well for himself, and acquired bicycle, television, sewing machine, and radio. Other peasants are exhorted to learn from his example and to work for socialist construction and get rich.

An increase in the living standards of China's desperately poor peasantry must be one of the main concerns of any government, and there is no doubt that the Responsibility System is producing results. There is far more food around than there was a year ago when we arrived. The free market at the entrance to the campus, for example, used to consist of a couple of old women squatting by the gates with a few baskets of eggs and some limp vegetables. Now the market has expanded so much that they've had to move it outside the gates, because it was taking up too much room. There are meat-sellers, vegetable-sellers, beancurd-sellers, fish-sellers, breakfast stalls, where you can buy rice pancakes and doughnuts as alternatives to the college breakfast, and even a couple of small restaurants in tents.

Some people have taken things further. A headline this week proclaims: PARTY BACKS BOLD MANAGER ACCUSED OF GOING CAPITALIST. Manager Bu Xinsheng introduced the Responsibility System into the Haiyan County collectively-owned shirt factory and thereby increased production by 400% 'paying great attention to the demands of the market'. Some Party members said that 'Bu's was the capitalist way, and should be stopped', but the Provincial Party 'endorsed him as correct and called on cadres to follow his example in initiative.'

A cartoon which surprised me last week showed two adjacent fruit shops, one labelled 'State Fruit Shop', the other 'Individual Enterprise Fruit Shop'. The state shop was empty, with a sign saying 'Sold Out', while two men were busy carrying baskets of apples from it to the other shop, where they were being marked up from 50 *fen* to 1 *yuan* a *jin*.

I'll end on a flippant note with the quote of the week, from a note appended to an essay: 'Jill, Enlish ability very poor, but when I make much progresses, I like to tell you about my village, people there was very interesting: example, The Ugly Blacksmith and his Lovely Wife, The Wicked Rover (or did he mean lover?) and the Pretty Girl.' (I can't wait!)

HU YAOBANG SAYS
I MUST INVITE YOU TO DINNER

Letter ten
HU YAOBANG SAYS
I MUST INVITE YOU TO DINNER

7 July 1984

Over a year now since we first stepped off the Beijing train into the steamy heat of Wuhan, and once again the temperatures are in the 100s, the pale pink 'powder puff' trees, gardenias, oleander, fuschia and hibiscus are in bloom all over the campus; there are brilliant turquoise dragonflies and huge swallowtail butterflies everywhere, hens are taking dust–baths and gawky adolescent chicks are running around. Since June 1 skirts have made a reappearance, and the female half of the college are now in a summer uniform of pastel cotton frocks, kindergarten-style with puff sleeves and sashes, white ankle socks, and lurid plastic sandals. Technicolour vests have also made a comeback. Coming as we did in the middle of summer last year, we missed the full impact of the re-emergence of bodies from their winter cocoons, and of the sudden dazzle of colour, brilliant reds and yellows of the flowers and luminous green of the young rice, after months of winter monotony. Less pleasant aspects of summer are the Reappearance of the Mosquitos and the Wakening of the Cockroaches, sweaty lessons, and mould on shoes and clothes, but we find the summer far easier than the winter, and don't seem to feel as hot as at equivalent temperatures last year.

Thinking back over the year, and more particularly over the changes that we have seen during the year, we realize that China is going through a very profound metamorphosis. Economically, things are becoming more and more liberal, with emphasis on free enterprise and individual initiative. Several new Special Economic Zones have been opened up to trade with the West: 20th century-style treaty ports – on Chinese terms. Foreign businesses and what Professor Zhang calls 'Joint Adventures' can be started up in these zones, which have different economic rules from the rest of China, allowing foreigners both to invest money and remit the profits abroad. Chinese graduates are being sent to business schools in America, profit is no longer a dirty word, and the Responsibility System seems to be overflowing from the countryside into industry. The papers are full of reports of factory manager Zhao who made X million *yuan* of profit by introducing the Responsibility System into his factory, or of commune member Dong who has built himself a house with the profits made from his sideline goods. Posters and headlines proclaim IT IS GLORIOUS TO GET RICH and those few who do make small fortunes are held up as shining examples to all in the national press. Does the prospect of a widening gap between rich and poor bother people? Some of my students confessed themselves disgruntled with their lot. As state employees, college teachers or research scientists, they are on fixed salaries ranging from about 50 *yuan* for a new teacher, to maybe 150 or 200 *yuan* for a top professor, with no chance of earning more. There is now a real discrepancy between state employees and those few peasants or entrepreneurs who start up small enterprises and strike lucky. Despite this, they say that the government is taking a 'correct line' with the peasants, and are quick to point out that China could never revert to the bad old landlord and peasant days, since the state still owns the land, and merely allocates it to the peasants. The government itself seems sensitive to criticism that the gap between rich and poor is growing. A cartoon for *Liaoning Daily* shows runners heading for a finishing post marked 'Prosperity for All'. Some are lagging behind or running out of breath, while a cynical onlooker remarks 'Do I detect a tendency towards polarization?'. The accompanying article in *China Daily*, however, under the headline 'More for the Rich and More for the Poor', is careful to refute this criticism, expounding the trickle-down theory of wealth. It admits that 'it is true that the gap between rich and poor is getting wide', but adds that 'with a closer look, one may see that this is a blessing in disguise', and concludes that 'the rich are becoming richer, but the poor are also getting better off – they are not competitors' Here is a miscellany of signs of the times culled from *China Daily* over the last six months:

Some of the new-style People's Heroes:

> Peasant contractor Zhang Weihua of Asche Commune in Acheng County, Heilongjiang Province, enjoys a happy moment with his family as they decide who should answer a call on their new telephone. The family had the phone installed this month to facilitate their new upholstery business which has brought them an income of 12000 *yuan* in two years.

> Li Xue of Chengbei village in Jiangsu Province could afford to buy a motorcycle as his family earned more than 8000 *yuan* last year.

> When Huang Meqing of Wuxi County, Jiangsu Province heard that ground beetles were in great demand for use in medicine, he decided to have a try. He faced great difficulties . . . But his chief difficulty was the uncooperative attitude of his wife, who considered breeding beetles 'a waste of time and money' and would throw away his books, tools, and larvae. One thing she did not throw away: the 8000 *yuan* Huang made from a successful crop of beetles two years later.

> Fang Jinhai and fifteen partners signed a contract last spring to take over the fish farm from Baoying County for three years, agreeing to pay a rent of 21000 *yuan* each year. Since then they have invested a total of 10000 *yuan* to develop fish-breeding and melon and reed planting in the lakeside marshes. They earned a total of 52000 *yuan* last year from their crops of fish, crab, shrimp, melon, and lotus fruit which were sold to state agencies and at local free markets.

And currently the most famous lady in China:

> Sun Guiying, a Beijing chicken farmer, this week became the first peasant in China to own a car. She is pictured here beside the silver *Toyota* saloon for which she paid 9300 *yuan*. She and her family have sold this year 32000 kilograms of eggs at a profit of 37000 *yuan*.

The government have introduced a system, mainly to cope with the problem of unemployed urban youth, whereby people can combine in small cooperatives to start small businesses. Many people have taken advantage of this new policy, and the streets are crowded with hawkers and vendors of all kinds. Now, most of these probably barely eke out a living, but some apparently get quite rich. One human interest feature describes a girl who 'dreamed of becoming a doctor or an artist' but after years of waiting in vain for a state-assigned job, became self-employed, and started her own *jiaozi* stall, selling steamed dumplings:

Xu, who earns about 200 *yuan* a month, said 'Good service attracts customers and brings in more money, but good service also leads to good human relations and helps improve the general mood of society. Money is not everything, though it is indispensable. I often do free service, or move my stall near where entrance examinations for college or high school are held . . . I owe all my success to the Party's and the government's new policies of allowing individuals to open businesses of their own . . . I don't want to quit because I know that self-employed and state factory workers have equal responsibilities to society'.

A wonderful combination of private enterprise and socialist ethics!

These new reforms have brought other social developments in their wake:

The 'Help Wanted' ad is coming to Beijing. Coupled with examinations, it will be used to recruit workers for state-run enterprises.

Bank loans are to be extended to help urban house-hunters buy houses.

Although the employment of household help was criticized as gentrified and bourgeois or exploitationary during the Cultural Revolution . . . in reality, such employment cannot be abolished.

Chinese peasants are now officially allowed to buy and own motor vehicles . . . Individual households bought more than one million tractors since the policy of encouraging rural prosperity became official.

And a leader article forecasts future trends:

The economic reform that has proved so successful in China's vast countryside is spreading into the industrial sector at an ever-quickening pace. The Responsibility System, which has brought immediate results in rural areas, not only provides lessons that could be adapted to the urban economy, but has also served as an eye-opener and inspired confidence in city reformers . . . A Responsibility System will be enforced [I like the turn of phrase!] with executives held responsible to the state, and mid-level cadres in turn responsible to the executives and so on. Personal income and promotion will be linked directly to management and production.

Individual quotas will be governed by contracts, with only minimum wages guaranteed and no ceilings set for bonuses, so that each will be paid strictly according to his or her work.

All this industry and increased prosperity has meant a great increase in the amount and variety of goods available in the shops. A walk down *Zhongshan Da Jie* or Sun Yat Sen Street, the main thoroughfare in Hankou, is very interesting compared to the same walk only six months ago: there is much more on display, from variety of foodstuffs to colour television and stereo cassette recorders to flashy clothes.

There is also an increase in advertising. It surprised us, when we first came, to find any adverts at all in China, but they don't seem so incongruous now. Along with posters for the One Child Family, Party slogans, and admonitions about hygiene in kitchens, there are now hoardings advertising films, fridges, and cassette recorders just like at home, except that the contrast with the monochrome surroundings makes them even more startling, and they seem strangely irrelevant to the stream of cyclists passing below along the crowded street. A charming feature is that they are all hand-painted, so the art of the signwriter is thriving in this new consumer society, as it was in Europe before the war. Some artists are inevitably better than others, and perspective can play strange tricks with the shape of a *Toshiba* TV or a bottle of *Coca-Cola* (in Chinese *kou ke kou le* meaning 'Taste Good, Feel Happy').

Colours are also unbelievably lurid. *China Daily*, the English language newspaper, though of course aimed mainly at foreigners, has countless examples of the increasing consumer choice available to people. An advert for furcoats I saw recently reads 'GOLDEN SWALLOW: This luxurious fur coat can protect you from the cold, and its value could be worth more than your savings.' Is this really China? Chinese adverts are written in a language all their own, curiously naive and artless with a strange period feel to them. Here are a few examples:

DRAGON TEA BAGS are blended from selected black tea. They are strong and brisk in taste, bright in liquor, and attractive in packing. Orders are welcome.

PANDA BRAND rubber shoes. Everybody loves Panda. Everybody loves to wear Panda Brand rubber shoes.

SEAGULL torches. 'Second to None'. Seamless body. Exquisite design. Fashionable style. Super quality. Ready market at home and abroad.

DEER BRAND BEAUTY SOAP Best choice for quality and price. You think soap leaves your skin soft? You haven't tried DEERS.

TIANJIN CARPETS: our hand-knotted carpets are the only ones which won the nation's gold medal.

A basket advert: 'Economic and Practical. Long History. Elaborate Weaving. Bright Colours. Various Patterns.'

SHANGHAI ESPADRILLES: Fashionable design. Complete Specifications. Excellent Workmanship. Comfortable to Wear.

Want to keep in good health? Have you tried EXTRACT OF SPOTTED DEER ANTLER? Pilose antler is one of China's most precious and superior tonics. Spotted deer antler is the best. Our Spotted Deer Antler Extract is a drink refined from such antlers. It can invigorate the blood, stimulate the appetite, improve sleep, ease fatigue, enrich blood, and warm male genitals.

And finally, one that the makers themselves don't sound too sure about:

BEE AND FLOWER BRAND Sandalwood Soap. So delightful to your skin! Our BEE AND FLOWER Sandalwood Soap, made from selected materials, gives you delightful and lasting fragrance. It not only possesses all the merits that a sandalwood scented soap may have, but it also does no harm whatsoever to your skin. Just try it, and you will see our sincere recommendation is rather convincing.

Does all this increase in economic freedom mean an increase in political freedom? There are some signs. From an article in *China Daily:*

NOW WE FEEL FREE AND HAPPY TO GO TO CHURCH: There are now 16 Catholic and 17 Protestant churches reopened in the city (Shanghai) in contrast to the chaotic decade of the Cultural Revolution, when religious activities were banned . . . It is expected that more churches will open up in the future . . . Efforts are being made to train more priests. In 1982 a Catholic seminary was set up at Sheshan, about twenty miles from Shanghai. 'I feel very optimistic about the future of Chinese Christian churches,' said Pastor Shen Yifan, 'as I am convinced that today's religious policy in China is not an expediency, rather a basic long-term policy.'

Another paper in the same month was more cautious:

Religion under Marxist theory, should die a natural death, if not in ten years, then in one hundred, maybe longer, even a thousand. Until then the government sees no harm in the continued freedom to practise religious beliefs of whatever kind.

People and rules seem more relaxed than in the Spiritual Pollution period. The students have started dancing again, and notices go up on the board from time to time advertising 'DANCING PARTY WITH CHARMING MUSIC.' But by far the clearest indication we've had of a relaxation in attitudes occurred when our *Waiban* (Foreign Affairs) official said to us: 'Hu Yaobang says I must invite you to dinner.' He didn't look overjoyed at the prospect, and neither, to be honest, were we, as we stuttered hastily, 'Please don't feel you have to.' It turned out that Hu Yaobang (the General Secretary of the Party) had made a speech saying that foreigners were to be made welcome, and that it was now permitted for Chinese to socialise with us. Well, we didn't get an invitation from our *Waiban* man (I think that he had a modal verb problem, and meant 'may' not 'must'), but the next day, the students were lined up and told to clean their dormitories, because now the foreign teachers would visit them. As a seasoned dormitory visitor, I wasn't aware that it could have been frowned on – but then there is so much that we are not aware of. That same night, several students came round to visit us – no-one had ever just dropped in like that before. Among them was my friend of the abortive cookery lessons episode. She had brought her daughter with her, dressed in her best white frock. They had all brought presents. 'We have come to celebrate the fact that we are now allowed to visit you', they said.

But all is not sweetness and light and the jingle of money, as any two minute glance out of the window, or stroll down the street will show. And the darker side, which affected our outlook all winter, is still present. The Crackdown on Crime still

157

continues, and according to the papers is having the desired effect:

CRIME CUT BY HALF SAYS BEIJING MAYOR. The average monthly crime figures dropped 58% over the previous seven months . . . The municipal government has severely punished grave criminal offences since last August. Most bad elements have been rounded up, crushing blows administered to criminal gangs, and the number of criminal offences undermining public order has been greatly reduced.

When I was arranging a debate for an evening activity a week or so ago, the motion 'Capital Punishment Should Be Abolished' (that old chestnut in the West) was suggested by someone, but rejected by the group as a whole. 'Why?', I asked, as if not understanding. 'Too political', they said. So we had the apparently safer topic of 'Young People Should Not Take Any Notice Of What Older People Say', but even that, recently, could have been interpreted as too political. You never really know where you are here. So we are watching and waiting to see if all this will last, as are the Chinese themselves, with infinitely greater concern lest there should be a swing-round, a volte-face back into the dark old days of only a decade ago.

This seems such a placid, well-ordered society, compared with the tube muggings, rapes, and murders of Britain – in fourteen months here I have never felt less than totally safe on the streets or cycling home late at night – that it seems difficult to connect the peaceful streets with the reports of violence and crime in the papers. But a few weeks ago my bike was stolen from outside our house. I didn't report the theft, as I was worried about the penalties a foreigner's bike-thief might incur. But nothing is secret in China for very long, and at mid-morning break someone came up to me: 'It is said that your bike has been stolen.' So I had to make a formal statement to the police. The theft led to a delightful incident that could only happen in China. Charlie was away at the time, and a colleague deputizing for him was told, 'You should criticize Jill for having her bike stolen.' For having been careless, I suppose. He wasn't too keen on the job, and asked to be excused. 'Oh well,' they said, 'Charlie will just have to do it when he gets back!'

We've been on a couple of short trips since last writing. We spent one weekend in Shanghai, a city which is considered to be the most chic, trend-setting place in the country. Shanghai people have a certain *je ne sais quoi* and are admired, mistrusted, or envied for this by the rest of the Chinese. However, we were pleased to note that Shanghai's Nanjing Road, *the* street for shopping with its Number One Department Store and Number One Grocery Store, actually has very few flashing neon signs compared with central Hankou. Many more goods around in the shops though. One shop we saw was full of computers and calculators – something we've never seen in Wuhan. Other shops bulged with fridges and electric rice cookers and stereo cassette players. A lovely musical instrument store, and best of all, a wonderful old calligraphy shop with latticed windowed galleries and a treasure trove of brushes and carved inkstones, elaborately decorated ink-sticks and hand-made paper with designs of bamboo or plum blossom. Many shops in Shanghai have old-fashioned systems of payment. Overhead wires cross the shop, running from counters to cash till. If you are taller than the average Chinese, you frequently have to duck as bulldog clips with receipts, cash and change whizz over your head.

Shanghai is a fascinating place for a Westerner, as it reeks of the twenties and thirties, echoes of Somerset Maugham, and as you eat a meal in the Peace Hotel, overlooking the Bund along the river, you wonder where Noel Coward sat with flu composing *Private Lives*. In the Peace Hotel coffee bar, China's equivalent of Preservation Hall, a jazz band churns out the same weary tunes they must have played in the thirties, and you can still dance to the strains of *Tea for Two*. Still swinging, but not one of the players under sixty-five I'd guess. Buildings that could have come straight from London in the twenties and thirties are everywhere. The old hotels have wood panelled walls and art deco ceilings and are furnished with grand pianos, chandeliers, deep padded armchairs and aspidistra tables.

Although things have changed from Shanghai's days of sin and shady deals, the era when every third house was either a brothel or an opium den, when bodies were picked up every morning from the gutters where they had died, while the rich and famous danced the night away under the stars on the rooftop of the Peace

159

Hotel, and the crowds that throng Nanjing Road are now healthy, well-fed and well-clothed; it is impossible not to be conscious of Shanghai's past at every step you take, and the Shanghainese seem to have retained some of the verve and sophistication associated with that bygone age. Shanghai businessmen look much slicker than anywhere else in China, the girls are more fashionable, city life moves at a faster pace. It's not like Guangzhou, though, which was distinctly seamy, with a flavour of fast practice and underhand deals. Shanghai has style. It is a cosmopolitan city in a country where every other city, including the capital, feels like a provincial town.

The Shanghainese seem to know how to enjoy themselves too, more than other inhabitants of China's cities, and on a grander scale. There are some superb restaurants, and all those we went into seemed to be full of banquets and parties. All five floors of one we tried were full of a wedding party with five hundred guests, women fashionably dressed, men in Western suits and ties, with red flowers pinned to their lapels.

They seem equally enthusiastic about simpler pleasures. One of the most interesting things to do – and free – is to go to the People's Park, early in the morning, about 6.30 or 7 o'clock. Hundreds and hundreds of people all doing their exercises. Some alone, some in big groups. *Taiji, gongfu,* meditation, fencing, poetry reciting, English 'chat corner' (which we just managed to avoid – the last thing we wanted to do on a precious weekend away was to get involved in a discussion of people's 'weak points'). The strangest exercise we saw involves propping your foot up on a rock or in a tree and stretching back and forth. Our favourite old guy was doing three things at once, though I don't know if they all count as exercise. He had his foot in the lower branches of a tree, in one cupped hand he had his breakfast, some roasted peanuts, and in the other hand, with which he popped peanuts, he held a cigarette. So the morning exercise routine went: peanut, crunch, munch, stretch to the toes, back, crunch, drag of fag, stretch, back, peanut, crunch, munch, stretch, back, drag, stretch, and so on. Blissful happy way to spend the morning in the sun! But most of the people were doing *taiji* in groups of twenty, or reading books in groups of five, or doing

160

noisy, sweating, grunting *gongfu*.

For the May Day holiday, we went with a number of other foreign teachers from Wuhan on a *Waiban*-organized trip to Chongqing and back down the Yangtze through the famous Three Gorges. We stayed in the main hotel, a veritable multi-coloured wedding cake, the outside modelled on Beijing's Temple of Heaven, but the inside the usual vast Soviet palace. An ex-student invited us to his parents' flat for lunch. His father is a high-ranking cadre in charge of a grain depot, and his mother is a doctor in the local hospital. Our lunch date was preceded by a visit to her acupuncture clinic, where we watched her and the other doctors deftly inserting the fine silver needles, or burning herbs near specific sites on their patients' bodies: the technique known as moxibustion, which often accompanies acupuncture. The family of six lived in a three-room apartment, big by Chinese standards, overlooking the Jia Ling river. Mother, sisters and girlfriend all cycled over to join in the festivities in their lunch hour. The father had been at home preparing the food all morning, and now began to cook. Sichuan food is hot and spicy. The father said, with a twinkle, 'As you are foreign and perhaps not used to our food, I prepare something mild.' The meal was still quite a challenge! Dish after dish of hot red peppery Sichuan food, delicious but fiery. Our eyes were watering, and our student, after six months of bland oily Wuhan food, also had tears in his eyes. All washed down with the local *Five Grain Spirit*, as strong as the food was spicy.

We slept it off in the late afternoon, before an evening walk round the city. Chongqing is built on a hill at the confluence of the Yangtze and Jia Ling rivers, and the views are superb, over tumbledown crazy roofs, all coal-blackened and connected by steep staircase streets. The sight in the evening from the highest point of this hilly city, of the lights of the town spread out below and reflected in the water all around, with fainter lights from boats and craft on the river, is splendid, and the hilltop park is full of people: families out for an evening stroll, young lovers, workers at the end of their day, old men having an evening pipe, all taking the evening air and admiring the view.

The trip through the Gorges was spectacular. The river flows fast, and navigation is difficult. It takes five days from Wuhan to Chongqing upstream, but only three days back. The river is propelling the boat, the size of a Channel ferry, downstream at about 12 knots, with the engine adding another 15 or 20. So the banks, rocks, shoals, cliffs, mountains, swing past at an alarming rate, and the crunch would be hard if the captain didn't know his job. We spent hours watching him watch the river, and managed to sneak up onto the bridge behind him. He was really reading the river, staring straight ahead of him and giving very complicated hand signals to the helmsman beside him. His eyes never left the river. For two days we watched these hand signals, but could not decipher them. We were going through at a period of low water; presumably this time last year, with the floods, the trip would have been even faster! In the Tang Dynasty, the trip upstream through the Gorges could take something like twenty-five days, each boat hauled by teams of hundreds of coolies straining on bamboo plaited hawsers, along tow paths cut in the rock. There are still a few sailing junks, keeping to the slower side-waters. At certain points going upstream, the crew of these smaller craft still have to get out and haul their boats. We steamed straight down the middle, hooting imperiously at shabby junks and sampans. The Gorges themselves are perhaps best described by the little leaflet we were given as we boarded the boat:

> Visitors either cruising upstream or downstream would certainly cry out in admiration at the sight of the gorges which seem to be an excellent rolling picture. In addition, along the gorges there are a lot of historical relics and native places of famous figures, about which charming folk tales and legends are told. All these, like glittering gems, attract many visitors, who would feel that the boat tour along the gorges is like wandering in a long historical gallery as well as among the mountains and water. Oh! What a taste! How excited . . .!

What next on the travel front? In a few days we are off for the summer, to the far north-west, along the old Silk Road, via Xian, ancient capital of China, and home of the 'terracotta army'. The government has recently opened more towns to foreigners, so we should be able to get as far as Kashgar on the Sino-Pakistan-Soviet border, and almost halfway back to Europe. Oh! What a taste! How excited!

Letter eleven

DOWN THE OLD SILK ROAD

Letter eleven
DOWN THE OLD SILK ROAD

15 September 1984
Our journey began two months ago when we got a midday train
to Xian, an overnight journey of about twenty hours. After so
much train travel in China, that does not now seem particularly
long to us. Xian was the imperial capital for thousands of years
and features on most guided trips to China, as it has most of the
archaeological sites that foreigners have heard about. It is rich in
history, but rather poor in hotels! The *Renmin Dasha* is a huge
drab concrete Soviet-style building, with minimum facilities and
poor food. However Xian itself is a rather interesting place. Right
in the middle is the Bell Tower, and a little further away is the
Drum Tower: 'Morning bell and evening drum.' Hence the
names (a phrase that crops up again and again in Chinese English
guide books).

We took a very slow local bus out to see the 'terracotta army'.
The first emperor of the Qin Dynasty began constructing a huge
mausoleum when he was crowned at age 13. The 'terracotta
army' guards the actual mausoleum, under a hill, which has not
yet been touched; you can only see a small part at present of what
must lie beneath the dusty loess soil. The soldiers, horses and
chariots unearthed so far are underneath a huge arched roof,
rather like a London station roof: the lines of soldiers, four
abreast, climb out of the earth, broken into pieces, with heads,
bodies, and legs strewn in and on the ochre earth, becoming, as
they climb, upright figures in serried ranks facing the main
viewing platform and a blank earth wall. They seem like a huge
ancient army on parade; or perhaps a crowd of Qin Dynasty
commuters at Waterloo station, standing in line for their trains.
They all have 'earnest and steadfast' or 'brave and thoughtful'
expressions, they all have fine moustaches and are larger than life-
size, but every face is slightly different, with headgear and

165

hairstyles indicating rank. As we had gone out under our own steam, by local bus, we could look at them at our leisure, and we went back in several times. As Michelin might say, it is certainly 'Worth the Journey'.

We actually found the concentration of archaeology and museums quite tiring after an exhausting year of teaching. The Big Wild Goose Pagoda, to the south of the present city but to the north of the old capital, Changan, is where the Buddhist scriptures, the Tripitaka, finally ended their journey from India and were translated. (They are the reason for the journey told as *Journey to the West*, or *Monkey*.) A tall earth-coloured pagoda, with very narrow stairs, it was full of the Sunday thousands of local tourists. The city museum is excellent – full of Tang and earlier pottery, ancient bronze work, and a 'forest of steles' (stone inscriptions) which are very numerous, very old, very black, and to non-literates in Chinese, very dull.

Enough archaeology, and enough of the gloomy Soviet-style hotel; after three days we took a train westwards to Xining via Lanzhou. There was a terrific crowd pushing to get onto the platform. We had to queue for hours and then fight as the crowd surged through the ticket barriers. We ran towards the berth compartments. The stewardess said 'No room. Full up', but in fact there were twenty four empty berths in our compartment alone, and we got two of them. It is lovely to wake on a train and find yourself in a completely different landscape. Travelling from Wuhan to Xian, we had come into a land of dry loess, wind-blown Mongolian dust, carved by wind and rain into fantastic cliffs and canyons, with holes for troglodytes, hibernating locals, or weary peasants and their farm implements, or even for whole factories built into the cliffs. There were walls too, carved from the loess, and every building, every vehicle, every leaf, seemed to be made of loess too: coated in fine ochre dust. The Qin Dynasty army was the same colour too, a colour that remained with us for most of the journey to come. The temperature was a pleasant dry 80 degrees after the humid 100s we had left in Wuhan. From Xian to Lanzhou (capital of Gansu Province) the land became rockier and barer, with the Yellow River rushing muddy and brown between the cliffs. We saw more caves, more dust, with fewer

166

trees, but with watermelons and gourds among the wheatfields. The climb from Lanzhou to Xining, five hours hauled by a steam engine, was very impressive, climbing along a gorge most of the way. All along from Xian, we had been on a single-track line and as we were on a *zhikuai* (slow train) not a *tekuai* (express) we had to stop at every little station, pulling into sidings to let *tekuai* and goods trains past. At one such stop, looking out across the fields of watermelon, we were wondering why tents were pitched, or branch and straw shelters built, every 200 yards or so. Suddenly I saw an angry peasant leap up and run across the fields towards the train. Apparently two men had jumped off the train when it stopped, and run and stolen some of his watermelons. But it was no use him shouting and waving his arms; slow train or not, we had a schedule to keep to, and as we moved off he was left gesticulating angrily. Later we heard the culprits were workers in the restaurant car. They had got away, and the railway police seemed to do nothing about it.

In Xining, we managed to get onto a minibus trip to Qinghai Hu, also known as Koko Nor, which gives the province its name: *qing hai* means green sea. Before we reached Xining, we did not know that the lake was open to foreigners. Xining itself was only opened this year, and not much information is available on it. Koko Nor is a huge lake, about 150 kilometres long by 50 wide, and it is surrounded by grassland, mountains, and sand dunes. The temperature was in the 80s, but it is bitterly cold there in the winter. We looked around part of the Eastern shore, the scenery like barren wind-swept moorland in Scotland or Ireland – and then we met a lama. We spotted his purple robes flapping across the moorland, a strange sight in that desolate landscape, and waved to him. When he came across, we had a polite conversation in broken Chinese (his accent full of Tibetan 'sssh' and 'tchtchrrk' sounds) and then Karl-Heinz, one of our group, produced a rolled-up picture of the Dalai Lama and gave it to him. (He had brought it all the way from Germany, for the very purpose of giving it to a Tibetan lama.) Our lama knew a good thing when he saw one, accepted it and tucked it up the sleeve of his robe, all in one movement, and then strode off, robes flapping, across the moors again. We then all went to a nomad's yurt for tea. The local people are Northern Zhang, or Tibetans, and came to what is now Qinghai centuries ago. They wear wide-brimmed felt hats and very complicated black robes with the left arm in a sleeve, but the right arm out, the sleeve slung over the shoulder to leave the right arm free for work. They herd yaks and horses. We squatted in the yurt and were given boiled yak milk tea, with *tsampa*: a mess of yak butter and barley meal with yak milk curd, all mixed with your fingers to a paste in a bowl. Yak milk and butter smell strong, but the tea was good, and the *tsampa* tasted to me like mashed up digestive biscuits with cheese. It is the Tibetans' staple diet, and they drink yak milk tea and eat *tsampa* all day. To one starved of cheese for many months, it was not bad, but many people found it hard to swallow.

The next day we went to the sand dunes – beautiful views over four layers of colour – brown and purple mountains, bright blue saltwater lake, bright green marsh, and yellow sand. In the evening we ate sturgeon from the lake.

The real point of this trip to Xining was not Koko Nor, but to visit Taersi. This is the Tibetan lamasery of Kumbum, which is where the Yellow Hat sect of lamaism started. Friends travelling in April and May had said how beautiful it was, but we were not really prepared for its particular beauty and particular atmosphere. Already we are planning to return next year. It is the kind of place you arrive in, and know you will never want to leave!

Old wooden beams painted in complicated patterns, prayer flags flapping from the maypole-like prayer mast in the courtyard, the reek of yak butter – that is the hotel we stayed in. It was really a courtyard within the lamasery complex, with cheap simple rooms, and good food. We planned to stay two days, but eventually remained for over a week. Prayer wheels creaking, monks flying past in their filthy red robes, black leather boots on the stones, the smell of yak butter . . ., of all the sense impressions it is the butter smell that remains in my mind. Butter seems to be used for everything: lamp oil, candles, to stick coins and silk cloths on bells and statues, as an offering, for sculptures (a gallery of Buddhist deities and in the middle a model of Tienanmen Gate in Peking, with the Communist Party logo on it!), and even for eating, in *tsampa*. Everywhere reeks – halls, cushions, hangings, clothes, hair. We talked to several of the lamas, old and young. The youngest are about ten years old, the oldest we spoke to was seventy-five. Some of their robes are bright new scarlet, others a dirty-rusty red, and others verge on purple. Monks scurry around, shaven-headed, in robes that must be very hot in the summer heat but are obviously needed in winter, at 2000 metres altitude. Six parts of the lamasery are open to the public, and are all very different in feeling. The Temple of the Lesser Golden Roof was perhaps the strangest, with its gallery of stuffed bison, bear, monkey, and inside, the stuffed white horse on which one of the former abbots rode. All these animals were rather mouldy and grotesque. They are intended to ward off evil spirits; it actually seemed as if the place was full of them. Outside, lamas were performing weird rites. One was striding round and round the Great Hall of Meditation, clapping sharply every five steps, taking 108 turns round the pillars. Each handclap is equal to 108 prostrations in front of the temple. We saw peasants and lamas perform complicated press-up prostrations; sliding on their hands, on boards worn smooth by generations of previous supplicants for 'long life and fat sheep and yaks' as a bemused bystander put it.

One evening we saw a girl and her mother walking up the dusty road past the lamasery: every four steps, they prostrated themselves face down in the dust. They wore beautiful complicated black skirts, jackets embroidered with red, and beads. Such girls, smelling of yak, with lovely long complex plaits down their backs, would gaze admiringly at Jill's long red hair (and vice versa).

In front of the Great Hall of Meditation we watched a 'catechism session', which lasted about one hour. In late afternoon sun, rows of young monks were sitting cross-legged, some with their yellow coxcomb hats on, others bareheaded, about fifty altogether, in lines. In front of them, standing, slightly older 'prefects' were firing questions, clapping their hands, pointing with left hand cupped upwards, at the same time transferring the bead bracelet from right to left wrist. The 'prefect' figure went from one seated figure to the next, firing questions and clapping. A lot of horseplay, and some favouritism, was in evidence, all rather reminiscent of school. An older monk, with a very wise, kind, lined face, was moving up and down the while, occasionally touching one monk on the shoulder, speaking gently to another. Suddenly, everyone turned, stood up, and ran over to the throne area, to sit in a semi-circle on the flagstones facing the platform, where now about twenty-five senior monks were sitting cross-legged, facing the throne. A series of chants began, monotonous but not unpleasant. At the end, after forty minutes or so, two women came in and prostrated themselves in the gateway. As the monks, running and pushing into two lines, left the yard, the senior monks actually walked on and over the bodies of the women.

We managed to get up early enough one morning to see all the monks having breakfast: they are summoned to breakfast and morning prayer at about four o'clock by the melancholy sound of horns playing a single long protracted notes, fading away into the darkness at the end. In one of the temples, the monks were sitting in two long lines on cushions at right angles to the statue of Buddha, under the heavily embroidered silk hangings called *thangkas,* which look like rows of elaborate flags. They were eating breakfast – *tsampa* of course – and chanting prayers to ringing of bells and clashing of cymbals.

One day we went for a walk right round the monastery. Thubten Jigme Norbu, the Dalai Lama's brother, who was abbot of Kumbum, records that he liked to 'measure his length' around the monastery as a ritual act of devotion. It was not very far, he said, only about three or four miles, comparing this modest excursion with the pilgrimages frequently made by people who would measure their length from Kumbum to Lhasa. As we walked round, we passed many people: monks, old peasant women, young girls, all measuring their length around the boundary. The more dirt-conscious among them carried a piece of sacking or leather which they spread out on the ground, before prostrating themselves. The monks were especially well-equipped, with wooden hand guards and sheepskin knee protectors. Some were alone, many were in pairs or groups, with a communal rhythm of stretching out, scrambling up and walking forward. Some used a rosary to mark the place where their outstretched hands reached, and to where they could walk forward to start the next prostration, others merely guessed. It startled us to find little noodle stands and tea stalls scattered along the way, with pilgrims refreshing themselves and chatting over an inter-prostration cuppa. I suppose pilgrimages are traditionally social occasions as well as acts of devotion, but this whole process seemed so arduous, like a self-inflicted penance, a mortification of the flesh, that we were surprised to find bodily needs catered to at all. For a while we amused ourselves by making up names for these impromptu cafes: The Teahouse of the 108th Prostration, Nirvana Noodle Stand, Merit Cakes, the Om Yoghurt Stall.

During the Cultural Revolution, the monastery was disbanded. The monks were all sent for 'Reform through Labour', but the actual temple complex was not harmed, but guarded by PLA men who used it as a barracks. The soldiers have all gone, but not very far away: there is a barracks just down the road, and the town is full of green uniforms. We saw a lot of soldiers in Qinghai actually; it is a highly militarized area, and also has many prisons and labour camps. Qinghai Province has a reputation as the Siberia of China. Our students were not a bit impressed when we said we were going there! It is interesting that it is open to foreigners at all, given its reputation, and in fact our bus to the lake went right past a labour camp.

Many of the paths leading from the monastery into the country had large notices saying FORBIDDEN TO FOREIGNERS, but one of the pleasantest things to do in the area was to take a small path that skirted the notices, and walk into the hills behind the monastery. Taersi is about 2000 metres high, so the snow-capped mountains we could see in the distance must have been about 6000 metres. In between were glorious rolling valleys, golden with wheat and bright yellow with rape flowers, and green hills where sheep were grazing. We went for long walks through the fields along the red earth paths linking monastery to village and villages to each other. Women wearing broad-brimmed white sun-bonnets were working in the fields, harvesting barley, wheat, and peas. A group taking their lunch break hailed us and invited us to join them. We were fed with fresh peas. Farmers taking their produce to market and traders drove laden donkeys along the path to the monastery. Sheep and horses grazed on the skyline. Skylarks, bees, butterflies and the rich colours of green and gold all around. We walked up to where we could see a tiny shrine on a hilltop, butter lamp in the shrine, prayer flags hanging listless in the hot sun. The summit of every hill in sight was decorated with prayer flags and offerings of sheep's wool. Then back down, tired, in the evening, to the homely smell of yak butter, and the shuffle of dusty lamas' boots in the dirt, fall asleep, and wake at 4 am to the blare of horns calling the monks to prayer.

We very nearly didn't leave this fascinating place. But after a week we made the decision to head back to Lanzhou, and thence northwards, retracing the steps of so many travellers along the Silk Route. Back down the hill in a freewheeling but seemingly brakeless bus, and a day in Xining, where, as a contrast to the lamasery, we visited the Taoist temple built into a cliff high up overlooking the town, and were fed lotus tea and buns by a gentle blue-robed priest.

Our next stop was Jiayuguan, the very end of the Great Wall. The twenty-hour train-ride took us up over a pass of louring Scottish scenery: dark clouds, gloomy peaks, pastures with sheep and horses, yurts, wild flowers in profusion, including heather. In the evening we ran into a dust storm on the other side, as the train chuffed through the stone desert, the south edge of the Gobi. Train signs since Xining had been in both Chinese and Tibetan script, and now they started to appear in Arabic script as well. A real sense of travelling beyond the frontiers. From the lush wet landscapes of central China, all around us now was gravel and stone. Not a dune in sight. Just sharp stone, and the dusty wind ripping at the trees around the small station where we got out. For centuries the north-west has been an area of banishment and exile, the wild frontier. It is easy to understand why.

At Jiayuguan, we arrived at 5 am to be told that our travel permit was not in order. Jiayuguan was not on it. We protested, showed him the pinyin transcription of the characters, but he insisted. By this time, the train had pulled out, and it looked as if we would have to wait on the station, but he finally said 'All right, just one night.' In fact, the Wuhan police had put down Jia-yu-guan, but had used the wrong characters to write it. There are so many homophones in Chinese that this must happen a lot.

In Jiayuguan it was wet and windy all day. The town is surrounded by high mountains, snowclad, but we could see nothing of them. We went to the fort at the end of the Wall, a really bleak place. It guards the pass, and is the old frontier of China proper. Beyond are the Gobi and Taklamakan Deserts. Taklamakan means 'go in, not come out'. Travellers going beyond Jiayuguan would throw a pebble against the wall of the main gate. If it bounced back, they would return safely. If not . . . We bussed out to the fort, and spent a miserable four hours walking round the battlements and huddling from the cold rain, waiting for the next bus back. The fort was full of green cotton-clad PLA men on an outing, soaked to the skin, cold tourists like ourselves. Beyond, the remains of the Wall, mud and straw lumps like rotten teeth, peter out into the stones of the desert.

Jiayuguan itself is a concrete-block town with an enormous empty traffic circle outside the leaking cement hotel where we stayed. Cold empty streets, uselessly wide roads, rain-dripped cement facades. As I had only packed T-shirt and shorts, expecting the desert to be hot, I went to buy some long trousers. I had a hilarious half-hour in a department store which was being repainted. To get at the clothes, they had to take polythene sheets off the cupboards, and as they were knocking plaster off the ceiling, we all got covered in little flakes of plaster. The best thing about Jiayuguan was the incredibly kind and helpful hotel staff, and the circus we went to on the other side of the traffic circle: a huge ripped and repaired big top, and some wonderful acrobatic and comic turns. Our favourite was a girl on a unicycle, who did a reverse strip tease. That is, she came in, circled around, and then proceeded to catch clothes thrown at her by the ringmaster: first a jacket, then some trousers. By the time she finished, she was wearing five or six layers. Not that she was exactly immodestly dressed to start with. This prudish country! Not so prudish was the horse that played dead, springing to life when pumped with air via the anus by a comic doctor with a bicycle pump. All good family fun!

173

Other memories of Jiayuguan: the early morning exercise music on the loudspeaker at 6.30 am as the station came to life, and a platform full of blue-uniformed guards all solemnly waving arms and legs in time to the music, and the Chinese scientist who had the room next door to us in the hotel, one in a long line of 'language con-men': people who start up a conversation with you for the sole purpose of practising their English or asking for a translation (in this case, it was a paper written in English that needed checking and correcting). At least he came to the point fairly quickly, unlike the best and most persistent in this line: a professor from Lanzhou with a plastic ear, who came and sat in our compartment for eight hours, despite repeated entreaties from the sleeping car attendant, whose sense of order was upset by having one of her passengers in the wrong place. At the end of nearly eight hours of somewhat strained and limited interchanges (during which he offered us a job in Lanzhou any time we needed one), he came to the real point of the exercise and produced a mini-cassette recorder and tapescript and asked us to make a recording for him. That done, he promptly disappeared and we never saw him again. Would anyone like a job in Lanzhou?

From Jiayuguan we went to Dunhuang, an eleven-hour bus journey across the desert, stopping at the occasional mud-brick oasis town for watermelon and green tea. The road follows the old Silk Road for a while, a narrow desert corridor between two high mountain ranges, then turns south across a wasteland of stones and burnt tufts of grass. The road is in a bad state of repair for much of the way and several times the bus had to leave it and lurch off across the desert, following tyre tracks for an hour or more before rejoining it. About an hour before Dunhuang, the bus broke down and we sat and contemplated the desert for about an hour and a half, during which time two lorries passed. I actually found the barren empty scenery wonderfully relaxing. China is such an enormous country, but nowhere in eastern China do you get a sense of that vastness: the landscape is tamed, domesticated, parcelled up into little plots of land, miniature fields: the general impression is of minuteness and detail. North-west China was where I felt the size of the country for the first time.

Dunhuang itself is a dull grey town in the middle of a lush oasis, but about an hour's journey from the town are the fabulous Mogao caves with early Buddhist murals and statues. The caves are at several different levels in a cliff that runs along one side of a dried up river bed. They have been connected with concrete walkways and stairways, and given numbers so that the whole thing looks like a kind of prehistoric motel. A sign says BUDDHA IN NIRVANA THIS WAY PLEASE. All the guide books wax lyrical over Dunhuang. However what they neglect to mention is the lack of freedom to wander and gaze at will. To see the caves properly, you need time, but this you do not get, as all the caves are locked, and only some are open to the public anyway; you are marched from cave to cave by a guide who locks and unlocks doors. So our overall impression is one of dazzled bewilderment at the amount of beauty packed into the caves, and frustration at not seeing it better. A glimpse of Nirvana perhaps. It must be said that we couldn't have had a better guide. She was studying ancient history, knew her facts backwards, and was very patient when we wanted to linger. Others were not so lucky: most Chinese guides are fairly perfunctory. The fault is really ours for not staying there longer, or having had the wit to read up about it beforehand.

Each cave is minutely decorated on all walls and ceilings with tiny detailed murals, showing scenes from Buddhist stories and 'glimpses of the heavens' in a wide variety of styles, as the work began in the 4th century AD and continued through the Tang and even later. The sculptures also show a wide variety of styles. There is a clear Indian influence (this was a stopping place on the Silk Route) and there is a wealth of information about daily life in the various periods, from the scenes of city and country life in the background. There is also alarming evidence of the rapacity of us 'Foreign Devils', or at least of our grandparents and great grand-parents! Holes, spaces, empty plinths: witness to the fact that many of the best pieces of Dunhuang art now reside in museums all over the Western world. As if the contents of the Uffizi or the Prado were seized and taken to Beijing! The caves were part of a monastic settlement which was abandoned some time in our middle ages, and only rediscovered in the early 1900s by a monk who was fleeing from famine in eastern China. By accident, he tapped a wall when sleeping in one of the caves, made a hole, and discovered the treasure trove. He tried to interest the government of the time, but they told him to seal it all up again. But British and French and German explorers got wind of it and came and took away art by the cartload. Looking at this from the distance of a century or so, you find it hard to imagine a) what the monastery was doing there in the first place, b) how it was ever discovered – why flee from famine to one of the driest places on earth?, c) how Europeans ever got there, and d) had the nerve to do what they did.

The *xiao* style was our favourite. Row upon row of figures, with faces that look like the Chinese character for 'small', *xiao,* or

小

– hence the name. Faded green-blue with vermilion that has oxidised to a deep brown-black. These are from the Wei Dynasty, the earliest murals in the caves. Later Tang Dynasty murals are more flowing, with indistinct shapes swirling, long hair and ribbons floating behind: flying goddesses from the Western heaven. Successive occupants of the caves painted over and over the murals, so later dynasties used the earlier caves and started again. All the caves are unlit, and there is an eerie mystery to them, particularly when there is a large altar in the middle, round the back of which you creep in darkness, exploring the paintings with a torch. Buddhas and boddhisatvas of all shapes, sizes and expressions. The statues have had their hands and hearts cut out by marauding Moslems, exposing their wooden framework covered in straw and mud. There is a huge beautiful Sleeping Buddha: Mona Lisa-like, a strange bisexual figure with watery, clinging robes. There is a complex system of signs related to the way Buddhas hold their hands: attitudes for 'teaching' or 'subduing temptation', but this variant of Buddhism seemed uncomplicated, compared to the rites we had seen performed at Taersi. (I wonder what puzzles a Chinese tourist wandering around a European cathedral.) Like many cathedrals in Europe, this place is a museum: it is not a religious feeling that you receive, but a sense of awe at the past, at the skill of the artists. It is now a tourist site, not a place of worship: state-run, state-repaired, state-locked-up. Safe from acquisitive foreigners now.

From Dunhuang to the railway at Liuyuan, by very bumpy bus. The mid-morning train we'd planned to catch only ran on alternate days. This wasn't one of them. We could get another train in the evening, but no-one seemed to be able to say what 'evening' meant. So we settled down gloomily for a whole day in coal-black dusty treeless Liuyuan, whose name ironically means 'willow grove'. A one-street town, running downhill from the station yard between battered stalls and empty shops, men with handcarts piled high with dusty coal, straining and grunting uphill, but gliding downhill with their legs in the air, balanced on the shafts of the cart. We kicked our heels and waited, conscious that we could have been spending another day at the caves, got into ticket queues, only to be told that they were the wrong queues, sat on the steps, only to be ordered back into the noisy crowded waiting room. I think Liuyuan wins the title of Least Favourite Place in China.

The train that was eventually announced was three hours late, and came all the way from Shanghai, so we were not hopeful of getting more than standing room for the fifteen-hour journey to Urumqi.

But, miracle, we got a place in a sleeping car. And, having eaten nothing but melons of different sizes and colours for over twenty-four hours, it was especially pleasant to watch a huge red sun setting over the desert plain after a good train dinner, talking to the cooks and train security police about the *O-Li-Pi-Ke-Se* which were on in Los Angeles, where China had won golds for shooting. Train number 54 plies the Shanghai-Urumqi line, a journey of 4097 kilometres, taking four days. Quite a little community in the dining car.

'Nobody likes Urumqi' says one of the guide books. Actually, we did. It is a huge sprawling place with ugly industrial outskirts, dusty polluted air. But it is the most inland city in the world (nearest sea is the Bay of Bengal, about 2000 kilometres south-wards) and it is not at all Chinese in feel – except for the modern grey cement architecture, the rumbling buses and the jangling bicycle bells. The majority of people are Uighur, Moslems of Turkish origin, who dwarf the Chinese in stature and girth, some of whom have fairish, even reddish hair, coloured eyes, hooked noses — who, in short, look positively European, or at least Middle Eastern. The Han Chinese are immigrants, colonizers, who are sent there from eastern China, just as in the old days when people were exiled beyond the Wall at Jiayuguan. To get people to work in Gansu, Qinghai, Tibet and Xinjiang, all the 'Wild West', the government has to offer inducements: more pay, better holiday allowances. Most of our students shudder at the thought of having to go there. Yet on the train we met a woman who worked in a bank in Kalamayi, further west from Urumqi, 40 degrees above in summer and 40 degrees below in winter. She had been there twenty-five years, claimed to love it, but still described herself as 'from Shanghai'. The problems of food for the Chinese in Xinjiang (no rice, but unleavened bread, no pork or fish but plenty of mutton kebabs) were a pleasure for us. To get our teeth into charcoal smoked grilled fatty mutton, catching the drips on delicious flat bread after so long without even a whiff of New Zealand lamb! We used Urumqi mainly as a staging post on journeys back and forth to Kashgar and Turfan, but liked it, not least because the hotel staff and travel desk went out of their way to be helpful, making promises that were not merely ruses to get rid of us. Quite a change from the usual service!

Bogda Fen is a peak of 5445 metres, snow clad the year round, the highest part of the Tianshan range, which runs east from Urumqi. All around is dry stony desert, dunes, the only agriculture thanks to post-Liberation irrigation schemes. At the foot of Bogda Fen is a beautiful lake, Tian Chi or Heaven Lake. You could be in the Tyrol, except for the nomads in yurt villages, looking after their grazing animals, and the hordes of Han and Uighur tourists who come up in buses at midday every day and depart at 4 pm leaving behind piles of watermelon rind, shards of broken pop bottles, cans, and cigarette packets. We went up there one morning in one of a horde of buses. It is three or four hours from Urumqi, and our bus was overtaken by every other one in the horde. It is really an incredibly beautiful place, made the more

178

so by the contrast with the desert dryness of the plains below. We decided to stay overnight in one of the little chalet-style huts on the hillside and in the evening when the last bus had gone, we sat drinking wine by the lake with some German friends, watching the moon rise over Bogda Fen.

The next day we went for a long walk towards the high mountains at the far end of the lake. We sat and talked to a nomad family in their yurt. Ten or eleven bodies must lie down on the earth floor around the central cooking fire every night. The woman said she had nine children. The eldest daughter spoke some Chinese. Fascinated by rings and jewellery, she tried to swap Jill's wedding ring for her brass earrings, but accepted some foreign stamps and a Hong Kong dollar coin as a souvenir instead. The kids had a fantastic fight involving a giant puffball mushroom the size of a football, a couple of big rocks, a pole and lots of fists. The daughter asked Jill polite questions about marriage and England, while cuffing and kicking her two little brothers who were out to kill! It ended up with the mother and daughter putting all their weight on the tiny little door to prevent another brother from breaking in, while he hurled rocks at it with all his strength. A peaceful life, the nomads! The men all have daggers in their belts, and I'm sure they know how to use them for purposes other than slicing up melon.

Back down from the lake to Urumqi, tired and burnt after too much sun at high altitudes. Although this is a sort of extended traveller's tale, we now have a terrible confession to make. A 'traveller' we now know, after two summers' experience of them, is someone who travels as cheaply and as hard as possible, only to relax in a hotel afterwards and whine about the discomfort and brag of his bravado. Thus the people who bussed it all the way to Kashgar. We flew, an awful confession, as our journey took a mere four hours in a little twin-engined Russian plane, as compared to the three to four days it takes by bus. Had we had the time, actually, we would have taken the bus, if only to have the sensation of distance: distances are so unreal in a plane. But we had stayed too long in Taersi, and our days were numbered. The plane journey was not without its charms. About halfway, at midday, the plane touched down at Aksu, a little desert township. The airstrip was in the middle of the desert, dust clouds all around, and nothing in sight except the small low building at the end of the runway. Everyone got off the plane and made for the building. We followed. Inside, there was a noodle stall. Everyone including pilot and cabin crew was queuing eagerly, buying, and wolfing down the hot spicy noodles. We did the same. Twenty minutes later, lunch over, everyone got back on the plane, and we took off again.

Kashgar is a long way from anywhere, almost halfway to Europe from Shanghai, on the Chinese side of the Pamirs. Only 3% of the population is Han Chinese. Perhaps that is why the city authorities have erected what must be the largest Mao statue in China, on the main street. A desperate attempt by government to make the place Chinese. It isn't. It is also the most fascinating place I've ever been, as well as the driest, the dustiest, the dirtiest, and the slowest and most tiring place to visit. But I would love to go back. The mix of peoples is so strange. It feels like the home of every race, and I believe that the Pamirs were the cradle of civilization, according to some anthropologists . . . We needed the *Observer's Guide to Ethnic Minorities,* or *Noddy's Guide to Tribal Costumes.*

The sky was mud-coloured all the time we were there, full of dust kept down by low heavy cloud. The dormitory hotel was a good three-mile donkey cart ride out from the town and main bazaar areas, and it was hard to find anything to drink. The market was full of Pakistan-manufactured cigarettes and the old men spoke Russian rather than Chinese. Peter Fleming (*News from Tartary*) came through Kashgar on his way to what was then north-west India, and is fascinating on the Great Powers' interests in this frontier area, which is now Chinese on one side and Russian on the other. Its proximity to the border probably explains why we could not get outside the city itself. A hotel clerk promised to rent us a jeep and to take us out towards the Pamirs to visit an old ruined city and some Buddhist cave paintings. We waited three hours on the agreed morning, only to be told by Public Security that unfortunately the road was broken so our trip would have to be cancelled. We suggested that the jeep take us in the other direction just to have a look. But, no, apparently there were 'floods' in that direction. Looking down at the bone-dry, cracking earth, and up at the dusty sky, we found this hard to believe. Rumour had it that someone had tried to cycle out towards the Pakistan border, and since then all bike hire and expeditions of any kind had been stopped, but then rumour has a lot of things besides the truth.

The best thing in Kashgar was the bazaar in the little streets and alleyways radiating out from the main square with its big mosque. Each alley was specialised, so there was a whole street devoted to boot makers and leather workers of all kinds, another to rugs and carpets, another to carved and bejewelled daggers, and another to richly embroidered hats and caps for the men, different designs and colours according to race and creed. On Sundays the market was huge, taking up the whole of the city south of the main square. Camels, donkeys, sheep, all for sale, and every kind of craft work, fruit and vegetables: green melons and grapes, bright red oval tomatoes, the smell of sizzling kebabs and baking bread, noodle makers with long strips of dough which they pulled out with both hands, twisting the rope of dough over and over, like a skipping rope, to stretch it, then doubling it up and repeating the process again and again until the noodles were fine enough, keeping the strands separate between their fingers. Traffic jams of donkey carts and shouting proud-faced people: Uzbeks, Uighurs, Kazakhs, all with different headgear, clothes, daggers and footwear. Men in fur-trimmed Russian hats and knee boots, swirling black coats, putting stallions through their paces at the horse fair. Prosperous pot-bellied shopkeepers in long striped Arab robes. Glint of gold in a smile, sharp quick eyes, green skullcaps, black skullcaps, embroidered skullcaps, pink and purple voile scarves or brown veils over the faces of the broad-beamed women. Small children everywhere, barefoot in the dust, greeting you with 'Bye-bye'. If you say 'Hello' they take it as a word of farewell, so all Xinjiang now talks a sort of topsy-turvy pidgin to foreigners. The bazaar was of course much closer in spirit and feel to the Arab world than to China, and made us wonder at the vast extent of Muslim culture.

The railway to Urumqi was only completed in 1960. It used to take the best part of five months to travel from Xian to Kashgar, by lorry, horse, mule, camel. We took five weeks, with plenty of dallying on the way. Sure, but it's a wonderful thing, modern transport! It enables you and me to go to places like Kashgar, to find that the local people don't much care if you're there or not. They carry on with their own life, as they have lived it for centuries, whether they are ruled by their own people, or Chinese, or Russian. Despite the size of the Mao statue, the place feels untouched by outside influences, or by the 20th century. Miles from anywhere, miles from the sea, once on a very important trading route, but now a far-flung outpost of the Han Empire. The people are poorer than the Han Chinese, but proud. We have heard rumours of uprisings and rebellions against the Chinese throughout Xinjiang over the last decade, including, apparently, last year, but have no confirmation. Certainly if I were a Han Chinese, I would not want to go and live in the 'Wild West'.

Having got as far west as we could, we could only turn and retrace our steps. The Afghan and Soviet borders are obviously closed, and, despite the Pakistani cigarettes in the bazaar, I doubt if that border is available to us as a crossing-point! So we flew back to Urumqi (with another noodle-stop at Aksu) and then took the bus to Turfan, with Bogda Fen's snow glinting to the north, over a pass and down into the oven of the Turfan Depression, at 155 metres below sea level the second lowest point in the world, and the hottest place in China.

We left Turfan till last, as everyone said how relaxing and beautiful it was. It is. Not the town itself, which is a simple crossroads of dusty streets and after Kashgar, a rather dull market. But the hotel, with basic accommodation and simple food, has a vine-trellised courtyard and a huge fridge full of COLD BEER, rare anywhere in China. And, stretching out of town are fascinating lanes of houses and mosques and vines and water everywhere, gurgling unseen along conduits from the Tianshan mountains. Beyond the oasis, fields, dust, and a beautiful mud mosque, empty, with a single cigar-shaped minaret, decorated with complicated zig-zag brickwork.

One day we went out to the Flaming Mountains: a cliff

swirling with dried up rivulets of eroded rock, like an enormous lava flow, which according to the guide books, glows ruby red in the sunset. We went at midday – the only time you can get to see it. So much for guide books! We also went to the Thousand Buddha Caves at Bezeklik, a smaller, and less well-preserved, but equally well-looted version of the caves at Dunhuang. A very impressive sight, perched above a gorge on hot, dry cliffs, a green strip of wheat winding below in the valley. The contrast between greenery and dry sand is beautiful to see. 'Oasis' is now much more than a mere word to us.

The whole Turfan Depression, fed by underground water channels, is an oasis, and has a long history, as it was a major stopping place on the Silk Route. Beyond Turfan, to the east and west, are two huge abandoned cities. Gaocheng is the larger, to the east. The city wall is still about five metres high and stretches round a circumference of about six kilometres. Different guides and books tell different stories, but I believe it was destroyed by the Mongols (Genghis Khan and Co). It looks as though the whole city has melted in the fierce sun and been deformed by the heat, the mud-brick construction of six or seven centuries slowly turning back into desert. All the streets, squares, houses, temples, alleys, are clearly visible still, and by climbing up onto walls and looking down on the ruins, it slowly comes back into focus. A horrible picture of bombed 20th century cities comes into mind. However, the people of Gaocheng were not exactly peaceful themselves, being almost perpetually at war with their neighbour Jiaohe. This city was on a much more impressive site, on a rock promontory between two dried-up rivers. We took two and half hours on a donkey cart to get there, and it was worth the jolting. At the highest point, is a huge ruined temple with statues still clearly discernible in niches high up. Black stains on the brickwork show where chimneys were. According to the official guides, both Jiaohe and Gaocheng were Han nationality states (present day propaganda). According to some, Gaocheng took over Jiaohe, and when the rivers dried up, Jiaohe was abandoned. According to others, both cities were destroyed by Mongol, Horde, and Co. Whatever the truth, rumour and a romantic ruby sunset made Jiaohe much the more impressive of the two. After

Turfan, time was running short. Beijing seen through two pairs of eyes, has not changed. Since the holiday, of course, the Hong Kong agreement has made headlines, and it coincided with a very National Day on October 1. On all that you will have to wait for the next newsletter, which we hope will not be too long appearing!

Letter twelve

REFORM, RECTIFICATION, AND
REUNITING THE MOTHERLAND

Letter twelve
REFORM, RECTIFICATION, AND REUNITING THE MOTHERLAND

3 December 1984
Some headlines from *China Daily* over the last couple of months:

MONOPOLY OF BANKING BY STATE CRITICIZED

HARD WORK – RIGHT CHANNEL TO WEALTH

PROMOTING ABLE PEOPLE IS KEY TO SUCCESS – DENG

MARXIST THEORY: NOT A DOGMA BUT A GUIDE TO ACTION

CALL FOR WRITERS TO BE GUARANTEED LITERARY FREEDOM

STANDARDS SHOULD NOT REST ON CONFORMITY

DEMOCRATIC SYSTEM URGED FOR ELECTION OF SENIOR OFFICIALS

SHANGHAI NEEDS TO OPEN STOCK MARKET

BANK LOANS HELP HOUSING

COMPETITION SPURS PROGRESS

As you can see, things are changing here! The news that has been on the front pages of the papers, and one of the main topics of conversation for the last month or so is the 'Economic Reforms'. These were decisions adopted by the Central Committee at its plenary session at the end of October, and for which the ground had been well-prepared for months before by articles in the Press announcing the success of the Responsibility System and the birth of the New Prosperity ('Peasant Dong earns 10000 *yuan* a year'). There is no doubt that the system is leading to increased production and greater prosperity. Even if you sneer at the production figures and stories of *Toyota*-buying chicken farmers in the papers, you only have to look at the shops. The campus shop, for instance, which contained nothing but a few dingy packages and a barrel full of rotten apples when we first came, now has shelves and shelves of tins, bottles, and packets – and the latest addition, just in time for Christmas, liqueur chocolates!

What the Economic Reforms propose to do is to extend the Responsibility System to industry, and also to 'reform prices', which seems to mean releasing them to market forces. The document itself, *On Reform of the Economic Structure*, after a long preamble about how truly Marxist these measures are ('Socialism does not mean Pauperism', 'Left-deviationist errors result in correct measures being regarded as capitalism'), lists seven measures to invigorate the economy and reform the 'irrational price structure'.

Factories and enterprises will be much more autonomous, though still, of course, owned by the state: 'It is a mistake,' proclaims the document, 'to equate ownership by the People with operation by the State.' Accordingly, the role of the state is to change from controlling to guiding. The state will be responsible for guiding production, taxation, appointing managers, deciding what is produced, and opening, closing, transferring, or merging enterprises. The enterprise itself will plan production, manage its supply and marketing budget, recruit personnel, decide the price of its products and decide what to do with the profits.

This effectively means an end to the quota system and planned economy and a shift to supply and demand economics. 'A planned economy can avoid the anarchy of production and the cyclical crises of a capitalist society,' says the document, 'but if we try to implement planning in disregard of the market, our plans will be out of step with reality. A planned economy by no means excludes the law of the market.' The difference between a communist and a capitalist society, it goes on to say, has nothing to do with whether the economy is centrally planned, or ruled by market forces: it is a question of ownership.

The upshot of all this is that there will be three types of enterprise: the major industries will remain under state control, other enterprises will receive 'guidance planning', but prices and quantities produced will be according to supply and demand. Finally, there will be a free market sector covering cooperative enterprises and individual businesses (who owns those, I wonder, or have I misunderstood something somewhere?). Workers' pay will be decided on a Responsibility System – 'to each according to his work.' Profit delivery to the state, and a fixed wage scale (at present, there are eight grades of workers' pay according to seniority and length of service) will be replaced by bonuses for hard work, and a taxation system: an end to the 'Eating from One Big Pot' system, where everyone received the same, regardless of work done.

An end, too, to the 'Iron Rice Bowl', whereby workers were guaranteed a job for life. Enterprises can now advertise jobs, and hire and fire personnel. And competition between enterprises is to be encouraged in the hope that 'only the best will survive'. Don't start thinking that this sounds like cut-throat capitalism though, because 'competition between socialist enterprises is fundamentally different from competition under capitalism, where the law of the jungle prevails'. If any 'undesirable trends and unlawful acts' appear 'in the course of competition', the relevant 'leading organs should keep a clear head and strengthen education and tackle such problems earnestly'.

What all this will entail is a reform in the 'irrational pricing system'. This can be roughly translated as inflation. The document defines irrational pricing in three ways: inadequate price differentials according to quality (that's true – shoddy bikes cost just as much as *Flying Pigeons* or *Forevers*, they're just easier to get), irrational price differences between commodities (that's also true: we have for a long time been puzzled by Chinese prices), and retail purchasing prices that are lower than state purchasing prices – in other words the government wants to put an end to food subsidies and release prices to the laws of supply and demand. But to make sure that income and purchasing power don't go down, they are going to increase pay. Teachers have already been promised a rise. In effect what will happen is that food prices will rise but the price of consumer goods will come down, reflecting increased productivity. All this is on no account to be called infla-tion: 'It must be widely publicized among the people that such reforms will never bring about a general and spiralling price rise.' Anyone who can remember pre-Liberation days is scared of the word inflation. Then, prices rose so crazily that in the last days of the *Guomindang* it was necessary to take a whole suitcase full of banknotes to pay for a meal in a restaurant.

Further economic reforms include continuing the Open Door policy of opening up to the outside world, 'using foreign funds and attracting foreign businessmen' – a 'long-term strategic measure to promote our socialist modernization'; continuing the policy of opening up Special Economic Zones; and promoting 'a diversity of forms of economic management, drawing on the world's advanced methods of management, including those of capitalism'. 'This,' the document informs its readers 'is not retrogression'.

The last section of the report deals with something that has been in and out of the news all last year and now is to be stepped up: Party Rectification, or reform of the cadre system. It calls for the 'reshuffling of leadership in enterprises' by the end of 1985 and the 'replacement of veteran cadres who are getting up in years (sic) with new blood'. 'Party committees must not be fettered with outdated ideas and conventions.'

Re-reading the above, I realize that my tone may sound a little Left-deviationist, but the big question – and not only the West is asking it – is 'Is this really Marxism?' The Economic Reform Document does at times read a bit like a Fundamentalist quoting bits of Darwin to prove that he too believed in Adam and Eve. We missed the glee in the West that greeted the *People's Daily* editorial which proclaimed that 'Marxism cannot solve China's problems', but it caused a lot of embarrassment here, and the *People's Daily* subsequently carried a correction which added the little word 'all' to the blunder: 'We cannot expect Marxism to solve all China's problems.' An editorial in *Ta Kung Pao*, the communist Hong Kong paper, explained: '. . . just because of the omission of the word 'all', the article could lead to a misunderstanding. But if one has carefully read the article . . . one would come to the conclusion that the addition was neither an afterthought nor second thoughts . . . rather it was the adding of a key word which was inadvertently missed out, and this omission led to widespread misunderstanding . . . A careful reading will show that there is really very little that has not been said by Chinese leaders or printed in the press in the past six years or so. In fact the article itself quotes Mao Zedong's having said, 'Even now there are not a few people who still regard odd quotations from Marxist-Leninist works as a ready-made panacea, which, once acquired, can easily cure all maladies. These people show childish ignorance, and we should enlighten them.' It was in this spirit of facing reality that Mao and the Chinese Communist Party perfected the strategy of the revolutionary war and carried it through to victory.'

When I asked my students whether all this sounds like communism to them, they gave the official line: 'It is socialism, because land and the means of production are in the hands of the state.' This has come to be the new definition. From *Ta Kung Pao*: 'Whether or not a society is socialist or not depends on one and only one factor, i.e. whether the key and important sectors of the economy are owned by the state.' When I asked the students if they now resented the fact that some people could now become much richer than others, they again gave the stock answer: 'No, it is a good thing, they will be an inspiration to the rest.' Some, however, were a little dubious about the ideological pedigree of the reforms, and some were worried about some of the developments that could result: the growth of competition for example, or gross inequalities in living standards. But most are very enthusiastic about the reforms, seeing in them the promise of new prosperity for all. A friend in whose flat we had dinner recently – a flat so cold that we had to wear our thick padded overcoats through dinner, and the chopsticks fell from our numb fingers – said goodbye with the words: 'Our country has a promising future. When you visit China again, I will not have to entertain you in a cold house. And, maybe, who knows, I'll be able to visit you in your country.'

The other big questions are, of course, 'Will It Work?' and 'Will It Last?' My students' opinion: 'The economic reforms won't work without reform of the cadre system.' As research scientists, they are constantly stymied and frustrated because Party officials who know nothing about science are in charge of their research programmes and can dictate what can and cannot be studied. We have for a long time been worried about the fact that some of our students do not go abroad, but return to work in their units, and recently learned the reason from one student, who said: 'The trouble is, I am young and my unit leader is old. He is afraid that if I get sent abroad, I will be better qualified than he is and I will take his place when I come back.' Modern China claims to have replaced the feudal system with a new social order, but in many ways, the organization of society still seems feudal – each work unit is a separate kingdom, with the party cadres in complete control. The organization of Chinese society is like a lot of little islands, all controlled from above, but with no connection between them: the organization is vertical but not horizontal, and this can lead to tremendous complications: one scientific research establishment might be doing work that is duplicated by another, for example, and because of the lack of free flow of information and connection between institutes, they will not know about each other. In theory, all is controlled from above, but it takes such a tremendous amount of time for information to travel up and percolate down the channels from work unit to central adminis-trative office and back again that nothing gets done. People are afraid to take decisions on their own, because they may make the wrong decision and get criticized, so there is endless referral upward and postponement, even of simple decisions. And there is such secrecy about information! Our preconceptions are that everything is public, unless you have signed the Official Secrets Act. In China, all official information seems to be secret unless there is a good reason for it to be made public. In the college, for example, the administration seem to see no reason for giving advance warning of anything from an opera visit to holiday dates to purchase of new equipment to policy changes about course organization. Well, you can see the implications for industry: lack of free flow of information, centralized control, a proliferation of bureaucratic and administrative systems. Can a free market economy be grafted onto a communist political system? It seems to me that China could get the worst of both worlds: competi-tion, materialism, self-seeking opportunism, combined with lack of free speech and restrictions on artistic creativity, though, of course, what is hoped for is the best of both worlds: enough initiative allowed to stimulate an increase in productivity and prosperity together with sufficient state control to curb the worst excesses of capitalism.

Some of the 'undesirable trends' mentioned in the report are already manifesting themselves in money grubbing and materialism. Take *waihui* for instance. We get paid, not in *Renminbi*, (RMB) or People's Currency, but in *waihui*, or Foreign Exchange Coupons. When we first arrived, many people in the streets didn't know what the money was, and were reluctant to accept it. Now, a flourishing black market has developed, and everywhere you go, people will approach you on the streets offering to 'change money'. In Guilin last year, the only place then where money illegally changed hands, 120 RMB were offered for 100 *waihui*. In Shanghai this year, a man approached us on the street and surreptitiously showed us the palm of his hand. On it was written: '100 = 150'. Reports are that in Guilin and Guangzhou the exchange rate has reached 190 for 100. We have sometimes been given gifts by people we do not know or scarcely know: mung bean noodles, lychees, a bag of oranges. The gifts are really bribes, to induce us to change money. Often luxury items, such as televisions, can only be bought with *waihui*, some can be bought more cheaply with *waihui*, or sometimes if you can offer *waihui*, you can jump the waiting list for some commodity or other. Some people are profiteering: buying items with illegal *waihui* and selling them again at enormous profit for RMB. Though where they got the capital in the first place, God only knows. Most people, however, just need the foreign exchange for private domestic purchases: radios, televisions, cassette players. Even respected members of the community are not incorruptible: a traveller we met in the summer, teaching in another province, reports that her bank manager, in the middle of a transaction took the opportunity to whisper, 'You couldn't see your way to letting me have 200 *waihui*, could you?'. The government is very aware of the problem, and articles denouncing 'corruption' appear almost daily alongside those denouncing 'bungling bureaucrats'. The success or failure of the reforms will rest not only on whether they can raise living standards and improve productivity, but on whether China can avoid the 'undesirable trends' mentioned in the report. Corruption is not an exclusively capitalist commodity, of course,

193

and there are several tales in the press of corruption of a distinctly socialist kind, cadres who accumulate privileges for themselves, or who show favouritism to relatives, for instance, but more freedom does inevitably open the door to corruption on a wider scale, or at least gives more people the opportunity to indulge in it.

So whether new freedoms will inevitably follow in the wake of the new reforms, and economic change will bring about, of necessity, political change, or whether the two systems will co-exist in harmony, or whether the whole thing will fall apart under Left-deviationist pressure, or after Deng's death, who can say?

'Will it Last?' or 'Will It Outlast Deng?' are questions openly asked in the West, but unspoken here. All you ever see in the papers, of course, are bland and self-congratulatory articles about the correctness of Party policy, but there have been enough articles affirming that there will be no change in policy, that the leadership is in good hands, that China is now on the right road, etc etc, to make you think that there must be a sizeable number of people who don't think the leadership is in good hands, question whether China is on the right road, and would like to see a change in policy. There is also a persistent Press campaign against 'Left-deviationists' and 'Bungling Bureaucrats' – whether the two are the same, I don't know. Deng is certainly trying to replace the 'veteran cadres who are getting up in years' with younger people who have more go-ahead ideas, and who are more sympathetic to his policies: the veteran cadres are probably relics from Cultural Revolution days, who oppose Deng's ideas, and the ongoing 'Party Rectification' campaign is designed to root them out.

Students and colleagues have certainly been more forthcoming with criticisms of conservative (i.e. leftist) ideas in recent months, but I don't know if that is because they have been emboldened by the new direction in Party politics, or simply because we've got to know them a bit better. So much uncertainty! But it is that very uncertainty which is so fascinating about Chinese politics: the amount of speculation involved, the suddenness of change, and the transience of supposedly permanent policies. In the eighteen months we've been here we've already been through one period of repression and seen the start of a period of liberalization.

The Hong Kong Agreement is the other big political event in recent months, of course, coinciding rather neatly with the National Day celebrations for the 35th anniversary of Liberation, and an outburst of patriotism that swept the country. The signing of the Agreement was announced on Chinese television on National Day, like a gigantic birthday present. Our students held a speech competition for National Day, and there were many stirring speeches with references to the reunification of the Motherland. Reaction in the Chinese press was predictably jingoistic, with immediate parallels drawn with Taiwan.

Reactions here ranged from curiosity to indifference. One student thought the situation was better left as it was. 'Now we all accept that we can't go to Hong Kong,' he said 'but when it's a part of China, how will the Government be able to explain to us that we're not allowed to go there? This will raise a lot of questions in the minds of the people.' 'Don't be silly,' said the others, 'you're already not allowed to go to Shenzhen are you? And that's a part of China.' Shenzhen is the border town between Hong Kong and China. If you take the slow train, you have to get out and go through customs at Shenzhen, crossing a footbridge over a river, and following an incongruous British Rail sign that says CHINA THIS WAY ➤—➤. It's been made into the most Special of the Special Economic Zones, and no Chinese can go there without a permit. Full of luxury hotels for foreigners and shops bulging with imported electronic equipment, the place is a boom town, with new tower blocks mushrooming up everywhere. In many places you can only pay in Hong Kong dollars. When I told my class I'd been to Hong Kong, they weren't really interested, but wanted to know if I'd been to Shenzhen. And the *Waiban* want to organize the next foreign experts' trip to Shenzhen. Not that there's anything to see there, but they want the chance to go themselves. The town is surrounded by a perimeter fence bristling with barbed wire like the fence round Hong Kong itself, or the Berlin Wall. The students thought that it was a smart move on the part of the government to prevent embarrassing questions being raised about access to Hong Kong when it becomes part of China – they will simply remove the border between Shenzhen and Hong Kong and then it's not a question of not being allowed into Hong Kong, but of not being allowed into Shenzhen, which is the *status quo* anyway. I have this heretical vision, not of the communization of Hong Kong, but of the gradual capitalization of China, with The Fence creeping northwards year by year until it becomes a new Great Wall of China.

This letter is all politics and not much personal news I'm afraid. Still, on a less serious note, I'll close with a few seasonal quotes from our students on the subject of the Christmas story:

THE GOSPEL ACCORDING TO CLASS TWO

This happened when the time dated back to many many years ago. Joseph and Marry were a couple, but they didn't mate. One day, on the way of going to Rome, Marry suddenly got prenancy. Actually, this was the God's will, which predicted that the saviour of human beings would come in the would. At the midnight on December 25, Jews, our great saviour was born in a pen. At this moment all the animals in the pen kneeled and lowered their heads. The stars were shining thinly, only Jews cry broke into the dark quiet sky. Before this time, Harold, King of Roman, used to have an awful dream, in which he dreamed that an another king was going to appear soon. He feared someone would take off his throne and ordered to kill all the children who were born during this time. So, with little Jews, Joseph and Marry had to leave to southwest Europe

. . . it was said that Jesus was a Jew. His mother, Mary, had been pregnant before she got married to his boyfriend Joseph . . .

. . . on their way to Bethlehem, Mary felt ill. She told Joseph that she had a visitor two months ago. It was an angel, a God, who told her that she would have a son. Joseph was angrily surprised to hear that and not quite convinced . . .

. . . the baby Jesus was lying in a manger. There are a lot of poor shepherds and not rich people looking on. That part of Palestine had pretty poor soil, so they raised a lot of sheep . . .

SOME ANCIENT ARTS,
SOME NEW TRENDS

Letter thirteen
SOME ANCIENT ARTS,
SOME NEW TRENDS

15 February 1985

Happy Spring Festival and welcome to the Year of the Ox! Spring Festival is late this year – February 20 – which meant that we had to remain in Wuhan all through the *Da Han* or 'Month of the Great Cold', instead of escaping south to warmer climates as we did last year. However, the cold doesn't seem to have been quite as great this year – a pleasant surprise, remembering last year's misery – though I'm not sure whether this is because we're better equipped with moonboots and down jackets and thermal underwear, or because we're better acclimatised (though how you ever get acclimatised to a place with a 50°C range in temperature I don't know), or because it's really been milder. A few days of snow, which decorated the bamboos and palm trees but didn't settle, and then, since January, a succession of bright crisp blue days, which have brought people out from inside their padded military green overcoats and from behind their white surgical winter face masks, and sent us cycling along the causeway into Wuchang or to East Lake at weekends. The countryside is still drab brown and dusty winter green, but there's some very exotic blossom on some of the trees. Maybe I've got used to Chinese monotones; certainly, although the winter scene is the same: dull blues, greens, greys, and browns on people and buildings alike, with the only splash of colour provided by the small children waddling along in their several layers of padding, I don't feel that same sensory deprivation and lack of visual stimulation as last year, and begin to understand the reaction of our Chinese friends to our room, which I filled with bright colours as a reaction against the outer drabness: red cushions, a woven rug from Kashgar, brightly decorated butterfly kites on the walls, 'How colourful!', they say, not quite approvingly, or 'This room is very . . . busy.'

199

How restless, fidgety, and mindlessly energetic we appear, I can only guess. Here is part of a letter from one of my students, now in the States: 'People seem always in a rush. They work hard, try to get more money, and they have adventure (not just have fun). It doesn't make one feel at ease even at the leisure time if he turns on the radio or TV. There is too much information, and worst of all, the rock and roll which seems invented to make people more restless. The same feeling when one visits the contemporary arts gallery at least it doesn't make me feel at ease at all. The sense of beauty is diminishing, what is left is the image of stress, sadness, strange and empty. I think you must have a very good knowledge of my country now. Now if I say to you, dear Jill, that our quality of life is not poor at all, do you agree with me?' He seems to be having culture shock in the reverse direction from ours: overload instead of deprivation. And his amazement at the hard work which American leisure time seems to involve is the reverse of Charlie's and my bewilderment at our fellow travellers, who seem quite content to occupy a twelve or fifteen-hour train journey with nothing more than staring into space, the occasional smoke, or sip of leafy green tea from a screw-top jar, while we plough our way through thick novels, write letters, scribble in our diaries, play chess, and learn Chinese characters.

Chinese pleasures, like Chinese painting, are minimal, compared to their Western equivalents. An evening walk down the wide dusty avenues of plane trees; in the country, a lovers' stroll by the lake; in the city, a family saunter down the dimly-lit streets; a game of chess, cards or *Go* in the park or in the street, the players squatting or sitting on low bamboo stools or squares of cardboard; an afternoon in the teahouse slurping the dark tea from cracked mugs, snoozing, listening to the storyteller, endless refills for a few *fen*; family life: families and neighbours sitting at the doorways of their houses, chatting, admiring the babies, making music on flutes and *erhu*, singing. Chinese celebrations run on peanuts, sunflower seeds, sweets, plum juice or fizzy pop, the occasional bottle of beer or wine, and a lot of talking. Usually, everyone has to do a turn, like a Victorian evening – a song, or *erhu* recital, or recitation of a poem. Festivals are marked by firecrackers, cheap, noisy, and simple. The park is an important part

200

of Chinese life, and on Sundays the parks are full of young couples walking side by side, not holding hands, families strolling along the pathways or renting boats on the lake, fathers and sons playing football, storytellers entertaining squatting circles, musicians, chess and *mah-jong* games, young boys swimming in the lake, peanut and melon sellers. Even the opera, that most incongruously elaborate of Chinese pleasures, is a curiously informal occasion: the audience, mainly old men and women, come in late, crack and spit sunflower seed husks, chat, get up and shuffle around throughout, and when the curtain falls, get up straight away and leave without ceremony.

How fast all this will change, I don't know. Things seem to be changing very fast indeed. The evening walk seems as popular as ever with young couples and families, but there is a growing number of families now with TV to lure them indoors and off the streets, altering the traditional pattern of family life here which is lived on the street as much as it is indoors, and in the community as much as within the family. For young couples, there is competition for the evening walk from the dance halls which have sprung up over the last months. When we first arrived, dancing, strictly forbidden of course in the Cultural Revolution as bourgeois, frivolous and decadent, was just beginning to catch on, and the students would spend a lot of time rehearsing sedate waltzes and two-steps. The Spriritual Pollution Campaign put a stop to all that, but when that campaign disappeared as suddenly as it had come, the waltz and quickstep music reappeared and with them, the advent of the dance hall. The roof of the Fun Palace, which used to hold a small circus with performing dogs and bears, has been transformed, and on Friday and Saturday nights is crowded with couples waltzing and tangoing under the stars. Dance halls have even received official approval in a recent article in *China Daily*:

> Young Chinese are putting on their dancing shoes and stepping out to the music without fear at public dance parties. Thousands of people in Shanghai flocked to the city's 70 makeshift ballrooms. And dancing fever swept Beijing as dance parties were held over the New Year holiday by various organizations. Two or three years ago, people were only able to dance at private parties, and then with some trepi-

dation. But early last month workers at the Beijing Mass Recreation Centre gathered in a shabby hall and there were many worried faces. They were holding the first ever city-wide social dance competition but were not sure about the official response. When a man wearing a worker's hat entered the hall, the organizers and participants relaxed immediately. He was Beijing's Mayor Chen Xitong, and he was there to give official blessing . . . Dancing now seems to be encouraged by government officials . . . The China Central Television has just started a series of lectures and demonstrations on how to do various dances . . .

The latest craze is disco! Our students beg us to teach them, and during the cold weather held 'disco practice' sessions in the classrooms during the breaks to keep warm. The loudspeaker seems to be churning out some pretty boppy music lately, a headline in *China Daily* heralds 'China's first disco music concert tour', and a recent letter in the opinions column defends disco: 'A disco dancing couple have little or no body contact and the movements are not unwholesome'. A far cry from the days when I was assured of medical evidence of the immoral effects of such music!

Actually, one very important function of the dance halls is to bring young people together – there aren't very many opportunities for this in China! It's surprising how many young couples are still brought together by matchmakers – the idea of meeting someone and falling in love is a new one in China, though one that's caught on very successfully! Modern Chinese stories are full of the arranged match v. true love dilemma, and true love usually wins. Anyway, dance parties in Beijing started out as 'matchmaking opportunities for the lonely hearts, particularly single people over thirty', according to the *China Daily* article. Single people over thirty are one of 'Modern China's new social problems'. A lot of them are people who were sent to the countryside for re-education through labour in the *xiafang* movement in the Cultural Revolution, and spent the years when they were ripe for marriage planting rice in the paddies and failing to find a soul mate among the local villagers. Though some, like my student Huang, who was sent to dig paddies in northern Jiangsu and found himself working alongside a pretty student from his home town, actually met their husbands or wives while being educated through labour. I don't think many townie-peasant marriages took place though. Class barriers between intellectuals and manual workers, town dwellers and peasants, are pretty strong, despite 25 years of constant revolution. Life is also immeasurably easier, pleasanter and more comfortable for the city dweller than it is for China's 800 million peasants, and the horror at having to spend the rest of his life in the countryside and relinquish the hope of returning to his home town, would probably be enough to keep an urban worker's head from being turned by even the prettiest peasant girl. Anyway, the 'returned from the countryside youth' as they are called, are presenting a new type of problem in Beijing. At thirty, by Chinese standards, you're past marriageable age. Well, a man might have a ghost of a chance, but a woman is well and truly on the shelf. And the problem has got to such a size in Beijing that the normal match-making channels of friends and neighbours don't work and the city has opened marriage bureaux! And now dance halls!

A short story I read recently called *The Marriage Bureau* deals with the efforts of a man approaching 'that sensitive age of twenty-nine' to find a wife, and describes the unsuccessful encounters arranged for him by neighbours, friends, and the marriage bureau. It ends with the heartfelt plea: 'Create a better life for single people. Let them have more opportunities to meet each other. You should organize tours, dances, get-togethers. In my opinion, that's the best way.'

But it's precisely because the dance halls have this function that they still meet with disapproval in some quarters: dancing might encourage loose behaviour. A sobering thought that if there were another Cultural Revolution, or if there were a swing to the ultra-left, the author of even such an innocuous statement as that which ends *The Marriage Bureau* could find himself a candidate for re-education. Does that sound like exaggeration? I've been reading a collection of stories published in 1956–7 in the Hundred Flowers period, and later condemned as 'poisonous weeds', and am chiefly astonished at the mildness of the criticisms they make. One story, which showed bureaucratic bungling in a Party Recruitment Office, seen through the eyes of an idealistic young recruit, earned its author twenty years in Xinjiang. Another describes the struggle of a young girl student in the 1940s between her commitment to the Party and her feelings for a handsome young *Guomindang* supporter. She makes the right decision and refuses to go to America with him, staying instead to serve the Party, but the author was condemned for daring to suggest that it was possible to have such feelings for a man who is not sympathetic to the revolutionary movement. Another author was condemned for the suggestion in his story that an unhappily matched couple would do better to part – the suggestion was regarded as immoral. By traditional standards, a woman belonged to a man for the rest of her life, once they were even engaged. This view still prevails: the word 'girlfriend' seems to mean 'my future wife' – for a couple even to hold hands seems to mean they have matrimonial intentions.

Most people only ever have one boyfriend or girlfriend: the custom of shopping around that we have in the West would be thought very shocking here, though we did have one student who, when asked where he had acquired his Chinese-English dictionary said sadly, 'It was given to me by my used girlfriend.' Assigned to work units in different provinces, they had decided, despite general disapproval, to break off their engagement rather than endure the kind of broken marriage that the state not only tolerates, but actually creates.

Sexual mores in China are the subject of much curiosity among Westerners, who find the transition from the sexual freedom of their own society to the Victorian prudishness of China hard to believe. When we first arrived, we never saw a couple so much as hold hands in public, though this is becoming a more frequent sight now. Couples saying goodbye at railway stations do not kiss or embrace each other. But it is not only the public display of emotion that is frowned on. I can remember a class of students very puzzled by the title of an article in the Western press: 'Is Marriage Out of Date?'. As the only alternative they understood to marriage was celibacy, they didn't think the subject merited discussion. When I explained, they were somewhat shocked. 'Oh, never in China', they said. Extra-marital sex was, I don't know if it still is, a punishable offence in China. I recently saw an article in *China Daily* urging stiffer penalties for co-habiting couples, so suppose it must still be against the law. A similar confusion occurred in another class when a student produced the sentence 'My sister is married, but my brother is a virgin.' 'I think you probably mean a bachelor', I said 'What's the difference?', they asked. I explained. 'So, what's the difference?', they said.

The unusual and rather cruel combination in China of taboos on pre-marital sex and government policy encouraging late marriage (part of the One Child Family campaign) must mean a lot of frustration. Many people don't get married until their late twenties. Our students recently held a debate on 'Marriage: the Younger, the Better' during which I was startled to hear the speaker for the motion announce, 'It is a well-known fact that in Western countries young people hold the sex experiments before marriage.' He was not suggesting that Western-style sex experiments be introduced into China, though, merely saying that, as this wasn't the case in China, the marriage age should be brought down.

I don't know if things are changing. You certainly see more couples holding hands or walking with their arms round each other, though kissing or embracing in public as couples do in the West would still be very shocking to the Chinese. I have never understood at what point a couple actually consider themselves married. There is no actual marriage ceremony in China: a couple will obtain permission to get married from their unit leaders and then go down to Public Security to sign a certificate. The real wedding celebrations, banquet, wedding photos, distribution of Happy Sweets, however, seems to take place when married accommodation is allocated to the couple by their unit and they can move in together. Sometimes this is simultaneous, sometimes months or even a year later. Up to that time the couple refer to each other as boyfriend and girlfriend, even though they are legally married. A friend told me that nowadays young couples will sleep together during that period, though this offends the older generation's sense of propriety. It must be difficult for a starry-eyed pair of lovers to find anywhere private in China, though. Many students have tactful reciprocal arrangements where room-mates will go out for a walk, visit a friend, or go to the library when one of them has a visiting friend or spouse, and I recently read a short story by Wang Meng, complaining about exactly this problem:

She could walk hand in hand with Jiayuan, although some people went crazy at the sight of young men and women together. But they still couldn't find a place to talk. The chairs in the park were always occupied. After trying hard, they eventually did find one, but it turned out there was a pool of vomit in front of it. They moved on to a large ramshackle park where loudspeakers hung from the telegraph poles beside every bench. The loudspeakers were blaring out 'Information for Visitors', '. . .fifty *fen* to fifteen *yuan* fine', '. . . will be sent to the relevant law-enforcing authority', '. . .conscientiously observe the regulations and obey the administrative personnel', etc. The regulations were so complicated a person wouldn't even know how to stroll in the park without first taking a week's training course. How could they possibly sit there and talk about their love? They left.

But where to? . . . What about going to a restaurant? Well, first you have to position yourself behind someone's chair and watch him eat, mouthful by mouthful, then light a cigarette and stretch himself. Not long after you take this hard-to-come-by seat, your newly-arrived successor places his foot on the rung of your chair. As he moves his leg, the diced meat and slices of tripe you're eating begin to dance in your throat. Should you want to go to a bar or a coffee shop, you won't be able to find one because these are decadent places. Taking a walk will keep you in trim and is a fashion in America. But in winter it's too cold. Of course, they did go out together in that cold weather, twenty degrees below zero, wearing padded coats, fur hats, woollen scarves and face masks. Hygienic and infection free. But what often happens to courting couples is that naughty children playing in the lanes burst out laughing or curse and throw stones at them . . .

For three years now they had spent their evenings looking for somewhere to sit down. They kept on looking and whole evenings disappeared. Oh, my boundless sky and vast land, on which tiny piece of you may young people court, embrace and kiss? All we need is a small, small place. You can hold great heroes, earth-shaking rebels, vicious destroyers and dissolute scoundrels. You can hold battlefields, demolition sites, city squares, meeting halls, execution grounds . . . why can't you find a place for Susu, 1.6 metres tall and 48 kilos in weight and Jiayuan, just under 1.7 metres and 54 kilos who are head over heels in love?

The West's liberal attitudes must be shocking to the Chinese who are exposed to them. I had a letter from an old student recently, describing what was on offer besides Chinese food in Soho: 'It is very terrible. There was a girl sitting by one door and a sign saying 'Two pounds for once.' ' We had an embarrassing time last summer, when two visiting technicians who had been doing some repair work left us a goodbye present of a bundle of Western magazines. In among the *Times* and *Newsweeks* we were horrified to find a copy of *Playboy*. This gave us an awkward disposal problem. I've already explained how difficult it is to do anything on campus without someone getting to know exactly what you're doing. Impossible just to throw it away. Even if we tore it up, the chances were that someone would put the pieces back together again and the next day someone would say, 'It is said that you have been reading pornographic magazines.' Even if we burnt it, someone would probably say, 'It is said that you were burning a magazine outside your house last night.' So we sealed it up in a plastic bag with lots of sellotape and took it on holiday with us, intending to fling it from a train window or leave it in some hotel where it couldn't be traced to us. But then we pictured a naive country boy or hotel chambermaid leafing through out of curiosity and being corrupted for life. Unwilling to have that on our consciences, we finally tore the pictures up into innumerable little pieces and threw them away a handful at a time at various points on our journey across China. We felt like murderers trying to dispose of a body!

Since we last wrote, we've been on another short trip, this time eastwards to what is probably the most typically Chinese part of China: Jiangsu Province, the 'Land of Fish and Rice', one of the most densely populated parts of China. We went to Suzhou, Wuxi, Nanjing, and to visit an old student in an officially 'closed' town north of Suzhou.

The Public Security Bureau in Suzhou were none too keen on letting us go there to begin with. 'How can we be sure his house is fit to entertain foreigners in?', they said. Finally they allowed us to go, but said there was no question of our getting the bus – we had to go there and back by taxi, 'for your security'. The buses, it appeared, though frequent, were too old, uncomfortable and dangerous for foreigners to travel in and besides, we might lose our way. Useless to protest that we had already spent two summers travelling all over China on just such buses, and that not only were we still intact, but also knew exactly where we were. 'For your security', really means for their security: they want to keep track of us. (Exactly the same formula is used by the college every time we renew our request to be allowed our own front door keys to the teachers' hostel. The sole key is guarded by a concierge who checks who comes in and who goes out. It's almost a game now, we know we'll never get keys, and we know why: they want to know who goes in and out, and they know we know why, but we still go on asking and they still go on politely refusing: 'for your security and protection . . .')

So by taxi we went. The taxi driver was a nice old guy who had lived in Brussels as chauffeur to the Chinese ambassador there, so we nattered on in a mixture of French and Chinese. We got back very late, but he refused to charge us extra, 'Been a pleasure gov,' he said, or words to that effect, 'and, seeing as you work for the Motherland . . .'. You still do find that attitude, but it's becoming rarer. Our first summer we often met officials, taxi drivers or hotel staff who would be extra helpful because we were 'working for China', but it seems to me now that all foreigners are coming to be regarded as dollar bills on two legs.

We had a lovely day and gluttonous lunch with our student and his family and it was useful having the car because we could all pile in it for an afternoon trip to see an old temple. The children had never been in a car before and were thrilled. In fact when we suggested taking some family photos, everyone wanted them taken not in the family living room or at the temple, but posing in front of the car!

Suzhou was our favourite of the three towns we visited, and probably our favourite town in China. The saying is 'Heaven above, Suzhou and Hangzhou below.' The town itself is enchanting, low white-washed buildings with grey-tiled roofs, backing directly onto the canals, Venetian style. The bridges resemble those in Venice too, with their high arches and steep steps leading up to the highest point of the arch. Perhaps Marco Polo took more back with him than the concept of the noodle. He was certainly impressed by the bridges. He visited Suzhou in 1276 and wrote enthusiastically: 'Let me tell you, in this city, there are fully 6000 stone bridges!' Although Marco Polo seems more interested in the bridges, Suzhou girls are famous too, with a reputation as the prettiest in China. Suzhou food is arguably the best in China, and the accent of the people is supposed to be the most charming ('Better an argument in Suzhou than flattery in Guangzhou.'). The city has an ancient reputation for culture, elegance and refinement: Marco Polo noted the 'capable merchants and skilled practitioners of every craft, and among them wise philosophers.' The town is famous for its silk, carved sandalwood fans, and exquisitely fine embroidery. But it is the gardens that are its main attraction.

A Chinese garden is quite different from the British concept of 'garden'. There is no grass for a start. Our passion for neatly manicured lawns seems equally strange to the Chinese. A Chinese scholar, visiting Britain in the twenties, speculated why we place so much importance on an expanse of grass, which, 'while of interest to a cow, offers nothing to the intellect of a human being.' Chinese gardens are all about making nature into an intellectual and aesthetic experience, and seem very artificial to the eye used to the tamed wildness of an English garden. They also seem to be more about architecture than plants: you wander from one pavilion to another along winding walkways, through corridors of stone with latticed peepholes, over arching bridges, across terraces and through moon doors, down twisting galleries. It's like a maze: a succession of small, interconnecting but distinct spaces. You get the sensation more of looking at a series of framed pictures in an art gallery, than of being surrounded by and communing with nature. The space between the pillars of a pavilion elegantly frames a view of a curving lake, the peepholes in the gallery or courtyard wall are placed to give you a carefully composed arrangement of plants, rocks, buildings, and water.

The plants and trees chosen to adorn the gardens all have a symbolic meaning. A landscape architecture student recently gave a fascinating talk outlining some of the symbolism. Here are some of the notes I made: Emperors planted pines, juniper,

209

magnolia, jasmine, peony, osmanthus, crab apple. Ordinary people were restricted to willows and poplars. Pines and junipers symbolize a long life, magnolia means nobility, crab apple means perfection, jasmine spring, and, by association, vitality, the peony is symbol of property and wealth and the osmanthus is indicative of status. Feudal intellectuals and scholars had their own particular preferences too. They favoured bamboos, lotuses, plum blossom, and banana trees. The bamboo is the symbol of the scholar: the hollow stem means modesty and the joints mean aspirations; the hollow jointed stems therefore symbolize high aspirations coupled with modesty. When the young plant is still under the soil, the joints are already formed. This means that intellectuals in low positions have high aspirations. However high the plant grows, the stems remain hollow. This means that scholars remain modest even when they reach the heights. Bamboos can't be blown down: intellectuals' opinions can't be changed. The lotus represents purity and cleanliness; it grows from the mud, but is not contaminated. Intellectuals are never pushy, like the delicate scent of plum blossom. Plum flowers open in January. This shows two qualities which all intellectuals should possess: originality – the blossom appears when no other flower is around, and courage – the flowers can withstand the snow. A poem describes how even when the petals of the plum blossom fall to the ground and are pulverized by the wheels of the carts, the scent lingers on the air. This shows how an intellectual under adversity will remain constant and true to himself. Banana trees don't seem to have a particular symbolic meaning, but are favoured because 'the scholars liked to hear the sound of raindrops falling on banana leaves and pine needles whistling in the wind.'

A Chinese garden is an exquisite experience, full of subtle pleasures. My favourite garden was the smallest: The Garden of the Master of the Fishing Nets – a magical secret place, that unfolds its secrets slowly as you are led across bridges and into pavilions. Best of all are the names of the various pavilions and resting points: The Hall Where One Smells Marvellous Perfumes, Pavilion Requiring the Utmost Respect and Admiration, The Pavilion of Gentle Perfume and Spreading Shade, Lotus

Winds on All Sides Pavilion, Scented Snow and Luxuriant Clouds Pavilion, Quiet Retreat Among Bamboos, Waiting for Frost Pavilion, and the delightful Kiosk Where One Questions the Plum Tree.

The gardens of Suzhou were mostly built by government officials at various times between the 11th and 19th centuries as quiet retreats from the cares of office and the gardens often bear the names of their founders. My favourite name was The Humble Administrator's Garden, which can also be translated as The Unsuccessful Politician's Garden. I suppose the modern equivalent would be Bungling Bureaucrat's Garden.

We spent four blissful days in Suzhou, lingering in gardens, watching the busy traffic on the canals from banks and bridges – and eating! The inhabitants of Suzhou are sweet-toothed, and the main street is packed with sweet and pastry houses, windows bulging with lurid confections. We found many of these too sweet and rather rubbery, but food in general was excellent, like Shanghai cuisine, slightly sweet. Delicious despite the menus which advertised such delights as Crap soup, Stare-fried shrip, Soap with Three Delicious Ingredients, Pork with Bamboo Shouts, Fried Nice with Three Kinds.

After Suzhou we went home, via Wuxi and Nanjing. We travelled 'soft seat' to Wuxi, partly to see what it was like and partly because we were attracted by the sign at the station which read 'Soft-Seated Passengers This Way'. Wuxi is also a canal town, but much more extensively rebuilt than Suzhou. We went for a boat trip on Lake Tai and watched the various fishing styles in operation there. Some fishermen had cormorants like those on the Lijiang River near Guilin, some on the bank were using poles with a hook on the end to pull in small nets attached to floats, others were using the traditional four-cornered fishing nets, but most were throwing nets out from their boats with a graceful circular motion, wonderful to watch. Fishing is a popular hobby with men of all ages in China: a way of escaping from the pressures of too much humanity and sitting for a while in your own silence.

In Wuxi, we also visited a silk factory: trays full of cocoons bobbing around in boiling water, and rows of women workers, the skin on their hands white and wrinkled from the heat, drawing off the slender silk threads from the cocoons and attaching them to whirling bobbins.

Nanjing we visited principally to see an old student, but while we were there we caught a bus out to the Ming Tombs and Sun Yat Sen Mausoleum. In heath-like and wooded countryside, rather like suburban Surrey, are two rows of twelve stone animals, like the tombs in Beijing, but instead of lining a tarmac road full of Japanese tour buses, these animals stand or kneel on either side of a grassy path surrounded by woods. I hope this peaceful place escapes the grandiose plans recently unveiled for the development of the Beijing Ming Tombs which include a luxury hotel, a golf course and a ski slope. I think that's a modernization they can do without!

Back in Wuhan, the days seem to be very full, and zip past unbelievably fast. We've taken up *taiji* and calligraphy as winter hobbies, though we're not very good at either. They both seem to require the same fluidity of movement and a kind of suppressed or tightly controlled energy, and we have the same difficulty getting our brushes round the complexities of Chinese characters and our bodies round such movements as 'Parting the Horse's Mane On Both Sides', 'White Crane Flashes Its Wings', or 'Wave Hands Like Clouds'.

Calligraphy is fascinating and I love the small refined and gracious pleasures it provides, from preparing the 'Four Treasures' (brush, paper, ink-stone and ink-stick) to grinding the ink-stick on the stone with a slow meditative tranquil motion, to loading the brush with the glossy black ink, to the slow sweeps and curves of the brushstrokes, the graceful application and release of pressure, energy flowing down the arm and controlled by the wrist.

Taiji I find more difficult and at the end of a busy day, head filled with random trivia, it is hard to concentrate. I find it curiously intellectual as a sport: my head is so full trying to remember whether 'Strum the Lute' comes after 'Find Needle at Sea Bottom' or 'Strike Opponent's Ears with Both Fists', that I don't find it at all relaxing, particularly as our routine is punctuated by our instructor's commands of 'A bit bow, a bit bow with the legs', or 'You should beautiful your movements and not ugly'.

LITERARY FLOWERS AND
POLITICAL LANTERNS

Letter fourteen
LITERARY FLOWERS AND
POLITICAL LANTERNS

5 May 1985

This will be our last letter from China, as in a couple of weeks we set off on our roundabout way home.

We've packed up our trunks to send home sea-freight, following the centre secretary's detailed list of instructions, which included getting the carpenter to make wooden boxes to pack the trunks in and writing lists in triplicate of everything we packed with its approximate value. These packing lists have been the subject of much earnest discussion by the secretaries and the technicians who are translating them into Chinese, as they wonder not only how to translate such items as One Buffalo Bell, value 1 *yuan,* or Three Joke Cakes, value 3 *mao,* or One Replica of Tang Dynasty Camel, value approximately 1 *yuan,* but also how on earth we acquired these things and why we are taking them back home. (The answer to both is that they were presents.) I imagine that the whole department, if not the whole college now knows exactly what we have in our trunks! I particularly like Xiao Li's final instruction, which reads, 'Then the Customs will come. The Customs is the difficult. We should patient.' The Customs came last week and her warning came in handy as we spent five hours ferreting about in our neatly packed trunks trying to recover obscure articles they expressed an interest in seeing, while they sat slurping tea, smoking, and looking officious. We packed and repacked one trunk three times as they demanded different articles for inspection. Finally, just as we'd thought we'd finished, some stamps fell out of a book we were repacking. One official pounced on them. 'Ah, stamps,' he said, his eyes lighting up greedily, 'have you got any more?' We had an album full, which was, of course, at the bottom of the trunk we'd just repacked for the third time. We produced the book and all three officials pored over it, turning the pages slowly, exclaiming

215

over the stamps. We had some old, and presumably quite valuable stamps given to us as presents by students. Everyone in China seems to be an ardent stamp collector. Our customs official was no exception. Closing the book, he said sternly, 'I'm afraid you are contravening the regulations. You are only allowed to export 200 stamps. You have at least 600 there.' Quick-witted Xiao Li knew how to deal with the situation better than we did and came to our rescue. 'Is that 200 per person?', she asked. 'Well, that's 400 for a start. And presumably they can take 400 stamps with them each time they leave China. Well, they've been out twice since they arrived, so that's 800 more they're allowed. That's a total of 1200 stamps, and they've only got half that so they're well within the limit.' Her fast talking did the trick. Fight regulations with more regulations seems to be the answer to a lot of bureaucratic problems. Grumbling, the official telephoned Head Office for instructions and grudgingly told us that as a special favour we would be allowed to keep the stamps. So customs clearance was obtained and the ceremony of Nailing Down the Boxes and Affixing the Seals eventually took place with great formality and a lot of glue.

Some weeks ago, on our return from the Spring Festival holiday, we went to Lantern Festival. This event, which marks the end of Spring Festival, was celebrated by an exhibition of lanterns in a muddy park in Wuchang. Some were made by individuals, others by various factories and work teams – a Chinese equivalent, I suppose, of carnival floats. The lanterns were a marvellous combination of traditional art, Socialist Realism and sheer kitsch. Some were in the shape of local Wuhan landmarks, like the Yellow Crane Tower, a recently rebuilt pagoda on a hill overlooking the Yangtze. Others represented scenes from famous folk tales and operas, such as *Journey to the West* with an illuminated tableau of Monkey, Pigsy and Sandy. Many were in animal shapes: there were a lot of dragons and, since this is the Year of the Ox, a lot of water buffalo. One display had lanterns in the shapes of all twelve Year animals. But by far the most interesting were the political lanterns: a real insight into popular interpretation of current political thought. One lantern featured a money tree with a cock underneath crowing 'Time is

Money'. Another lantern had a cock on top of a hill, crowing 'In competition, fight to get to the top.' Inside another brightly illuminated lantern, a black and a white cat revolved round and round on a disc, perpetually chasing a mouse: a reference to pragmatic Deng's famous saying 'What does it matter if the cat is black or white as long as it catches mice?' Another lantern proclaimed 'China is flying high', and best of all was a mechanical hen laying eggs that turned into trucks: a reference to the much-publicized chicken farmer who earned enough to buy herself a *Toyota*.

Another festival recently was also an interesting combination of revived traditions and socialism, and it too was a sign of the times. This was the May Day celebration in the college, which began with a Dragon Dance, heralded with noisy firecrackers, drums and cymbals. These old traditional festivities, banned during the Cultural Revolution as backward-looking, seem to be coming into their own again. Next on the agenda though was massed choir singing of a socialist anthem by the Young Pioneers, looking like a scout troop with red neckties and ankle socks. Finally was a stunning display of something only China could have invented: formation disco! Our students have never been able to understand there aren't any formal steps in disco; that you just do your own thing. Finally, they cottoned onto the idea that steps can be invented in time to the music, but they formalized this, with everyone doing the same steps in pattern formation. Formal or not, the dance was something that couldn't have taken place a year ago. The college loudspeaker is playing a lot of Hong Kong style pop these days instead of the slushy romantic, soul stirring numbers we used to get, and last week we were even woken up with an old Beatles' song!

There seems to be a lot of rethinking going on, and while there is not exactly an atmosphere of 'anything goes', the general feeling seems to be 'try it out and see if it goes'. The Clean Up campaign, or purge of leftist elements is still going on, and seems to have reached grassroots level: Party members in the college are having three evenings of meetings a week now and when we asked why Professor Han hadn't been around recently, the answer was, 'Oh, he's being rectified'! Something else that is being rethought is the government's position on literary and artistic freedom. I was amazed by a collection of cartoons I saw recently on this subject, and how openly they criticized censorship in art and literature. One shows a writer holding a potted plant. WORKS OF ART is written on the flowers, and FREEDOM OF THINKING is written on the leaves. A pair of distinctly official scissors appears out of nowhere and snips off the leaves one by one. Its leaves gone, the flower wilts. Another cartoon shows an artist painting a picture of a rooster. A cadre appears and protests 'Male chauvinism'. The artist obligingly adds a hen. The cadre is still not happy. 'Too much love', he protests. But when the artist tries to remedy this by adding some chicks, he nearly hits the roof. 'It's an attack on family planning', he yells. In a third cartoon an art class have a sphere as a model. They have all drawn circles. Their teacher is asking, 'Why have you all drawn circles?' In unison they reply, 'We didn't dare show any dark side.'

A recent headline had an element of *déjà vu*: 'Let a hundred flowers bloom: let a hundred schools of thought contend: call for writers to be guaranteed literary freedom.' The article goes on: '. . .Chinese writers must be free to choose their subjects and ways of expression and to air their own thoughts and emotions under the socialist system. Only in this way can writers turn out works [I love *China Daily*'s style!] that are moving and instructive at the same time . . . Leftist tendencies are a remaining shortcoming in the Party's leadership and they have resulted in too much interference in the field of literature . . . Freedom should prevail in literary criticism. Mistakes and faults in litera-ture, as long as they do not violate the law, should be solved through criticism, discussions and debates.' Sounds good, although the article goes on to spell out 'the law', which 'forbids writings that undermine the socialist system.' The promise of freedom isn't quite as empty as this makes it sound though. Writers may now point to faults within the operation of the system, or, like the author of *The Marriage Bureau*, make sugges-tions for improvements, though they must not question the system itself. The article claims that 'ever since 1979 there has been a situation where a hundred flowers were in full bloom in imaginative writing.' Not strictly true: there have been at least four periods of blooming and nipping in the bud since then, that I can count, and I have a very superficial outsider's view. For one thing, I can only read what gets officially translated into English.

A brief overview of the Chinese literary scene since the end of the Cultural Revolution, which placed such stringent controls on literature that most writers were scared off writing altogether (if they weren't already doing time in Xinjiang for what they had written), and the only works of literature produced were Madame Mao's eight revolutionary operas:

Phase One, following on the end of the Cultural Revolution, produced what came to be known as 'Literature of the Wounded' or 'Scar Literature', after the most famous story of that period, called *The Scar*. For the first time for twenty years, writers were allowed to express their criticisms. Criticism was directed at the Gang of Four, the stories exposed the sufferings of individuals during the Cultural Revolution, and each story ended with a predictable tag line: now that the Gang of Four had been vanquished, the Chinese people could look forward to 'a bright future' under the new leadership. Some sample endings:

> . . . the sweet fragrance of flowers and the twinkling stars overhead seemed to offer approval and encouragement . . .

> . . . Chen's heart thrilled to the knowledge that the majesty of the law had been restored.

> . . . The dream of the people will be fulfilled. The reactionaries will be smashed. This is historically inevitable.

Despite the glib endings, the feeling in the stories is real enough, and they make fascinating – and horrifying – reading. *The Scar*, for instance, describes the break-up of family relationships in the Cultural Revolution, where children informed on parents and friends betrayed each other in the collective madness that swept the country. In the story, a daughter rejects her mother who has been labelled a counter-revolutionary, and is in turn rejected by her friends and boyfriend because of her 'bad class background'. The best modern Chinese novel I have read, *A Small Town Called Hibiscus*, is also about how the Cultural Revolution affected human relationships – Gu Hua, the author describes political machinations and power struggles in a remote mountain village, but does it much better than most: the characters are more alive, and he shows how people used political means for personal ends, denouncing people politically because of personal grievances or out of jealousy. And the book is funny, not just bitter like the 'Scar' stories: it rises above vindictiveness into art. One of my students from a remote village in Sichuan told me Cultural Revolution stories like those in *Hibiscus*. I asked what people in the village were doing now and how they got on with each other, and he said, 'Oh, of course we all still live together and work together. People smile on their faces but not in their hearts.' What a horrifying thought: 400 people all forced to go on living and working with the people who had denounced them, or who they'd betrayed, after ten years of mutual mistrust, paranoia and hatred. Whenever I meet anyone over 30 or so, I find myself wondering what they did in the Cultural Revolution.

The phase that followed the 'Scar' period – just two years from 1979 to 1981 – was the most liberal period in Chinese literature since the Hundred Flowers, and produced the most outspoken criticism, not only of past mistakes, but also of present malaise, and also, in my opinion, the best writing since Liberation: characters in shades of grey instead of the standard black villains and shining white examples of revolutionary zeal. Some of the stories are actually about characters' moods, emotions, and inner life – any focus on the individual had previously been condemned as Western bourgeois liberalism – very unhealthy! Much of the writing is still about social issues, but startlingly honest in its analysis of China's social ills. No sweet fragrance or twinkling stars here, but fascinating glimpses into Chinese inner life: the tensions of a family living five to a small overcrowded room, for example, or the privileges enjoyed by cadres: the corruption and opportunism in a society where privilege and luxury (and even some essentials) are rare, and in the hands of the bureaucrats and cadres to dispose of at their discretion. One such story describes the amount of sychophancy, machination, and even bribery necessary for a family to get their name on a list for rehousing. Other stories describe the pressures placed on the individual to conform – Chinese society is controlled not by Thought Police but by what could be described as peer pressure groups: your co-workers in your work unit or your neighbours in your street committee are all alert for signs of deviant behaviour and ready to place persistent psychological pressure on you to return to the correct line. A woman expecting her second child, for instance, will be visited again and again by members of her work unit or street committee until she is persuaded to have an abortion. A recently-married student in my class last term completely broke down under similar pressure and suddenly started sobbing in class. She had become pregnant sooner than she had planned after her marriage and since then had been subjected to insistent pressure from two sides: from her work unit who were planning to send her abroad and wanted her to have an abortion, and from her parents-in-law who wanted a grandchild, particularly a grandson. The pressure from both sides was so insistent that she didn't know what she herself wanted any more. (The baby survived the debates on its right to exist and is due next month.)

Another means of keeping people in line is criticism or self-criticism. This, of course, was at its height in the Cultural Revolution, when so-called counter-revolutionaries or bourgeois liberals were subjected to criticism-struggle sessions, where they would be attacked verbally and sometimes physically, in gatherings of their co-workers or fellow commune-members, until they repented. This tradition is also alive today, though in much milder form. I asked one student what went on in a typical 'evaluation' session. 'Oh, not much,' he said, 'you try and find something nice to say.' 'Nice?' 'Well, harmless. You know, like, you haven't been doing your morning exercises this week or you should go to more study meetings. That kind of thing.' There is a generally happy and friendly atmosphere among our students though – since they come from different work units all over China, there is, as one student put it, 'no competition, no distrust, and no fear.' His words speak volumes for what goes on in the claustrophobic closed communities of the work units. There are two fascinating 'pressure' stories in the volume I've just been reading: one, called *At the Denunciation Meeting*, describes the feelings of an old man when he hears that his commune have called him to a struggle meeting to denounce him for 'taking the capitalist road' by selling ox-hides for personal profit. A horrifying detail: he shaves his head before the meeting to prevent his hair being pulled. The other story is by a writer I really like, Wang Meng, who spent most of the twenty years between the Hundred Flowers and the 'New Realism' in exile in Xinjiang for producing 'poisonous weeds', and, rehabilitated by Deng, started writing again in the Beijing Spring, as the new period of freedom was called, with a much sharper eye for detail and a much more acid wit. The story *A Spate of Visitors* describes what happens to Ding Yi, a newly-appointed manager, when he makes the embarrassing discovery that Gong Ding, the worker he's sacked for absenteeism, is a relative of the Party Secretary:

> I hope readers will excuse me if I depart from normal narrative style to publish some correct but well-nigh unbelievable statistics. In the twelve days from June 21 to July 2 the visitors who came to plead for Gong Ding totalled 199. 33 people telephoned, 27 wrote letters, 53 or 27% really showed keen concern for Ding Yi and were afraid he would run into trouble. 20 or 10% were sent by Gong Ding, 1 or 0.5% by secretary Li. 63 or 32% were sent by people approached directly or indirectly by Secretary Li. 8 or 4% were asked by Ding Yi's wife to talk round her stubborn husband. 46 or 23% were not sent by anybody and did not know Ding Yi but came on their own initiative to do Secretary Li a service. The remaining 4% came for no clear reasons.

Well, all this literary freedom came to an end during 1981, when the Democracy Movement activists were arrested, the right to put up wall posters withdrawn and the underground journals denounced. Towards the end of that year, an article was published in the paper *Red Flag* warning that bourgeois liberalism in the arts would not be tolerated. Why the clampdown, no-one is quite sure; maybe the critical voices got too loud even for Deng, or maybe conservative elements in the Party forced him to call a halt to the freedom. Shortly before the clampdown, the most outspoken essay on literary freedom, called *Rigid Control Ruins Art and Literature* was published in the *People's Daily*. Written by Zhao Dan, a famous film actor, from his hospital sick-bed about a month before he died, the essay claimed that:

Art and literature are the concern of the writers and artists themselves. If the Party gives too specific a leadership to art and literature, then art and literature will stagnate . . . Is there anyone who became a writer because he was asked to by the Party? Who asked Marx to write? Why should we invite so many cadres who know little or nothing about art and literature to lead artists and writers? May I ask which countries in the world are like ours where non-professionals hold such a high percentage of posts in artistic and literary circles? . . . A good work can never be produced by many levels of scrutiny. A vital work has never been the product of censorship. Each time there has been a debate on films I have wanted to speak my mind. Sometimes I tried to control myself and not speak out. But now I am not afraid of anything. I feel I have talked too much. Will this have any effect?

Well, the immediate effect seems to have been a tightening of control, and with the Spiritual Pollution campaign, a further clampdown, with an attack both on Western influences and on 'individualism' and 'bourgeois liberalism' in art and literature. The suddenness of that campaign, and the speed with which it came and went still leave me baffled. And uneasy. Having seen how suddenly repression can take the place of liberalization, I distrust the new freedoms announced in the press and begin to understand the wariness with which colleagues treat each other. The spectre of the Cultural Revolution is still present at the feast of liberalization. And now a second Hundred Flowers! I hope this lot of gardeners don't go the way of their predecessors!

So what else is new? There seems to be a consumer boom in the shops, notably a lot more Japanese imports. There were not many of these around when we first arrived: the occasional taxi driver very proud of his new *Toyota* saloon, the occasional *Sanyo* or *Sony* cassette recorder or TV. It was hard to get imported cassettes, or even cassettes at all when we first arrived, and then Chinese brands such as *Parrot* started to be rivalled by *Sony* and *TDK*. The situation became complicated when the Chinese manufacturers started to make their own *Sony* and *TDK* look-alikes, so a couple of times we were caught out by what was really a *Parrot* in disguise. We found *Tony* cassettes in one shop and *Shrap* calculators in another. Recently though, the situation has changed, and now few Beijing or Guangzhou taxi drivers would be seen dead in an old *Shanghai* saloon, but whizz around in smart new *Datsuns* and *Toyotas* with built-in air-conditioning and car radios. Japanese motorbikes are being built under licence in Chongqing and Japanese cassette players and televisions are for sale everywhere. Japanese goods have great prestige value. They are also much better made. Imports have soared, and the unequal trade balance with Japan has recently begun to annoy the Chinese leadership quite as much as it annoys the West. My experience though, with *Parrots* masquerading as *Sonys*, makes me wonder if the Chinese will start to beat the Japanese at their own game, and Chinese-style *Datsuns*, rechristened *Red Dawn* or *Autumn Breeze*, will soon be speeding through Beijing streets . . .

Prices have gone up, as the government forecast they would in October. Food is noticeably more expensive, and tourism is becoming prohibitively priced: prices of hotel rooms, taxis, and restaurant meals have all gone up. In general, people seem to be much more on the make. Wuhan's Friendship Store had a rather shady deal recently for foreigners who wanted to buy bicycles. The bikes cost 165 *yuan*, and payment, as for everything in the Friendship Store, had to be in *waihui*. But it wasn't as simple as that. To get your bike, you had to pay 500 *yuan* in *waihui* and have the change returned to you in *Renminbi*! The papers are becoming increasingly full of tales of 'corruption' in high – and low – places: embezzlement and swindling mostly.

Another news item, and quite a controversial one, is the abolition of the noonday nap in the name of efficiency in Beijing. The line is that the cut is necessary because of 'China's economic development and increasing contacts with foreign countries'. I bet that won't go down too well! Our students are pretty disgruntled and very sorry for themselves if their midday snooze is interrupted.

Fashion is also much in the news recently. There has been no discernible change in the typical cadre's uniform since Tian Jiyun, the Vice-Premier, put forward the suggestion that 'cadres should be fashion leaders' and 'help create a revolutionary change in the way people dress'. Hu Yaobang supported him: 'Clothing in China is still too dull and monotonous', and the old revolutionary

224

ideals of wearing clothes 'three years new, three years old, and three years patched' and that 'a woman should dress and look older than her years to show she is austere', have been overturned in the interests of boosting sales; 'How can we develop our textile industry if people keep on wearing the same clothes for nine years?' Well, cadres seem reluctant to discard their white shirts and blue jackets in favour of jeans and flashy jackets, but a good many other members of the population are beginning to. The free market in Hankou now has a whole street devoted to brightly coloured stylish clothes. There are some extaordinarily gaudy jumpers, check trousers, barrow loads of jeans, down jackets, baseball caps – and the latest hit item: printed T-shirts. Many of these have slogans in English, many of which are totally nonsensical. One girl I saw had a picture of a clock emblazoned across her chest, with the logo 'The Hands of the Clock Go Around and AROUND'. Another, on a man this time, bore the legend 'CINEMA', and underneath 'I'M INTEREST IN COSTUME ORIGINAL'. Yet another: 'URBAN FIT: THE SENSATION OF BEING FREE, SIMPLE AND FASHIONABLE'. My favourite was much in vogue last summer: a picture of an enormously muscular black man, flexing his biceps, muscles rippling. Underneath was printed 'VIGOROUS AND GRACEFUL'. On the chest of a small and bony Chinese, it looked incongruous to say the least!

More cautious attitudes prevail though. One of our students confessed she would love to wear jewellery, but just didn't dare, and one of our colleagues raised eyebrows in the department last week, when she went into summer frocks a whole month early, on May 1 instead of June 1.

I will close this letter with a short anecdote about an incident that happened a while ago, and which, to me, is a kind of cameo portrait of differences in attitude between China and the affluent West.

Two friends in a neighbouring college had a cat, acquired to deal with the mouse situation in their flat. The cat was called Rubbish, a free translation of her Chinese name, *bu hao chi*, or 'not good to eat', to deter any passing Cantonese who might otherwise regard her as a delectable morsel. Rubbish became sick, and since I had a vet in my class, my friends rang up to see if he could help. When I put the question to him, he looked distinctly dubious. 'Cats', he said thoughtfully. 'Don't know much about cats. Cows now. . . or pigs, no problem. But cats . . .' In the end he said if they brought the cat to the Vet Hospital that afternoon, he would see what he could do. That afternoon it was pouring with rain, and my friends, who lived forty minutes cycle ride away, came in a car and picked us up at my house. We were all already beginning to feel distinctly embarrassed. Most Chinese people do not have access to cars, which are reserved for officials and high-ranking cadres and other privileged people like foreigners. Most Chinese people would not have a car to take them to hospital – I have seen invalids being wheeled to hospital on a handcart. And here we were with a car for a cat! Our embarrassment increased when we arrived at the Veterinary Hospital, which was deserted. It was Thursday afternoon, which is Political Study Day, so all the vets were at a meeting. We hung around in a room full of enormous iron apparatus for holding cows down while they were being examined, while my student went to rustle up some help. He returned with half the staff of the hospital, including the Head Professor, who, when he heard that it was a foreigner's cat, had come on the run. What seemed like dozens of white-coated figures crowded around the recumbent Rubbish, who, by this time seemed, embarrassingly, to have perked up considerably. In the end, she was issued with enormous antibiotic pills. They were probably designed for cows. My friends, red-faced, drove off with a by now fairly cheerful Rubbish, and I, as it had stopped raining, walked back through the rice fields with my student. 'You must think,' I said miserably, 'that we're rather stupid to make so much fuss about a cat.' My student turned to look at me. He considered for a moment. 'In China,' he said thoughtfully, 'cat sick, get a new cat.'

226

Postscript
LEAVING

After a marathon session of farewell banquets, speeches, meetings, and last-minute presents (mostly given *after* we had packed up our trunks and boxes), we set off from Wuhan on a steaming green hot Sunday midday. Our driver was late, and after some panic, someone ran off to the car team, to find him curled up in the office, having a nap. As a result, we missed our train, but discovered anyway that we had been sold the wrong tickets for the wrong train from the wrong station. While we waited for the right one in the sticky May heat, our Chinese director worried about our proposed long journey home, overland through alien territory: 'India? They need a revolution! Moscow? Oh, terrible. Your journey is very difficulty.' She seemed even less impressed by the sight of us jumping hurriedly into a hard-seat carriage with all our bags and rucksacks.

We managed to upgrade to a hard sleeper, and celebrated the end of two years' work by watching the lush green paddies rock slowly past our window, and dreaming of travels ahead . . .

Two months later we left China, on foot. As we stumbled down the rocky track, negotiating landslides, and deafened by the roar of the Himalayan torrent, we could see the tiny border post above us getting smaller and smaller, until the red flag itself was swallowed up by the mountain greenery. Rounding a corner, we saw a frail bridge of wire and planks swaying over the swollen river. We crossed with great care, and set foot in Nepal.

We looked up, and caught glimpses of China, at a great height, through the swirling monsoon clouds behind us. Two years before, we had looked down through patches of cloud, and caught our first sight of land, as our plane approached Peking.

September 1985

Glossary

Some definitions of words and concepts used in the text that may be unfamiliar to the reader.

Cadre: (Chinese: *ganbu*) a word frequently used for officials and bureaucrats.

Criticism/criticism-struggle: group criticism of an individual often used (and abused) during the Cultural Revolution.

Cultural Revolution: or the Great Proletarian Cultural Revolution, launched by Mao Zedong in 1966 to spread 'permanent revolution'. Otherwise known as the Ten Years Turmoil, it finally came to an end with Mao's death in 1976.

'Eating from One Big Pot': the economic policy of the Mao years when everyone received the same rewards regardless of the amount of work done.

Erhu: a musical instrument. A bow runs between two strings and is pulled upwards to play the higher notes, pushed down to play the lower ones. Rather like a two-stringed violin.

Fen: unit of currency, one-hundredth of a *yuan*.

Four Modernizations: Deng Xiaoping's policy of modernizing key sectors of the Chinese economy: Science and Technology, Defence, Industry, and Agriculture.

Four Olds: old ideas, old habits, old customs, old culture. Often used as a rallying slogan during the Cultural Revolution, as things to be smashed.

Gang of Four: 'Madame Mao' (Jiang Qing) and her clique who are often now held personally responsible for all the chaos and misery of the Cultural Revolution.

Hundred Flowers: a brief period of 'liberalization' in 1958 when intellectuals were encouraged, after a speech by Mao Zedong, to speak out and criticize the shortcomings of the new society. In his speech, Mao said, 'Let a hundred flowers bloom, let a hundred schools of thought contend.' Shortly afterwards, there was a great crackdown on those artists and intellectuals who had voiced criticism; it is not clear whether this was Mao's intention or not.

Han: Most Chinese are of Han nationality, but there are scores of other nationalities within the People's Republic of China.

Iron Rice Bowl: policy during the Mao years of guaranteeing permanent employment.

Jiao: unit of currency, one tenth of a *yuan*.

Open Door policy: Deng Xiaoping's policy of opening up the economy to trade with the West.

Pinyin: the official standard system for transcribing Chinese into the Roman alphabet.

Red Guards: These young people acted as the vanguard of Mao's Cultural Revolution. They were encouraged to travel over the whole country and create revolution. Youthful idealism and high spirits became linked with violence and extremism, and bands of Red Guards would often bring terror, injury, and death to people who got in their way. Inspired by slogans such as 'Destroy the Four Olds', they also inflicted terrible damage on monuments and cultural relics throughout the land.

Renminbi: literally, 'People's Money'. Chinese currency. While we were there, one *yuan* was usually worth about 30 pence (or 50 cents) on the official exchange.

Responsibility System: Part of the far-reaching new programme for the Chinese economy, in which individual farmers are responsible for individual plots of land. As long as they fulfil their quota (their contract with the state), they can sell their surplus production for their own profit, and indulge in sideline enterprises. It seems a complete reversal of Mao's 'commune' system (see 'eating from one big pot').

Sheng: a Chinese wind instrument, consisting of a metal base, in the form of a globe, with pieces of bamboo, of different lengths, coming out of the top. The stops are holes or keys on the globe. Its sound is something like bagpipes.

Waiban: Foreign Affairs Bureau, the organisation responsible for relations between Chinese and foreigners.

Waiguoren: foreigner.

229

Waihui: Foreign Exchange Certificates, or convertible Chinese currency issued to foreigners and which most Chinese do not have access to.

Work unit: (Chinese: *danwei*) the basic organizational and administrative unit of Chinese society. Every citizen belongs to a *danwei*, and has a 'work unit card' or 'identity card'. This provides each citizen with an identity and is in many cases more important than the individual's name. The citizen is responsible to the state through the *danwei*; although the specific services provided by each *danwei* depend on its size and location. Our work unit (the college) was responsible for providing all the basic services (housing, work, shopping facilities, health care, education, etc.) for the people who lived and worked there. Much the same would apply to a factory.

Xiafang: 'rustication' – the practice of sending young people to work in the countryside.

Yuan: unit of currency.

Yurt: nomad tent.